TIM BELL is a speaker, writer and tour guide. Ra[...] travelled in the Middle East and North Africa a[...] Scotland to work with young people with special [...] Divinity at the University of Edinburgh in his for[...] a prison and later in the port of Leith. He began [...] tours under the banner 'Leith Walks'(www.leithwalks.co.uk) in 2003, and has since taken hundreds of people through the streets of Edinburgh and Leith, exploring Irvine Welsh's *Trainspotting* on location. Tim has lived in Leith with his family since 1980.

Praise for *Choose Life. Choose Leith.*:

Tim Bell's work intertwines the two themes of the working and lower working class history of Leith and through it of a major strand in the experience of the British working class and the art representing and explaining what that has meant for our collective culture with an impressive scholarship. *Choose Life. Choose Leith.* is itself a substantial contribution to our understanding of where we are now and of how we arrived here. I urge you to read it. PETER TAYLOR-GOOBY OBE FBA, Professor of Social Policy, University of Kent

Set against the culture of the 1980s and the backdrop of Irvine Welsh's *Trainspotting* this book is written with pace, insight and a broad scope. *Choose Life. Choose Leith.* is a must for anyone who wants the real story of this time & place. TOM WOOD, retired as Deputy Chief Constable of Lothians and Borders Police

Tim Bell's *Choose Life. Choose Leith.* is a very timely book. Well written, insightful, carefully crafted. BERT STEVENSON

Tim Bell 'gets' the dynamic that made *Trainspotting* a publishing then social phenomenon in the 1990s... the understated style of the author gently persuades the reader of the literary merits of the work and its various interpretations but also how it reflected the reality of its locations... Irvine Welsh has found the Boswell for his Johnson. GORDON MUNRO, *The Leither*

As entertaining as it is shocking, Tim's attention to detail and ability to bring the past back to life is fantastic. Highly recommended. STEPHEN BENNETT, Director of 1-hour BBC documentary *Choose Life: Edinburgh's Battle Against AIDS*

Many who enjoyed *Trainspotting* will be astonished at what is revealed here concerning all that lies behind Irvine Welsh's best known work. IAN GILMOUR

Praise for Leith Walks:

Top tour. SUNDAY TIMES

A vibrant event. EDINBURGH UNESCO CITY OF LITERATURE

Enlightening, entertaining and very knowledgeable, Tim really helps the place and the story come alive. COLM LYNCH, 14 JUNE 2018

If you love the book or the film or both this is a tour you need to take. LARS, 23 APRIL 2018

Tim will make you see the story with different eyes. ANJA, 15 JANUARY 2018

The man is a fount of knowledge, with rich political and social perspectives on the book and its location, as well as insightful critical views of both book and film. COLIN SALTER, 26 AUGUST 2017

[Bell] is at once warm, didactic, and encyclopaedic... he does an excellent job at describing selected scenes within the context of the surroundings. CAMILLE BOUSHEY, THE STUDENT NEWSPAPER

Praise for Irvine Welsh's *Trainspotting*:

Irvine Welsh's grimy novel of addiction has emerged as the public's favourite Scottish novel of the past 50 years. LIZ BURY, THE GUARDIAN

Irvine Welsh's writes with skill, wit, and compassion that amounts to genius. He is the best thing that has happened to British writing in decades. NICK HORNBY

The voice of punk, grown up, grown wiser and grown eloquent. SUNDAY TIMES

The best book ever written by man or woman... Deserves to sell more copies than the Bible. REBEL INC

An unremitting powerhouse of a novel that marked the arrival of a major new talent. HERALD

A page-turner... *Trainspotting* gives lies to any notions of a classless society. INDEPENDENT ON SUNDAY

CHOOSE LIFE, CHOOSE LEITH

Trainspotting on Location

TIM BELL

Luath Press Limited

EDINBURGH

www.luath.co.uk

First Published 2018
Reprinted with minor updates 2019
Reprinted 2021
This edition 2024

ISBN: 978-1-80425-109-6

This book is made of materials from well-managed,
FSC®-certified forests and other controlled sources.

Printed and bound by Ashford Colour Press, Gosport

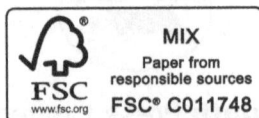

FSC
www.fsc.org

MIX
Paper from
responsible sources
FSC® C011748

Typeset in 11 point Sabon by Lapiz

To my dear long-suffering wife, Liz,
who makes many things possible.

And my younger friend 'Willy' who died
in 2023 after many years of addiction.

Bowie OD skag dole
Renton Begbie shoplift
Connery likesay
methadone radge
Muirhouse hit
HIV Leith needles
trainspotting
life Sick heroin
Dianne scam
HFC Dockers smack
Spud choose

Contents

Maps   10
Timeline   15
Preface to the 2nd edition   17
Introduction   21
Acknowledgements   24

SECTION I: By Leith Central Station They Sat Down and Wept   25

Chapter 1   Leith Central Station   26

Chapter 2   Leith Junkies   35

SECTION II: Composition, Threads, Tensions, Structures   47

Chapter 3   First Generation Episodes   48

Chapter 4   Second Generation   54

Chapter 5   The Bastard Twins   62

Chapter 6   David Bowie, Soren Kierkegaard and the Professionals   67

Chapter 7   The Music Trail   71

SECTION III: Trainspotting on Location and Character Profiles   79

Chapter 8   Leith, Edinburgh, Scotland   80

Chapter 9   There was an Irishman, a Dutchman and a Scotsman   95

Chapter 10   Maistly Rubble Nou...   107

Chapter 11   Meanwhile in the Schemes   122

Chapter 12   Welsh's Women   134

SECTION IV: Heroin, Dealers, Sex and HIV/AIDS   139

Chapter 13   God's Own Medicine   140

Chapter 14   From Eden to Leith   147

Chapter 15 Needles and Sex   152

Chapter 16 God's Own Wrath   161

SECTION V: **What sort of book?**   **173**

Chapter 17 Is Welsh Scottish?   174

Chapter 18 Influences, Context and Genre   182

SECTION VI: **Trainspotting the Play**   **193**

Chapter 19 In-Yer-Face Theatre   194

Chapter 20 Origins and First Year   198

Chapter 21 Analysis of the Play   202

Chapter 22 Aftershocks   212

SECTION VII: **Trainspotting the Film**   **219**

Chapter 23 The Making of the Film   220

Chapter 24 This Film is About Heroin   228

Chapter 25 Character   243

Chapter 26 Broader Appeals   253

Postscript   262

Glossary   267

Bibliography   277

Endnotes   279

Trainspotting

1. The practice or hobby of observing trains and recording the numbers of the seen locomotives

2. The act of injecting heroin; so called because of the mark or track line left on the affected vein

3. Referring to Irvine Welsh's 1993 novel *Trainspotting*, and its lasting legacy of the '*Trainspotting* Generation' – the over 35s impacted by the 1980s heroin and HIV era

Leith map: annotations.

1. 397 Leith Walk: formerly Boundary Bar.
2. 298 Leith Walk: formerly Tommy Youngers Bar. Renton meets Begbie in 'Trainspotting at Leith Central Station'.
3. 180 Leith Walk: formerly The Volunteer Arms. Scene for 'A Disappointment'.
4. 7-9 Leith Walk: The Central Bar. Taken to be the pub 'at the Fit ay the Walk' in 'Courting Disaster'.
5. 398 Easter Road: The Persevere Bar. Scene at the end of 'Na Na and Other Nazis'.
6. 31 Duke Street: The Dukes Head.
7. 13 Duke Street: The Marksman. Davie Mitchell boards the bus here in 'Traditional Sunday Breakfast'.
8. 17 Academy Street: Leith Dockers Club. Scene at the end of 'House Arrest'.
9. 2 Wellington Place. Irvine Welsh lived here.
10. New Kirkgate Shopping Centre. Renton shops here in 'The First Day of the Edinburgh Festival'.
11. Trinity House.
12. South Leith Parish Church (Church of Scotland).
13. St. Mary's Star of the Sea Church (Roman Catholic).
14. 58 Constitution Street: Port o' Leith. Bar where Welsh often met his writing group; clearly re-named Port Sunshine in *Porno*.
15. 44a Constitution Street: Nobles Bar
16. 63 Shore: formerly 'the dole office'. Spud sits near here in 'Na Na and Other Nazis'.
17. Cables Wynd House, better known as the Banana Flats. Sick Boy lives here (ref in 'House Arrest').
18. 23-24 Sandport Place: formerly The Black Swan.
19. 43-47 North Junction St: The Vine Bar. Presumably the pub referred to at the end of 'Station to Station'.
20. 72 North Fort St: formerly Halfway House.
21. 284 Bonnington Road: formerly The Bonnington Toll

Leith Central Station. The most emphatically identified location in *Trainspotting*. Scene of the ghostly figure's remark: 'keep up the trainspottin mind' in 'Trainspotting at Leith Central Station'.

Seafield crematorium and cemetery. Taken to be the place of the funeral in 'Memories of Matty'.

Leith Academy. Renton and Begbie attended school here.

Fort House. The Renton family used to live here before moving to a flat 'by the river' (Water of Leith) (ref in 'House Arrest').

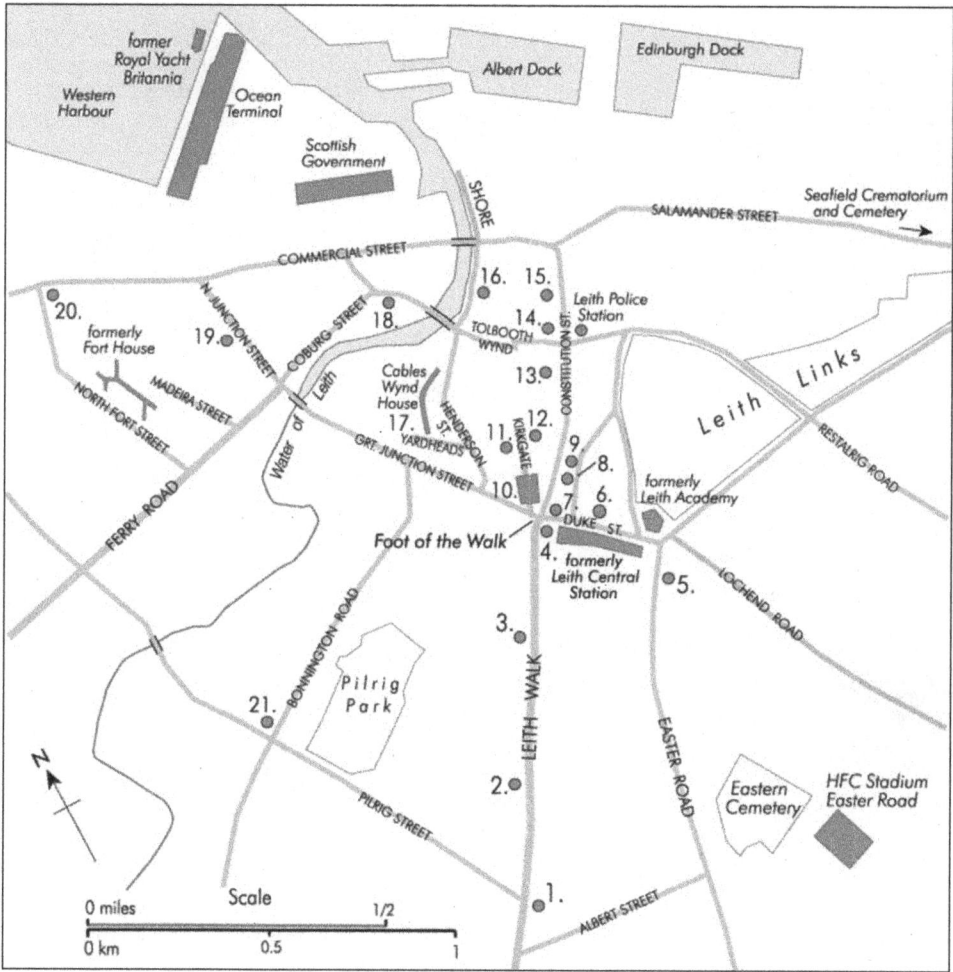

former
Royal Yacht
Britannia

Western
Harbour

Ocean
Terminal

Albert Dock

Edinburgh Dock

Scottish
Government

SHORE

SALAMANDER STREET

Seafield Crematorium
and Cemetery

COMMERCIAL STREET

N. JUNCTION STREET

20.

formerly
Fort House

19.

COBURG STREET

18.

16. 15.

14.

TOLBOOTH
WYND

Leith Police
Station

CONSTITUTION ST.

Leith   Links

MADEIRA STREET

Water of Leith

Cables
Wynd
House

13.

NORTH FORT STREET

FERRY ROAD

HENDERSON ST.

17.
YARDHEADS

GRT. JUNCTION STREET

11.

KIRKGATE

12.

10.

9.

8.

7.

6.

DUKE   ST.

formerly
Leith Academy

RESTALRIG ROAD

Foot of the Walk

4.
formerly
Leith Central
Station

5.

LOCHEND ROAD

BONNINGTON ROAD

3.

LEITH WALK

Pilrig
Park

21.

PILRIG STREET

2.

EASTER ROAD

Eastern
Cemetery

HFC Stadium
Easter Road

N

Scale

0 miles   1/2

0 km   0.5   1

1.

ALBERT STREET

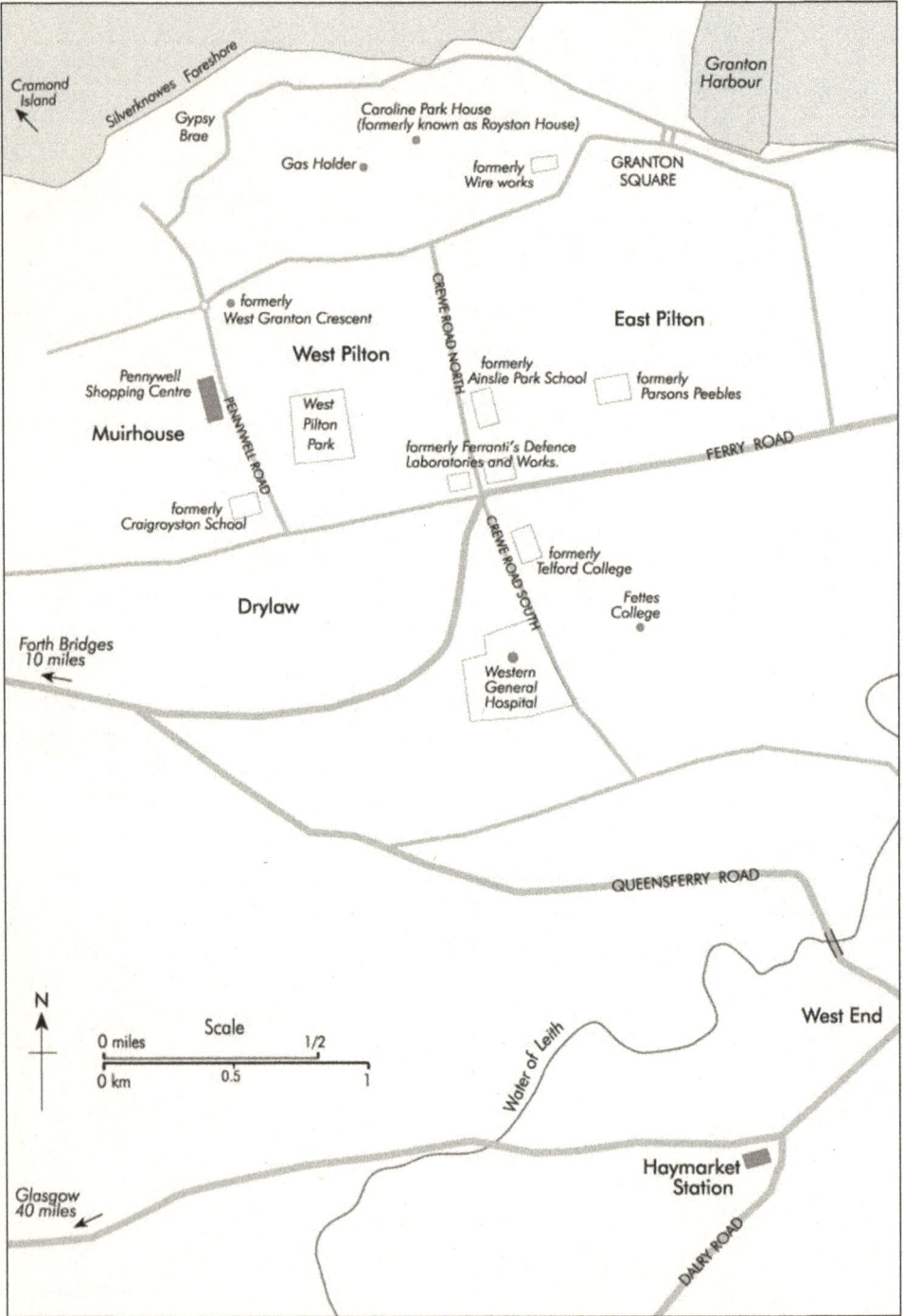

Cramond
Island

Silverknowes Foreshore

Granton
Harbour

Gypsy
Brae

Caroline Park House
(formerly known as Royston House)

Gas Holder

formerly
Wire works

GRANTON
SQUARE

formerly
West Granton Crescent

CREWE ROAD NORTH

East Pilton

West Pilton

Pennywell
Shopping Centre

formerly
Ainslie Park School

formerly
Parsons Peebles

Muirhouse

West
Pilton
Park

formerly Ferranti's Defence
Laboratories and Works.

FERRY ROAD

PENNYWELL ROAD

formerly
Craigroyston School

CREWE ROAD SOUTH

formerly
Telford College

Fettes
College

Drylaw

Western
General
Hospital

Forth Bridges
10 miles

QUEENSFERRY ROAD

N

Scale

0 miles   1/2

0 km   0.5   1

Water of Leith

West End

Glasgow
40 miles

Haymarket
Station

DAIRY ROAD

Western Harbour

Leith Docks

Newhaven

FERRY ROAD

GRT. JUNCTION STREET

Leith

SALAMANDER STREET

Foot of the Walk

Leith Links

Water of Leith

PILRIG STREET

LEITH WALK

ALBERT STREET

EASTER ROAD

LOCHEND ROAD

Eastern Cemetery

HFC Stadium Easter Road

MONTGOMERY STREET

LONDON ROAD

St Andrews Bus Station

Scottish Academy & National Gallery

YORK PLACE

St. James Centre

The Playhouse

Calton Hill

7.

6. 5.

4.

8. The Scott Monument

3.

GEORGE STREET

ROSE STREET

9.

Charlotte Square

PRINCES STREET

Waverley Station

CALTON ROAD

Palace of Holyroodhouse

Scottish Parliament

MARKET ST.

2.

WAVERLEY BRIDGE

SOUTH BRIDGE

10.

former Sheriff Court

COWGATE

1.

DRUMMOND STREET

Edinburgh Castle

11.

GRASSMARKET

LOTHIAN ROAD

BREAD ST.

EARL GREY STREET

Tollcross

formerly Edinburgh Royal Infirmary

Milestone House 3 miles ↓

The Meadows

Base Map © Openstreetmap contributors

Edinburgh/Muirhouse/Leith map annotations.

1. 3 Drummond Street: formerly Rutherford's Bar. Scene of 'The Elusive Mr Hunt'.

2. 17 Market Street: The Hebrides. Bar where Tommy meets Davie Mitchell in 'Scotland Takes Drugs In Psychic Defence'.

3. Calton Road exit from Waverley station. Renton begins his journey here in 'Trainspotting at Leith Central Station'.

4. Formerly the GPO (Post Office) on Waterloo Place. Kelly and Alison are here in 'Feeling Free'.

5. 17-23 Leith Street: formerly Housing Department advice centre. Kelly and Alison are here in 'Feeling Free'.

6. 43 Leith Street: Black Bull. The steps outside and the street alongside are the most accessible and recognisable Edinburgh location in *Trainspotting* the film.

7. 19 West Register Street: Café Royal. Seems likely to be renamed Café Rio in 'Feeling Free'.

8. 21 Rose Street: formerly The Cottar's Howff. Said to be the scene for 'The Glass'.

9. 124-125 Princes Street: formerly John Menzies stationery shop. Scene of Sick Boy and Renton entering to do some shoplifting in *Trainspotting* the film.

10. 435 Lawnmarket: Deacon Brodie's Tavern. Scene of the first celebration after the court hearing in 'Courting Disaster'.

11. 9-11 Grassmarket: Fiddler's Arms. Presumably the pub referred to on the bus to London in 'Station to Station'.

North Bridge/South Bridge ('The Bridges') and Royal Mile. Sick Boy cruises here in 'In Overdrive'.

Hibernian Football Club stadium. Derby match against Heart of Midlothian (Hearts) played here in 'Victory on New Year's Day'. Spud considers going in 'Na Na and Other Nazis'.

Albert Street. 'former junk zone' Renton refers to in 'Trainspotting at Leith Central Station'.

Montgomery Street. Renton lived here – see 'The First Day of the Edinburgh Festival'. See also 'The First Shag in Ages' and 'Trainspotting at Leith Central Station'.

The Playhouse. Renton walks past here in 'Trainspotting at Leith Central Station'.

St Andrew Square bus station. Main characters board the bus to London here in 'Station to Station'.

Charlotte Square. Venue of the Edinburgh International Book Festival.

Scott Monument. Sick Boy shows a photograph of himself and his girlfriend taken here in 'House Arrest'.

Former Sheriff Court House. Scene of Renton's and Spud's court hearing in 'Courting Disaster'.

Tollcross. Johnny Swan's flat is here in 'The Skag Boys, Jean-Claude Van Damme and Mother Superior'.

The Meadows. Scene of 'Strolling Through The Meadows'.

Milestone House, 113 Oxgangs Road. The hospice where Alan Venters lies mortally ill in 'Bad Blood'.

Haymarket station, Dalry Road. Renton and Dianne are here in 'The First Shag in Ages'.

Caroline Park House/Royston House. Source of the confusion of local names that puzzles Begbie in 'A Disappointment'.

West Granton Crescent or 'the varicose vein flats'. Renton visits Tommy here in 'Winter in West Granton'.

Pennywell shopping centre. Renton walks through here and loses his suppository in 'The First Day of the Edinburgh Festival'.

Craigroyston School. Spud attended school here (ref in 'Speedy Recruitment').

Timeline

1875	Hibernian FC founded.
1903	Leith Central Station opened.
1920	Leith amalgamated with Edinburgh.
1952	Leith Central Station closed.
1957	Irvine Welsh born.
1964	Leith Kirkgate demolished.
1971	President Richard Nixon declares drug abuse to be 'public enemy number one', subsequently widely referred to as the opening of his 'War on Drugs'.
1974	First new-style professional drug dealer charged in Muirhouse.
1979	Margaret Thatcher becomes Prime Minister.
1982	Nancy Reagan's 'Just Say No' first coined.
	April – June: Falklands War.
1983	Murder of Sheila Anderson, Leith.
	First two known cases of HLTV-3 (or Gay-Related Immuno-Deficiency Syndrome [GRIDS]) in Scotland.
1985	51 per cent of a sample of intravenous drug abusers in Muirhouse found to be HLTV-3 positive.
	HLTV-3 renamed Human Immunodeficiency Virus (HIV); and a group of symptoms that can result from an HIV infection named Acquired Immune Deficiency Syndrome (AIDS).
1987	'Don't Die of Ignorance' leaflet distributed throughout Britain. Edinburgh dubbed 'AIDS Capital of Europe' in a newspaper article.
	Needle exchange set up at Leith hospital.
1988	Waverley Care Trust founded.
	1 December established as World AIDS Day.
1989	Leith Central Station demolished.
1990	John Major becomes Prime Minister.
1991	Calculated per capita HIV+ people in England: 25 per 100,000; Scotland: 35 per 100,000; Lothian Region 144 per 100,000.
	Milestone House, Edinburgh, opened as an end-of-life hospice for HIV+ people.

1992	Forth Ports Authority (owners of Leith docks) privatised.
1993	*Trainspotting* the book (Irvine Welsh) published.
1994	*Trainspotting* the play (Harry Gibson) premiered.
1996	*Trainspotting* the film (Danny Boyle) premiered.
1997	Scotland votes in a referendum in favour of devolution.
1998	Former Royal Yacht berthed in Leith; now visited by around 300,000 visitors a year.
1999	Scottish Parliament inaugurated.
2003	*Porno*, sequel to *Trainspotting*, published.
2012	*Skagboys*, prequel to *Trainspotting*, published.
2013	Fort House, Leith, home of fictional Mark Renton, demolished. *Trainspotting* voted the favourite Scottish novel of the last half-century in a world-wide survey by the Scottish Book Trust.
2016	Hibernian FC wins the Scottish Cup Final, the first time since 1902.
2017	27 January *T2 Trainspotting* film released Cables Wynd House (the Banana Flats), Leith, home of fictional Sick Boy, awarded Category A List status. 934 deaths in Scotland caused directly by illegal drugs, opiates implicated in almost 90 per cent ; almost one-half aged over 35, thus from 'the Trainspotting Generation'. This is the highest per capita figure in UK and Europe. Almost 6,000 HIV+ people in Scotland, of whom 13 per cent are unaware; 368 new diagnoses in 2017; transmission by injecting around 14 per cent in 2017.
2018	Pennywell shopping centre, Muirhouse, demolished.

Preface
to the 2nd edition

So, in its author's words, a 'scabby wee book' with hard-to-read idiosyncratic spelling, highly localised both linguistically and geographically, was published 30 years ago. Some of the dozens of locations mentioned, unknown to non-locals, are used to help build an unstable structure. The literature on the page stands as it is, but appreciation of the on-location settings adds force and subtlety. Set firmly in a historical period, it bends historical sequences and comes to a fanciful ending which, it became clear later, was tacked on, at least partly, to act as the launch pad for the sequel. It contains scurrilous punk attitudes, a proliferation of foul and pejorative language, a scatter-gun use of voice, storytelling and philosophising, and no securely drawn character or plot.

Thirty years on, with a stage play which adapts as it goes, a blockbuster film and an expensive limited edition coffee table book on the making of it, lots of merchandise, my tours, over 20 editions, and many in translation, we have an audio book and an illustrated Folio Society edition with illustrations and a slip-case, retailing at £60. And a musical, due to launch summer 2024. The potential for all this wasn't spotted by the critics 30 years ago.

For ten years or more, Scotland has been home to an illicit drugs-related deaths rate per capita around four times greater than any other European country. Despite a small decrease in the last couple of years, the absolute number in Scotland is more than four times higher than in 1996, the year *Trainspotting* the film was released.[1] Illicit drug abuse is overwhelmingly associated with poverty and its close cousins, childhood trauma and neglect. Poor education and life prospects, also likely to cohabit with poverty, can have similar effects.

The UK has managed to create very favourable conditions for the illicit drugs trade to thrive. First, it hollowed out municipal housing with its Right to Buy policy in the 1980s. At the same time, it created an economy of easy money and over-mortgaging, resulting in 'sack-loads ay repossession orders

---

1 'Drug-related deaths in Scotland in 2022', National Records of Scotland

in the post'[2] and the crash of 2008. Welsh prophetically brings up both these factors in the book. Now we have too many unaffordable tenancies in badly maintained privatised properties. Inequality is firmly built into the socio/economic structures of a throw-away consumer society. As Welsh has said, the spurious Thatcher-inspired choices in Renton's famous rant in the episode 'Searching for the Inner Man', and magnified in the film, have turned out to be even more remote than back in the 1980s. The online world has fragmented local communities, drawing individuals into a vortex of potentially addictive remote virtual relationships.

In Scotland the illicit drug scene as a policy area is littered with short-term projects which clearly haven't worked. At the time of writing there are signs of some welcome policy initiatives emanating from Holyrood, but this comes with warnings. Just as Leith found in the 1980s, with its Tolerance Zone for on-street solicitations for sex workers, this can have a honey-pot effect. A distinctively Scottish law enforcement policy and provision of care resources – without matching measures elsewhere within the borderless area of free movement and markets that is the UK – is likely to lead to imbalances that can work against their best intentions. If these initiatives are not fully resourced and maintained, and do not enjoy robust political defence and support, they will join the trail of litter.

Far too much dirty money sloshing around the world, corrupting democracies and buying up our social and sporting heritage as cash-cows, has its origins in illicit drugs. Fearful politicians, with their political cycles on such short wavelengths, have good reason to be fearful. Beneficiaries of the industry have powerful ways of maintaining the phoney idea that, keeping the substances illegal, it should be a war zone and principally a matter of law enforcement. To take it out of daily politics, one suggestion in the UK is to form a Royal Commission that would research the whole complex area and recommend a strategy into which policies and provisions could be fitted. And as an international issue, ideally an overall strategy would be put into effect beyond these shores.

Nobody sets out to be an addict. It's easy enough to take the first shot.

If he could bind his eyes in wire
or cleanse his eyes in lime
he'd take back the fated curiosity
of that first time,
ignore the three little words
every lost soul yearns to hear

---

2 *Trainspotting* p230

Try this mate –
and seek his peace elsewhere.

… She adjusts the picture on the nightstand
of the wee angel she once knew
who love wasn't strong enough to save
though Lord knows she tried to.
BROTHER. UNCLE. SON. FRIEND.[3]

Why do people take mood- or mind-altering drugs? Because they are seductive and available. The starting circumstances vary widely from any combination of opportunity, experimentation, youthful delinquency, peer pressure and a search for the feel-good to self-medication against pain of whatever type. You might as well declare war on sex as prohibit these drugs. In the public policy arena sex is mostly a matter of education, health care and, where necessary, harm reduction. There can still be problems around sex – we are human – and we can't dis-invent harmful addictive substances. The damage to personal and community relationships goes way beyond individual addicts. The aim is no more ambitious than to reduce the harm and the pain.

Despite all I have seen here in Leith for 40-odd years, I wasn't prepared for the pain when it recently became personal. A fellow my wife and I had known since he was a schoolboy in the 1980s had a habit for maybe 20 years. Shooting up into his groin a few months ago, he hit an artery and the immediate cause of death was catastrophic loss of blood. It was a very sad funeral.

All this primes the situation for the projected *Trainspotting* the musical. The cause of drug policy reform as part of a more equable social/economic society needs a broad crusading revolution. Like mind-altering drugs, music dodges the forces of geography, orthodoxy and censorship. Music can be the anthem, the rallying cry for a cause, a campaign, a revolution. You can't derive a policy document from music, but music can find and generate creative spaces wherein lie insight, wisdom and truth.

Music can also be helpful in the rehabilitative process from the complex condition that is addiction. Rhythms, balances and melodies move differently from addiction's inexorable, unforgiving demands. Any words attached to music can have their meaning deepened and intensified. Music can bring solace and stiffen resolve. It can bond friendships and communities; it can help fetch the addict out of the depths of isolation.

---

3 From *Edinburgh '86* by Sophie Leah, in *The Darting Salamander*: www.leithwritings.co.uk

Don't expect the musical to be polite. If *Trainspotting* the book had not broken rules and caused offence, it would never have had the impact it has. The book tells of encounters with heroin in a particular time and place. The *Trainspotting* story took place in Leith, but the experience of heroin doesn't depend on time and place. It's a universal story. There is enough fuel in the raw honesty of the book to power another iteration.

The musical, in all its diversity, could have the power to unite the diversity of people who wish to drive change. Welsh has said that the musical will be 'darker' than the film, and, in view of his many remarks on how important this subject is to him, it is hard to imagine that it will not have a campaigning edge. Bring it on.

Tim Bell
Leith, March 2024

Introduction

...the greatest artists conjure an everywhere

out of a highly specific somewhere....

Howard Jacobson

SHORTLY AFTER MY arrival in Edinburgh in 1980 from my native rural Northumberland, I made half a dozen offers to buy a house for my family, and bought the first to be accepted. Enthusiastically I told my work colleagues we had somewhere to live. They were pleased for me. 'Where?' they asked. 'Leith'. Middle class Edinburgh eyebrows went through the ceiling, incredulously, pityingly. They never went to Leith. They had their reasons, of course. To them, Leith was a decayed port town, always rough and tough, now reduced to a gap site. It was the best move I ever made, and I'm still here with no plans to move.

I worked as a social worker with a non-statutory agency, going from professors' houses in the Grange to itinerant families in Muirhouse in the same afternoon. Briefly I was a part time lay chaplain in a prison, then a port chaplain in Leith, meeting seafarers on board ships. Imported Russian coal for nearby Cockenzie power station was stacked near the hoist that up to very recently had transferred local coal for export. This little cameo illustrates the collapse of Leith as the traditional port and working class town of which Irvine Welsh was writing. Now that the power station is demolished, both the hoist and the coal yard are unused and are surrounded by offshore vessels tied up during the slump in North Sea oil; a cameo that illustrates the further changes in Leith since Welsh's book *Trainspotting* was published in 1993.

I have only a dim memory of Leith Central Station, so important in Welsh's story. All I remember is the eastern gable end towering and glowering over the bottom of Easter Road. Talking it over with many others who lived in Leith during the 1980s, I realise that I am not alone in not registering the significance of this once mighty landmark edifice which had lost its power of attraction.

I was well aware, of course, of the arrival of HIV/AIDS, but, bringing up a young family and involved in neither the heroin scene nor the sex industry, it wasn't very immediate. In 1987 we were astonished to have a letter from friends in England who had read the headline describing Edinburgh as 'the AIDS capital of Europe'. Were we worried? our friends asked. Well, the plentiful junkies were very visible, and we knew all about the generalised anxiety and the apocalyptic warnings. Apart from our house being broken into a couple of times by junkies, like many of our neighbours, we didn't know it was worse here than elsewhere.

For a period around the turn of the millennium I was trying to cut it as a tour guide. I couldn't bear to be a kilted wonder on Edinburgh High Street. I needed a niche. My business name was Leith Walks. One day I had an email from a Dutch journalist. With a name like this, surely I did an Irvine Welsh tour of Leith? I didn't, but I researched it and created one. The write up was good, and I had found my niche. The more I looked into *Trainspotting* the book and interpreted it for visitors, the more I realised how much Welsh had spliced geography and history into his fiction. Now I think of it as something like fictionalised journalism or a first draft of history, with satire, humour and social commentary thrown in; and in some respects it's an autobiographical diary.

The publisher's blurb on the first edition ran through the main issues: '...What with vampire ghost babies, exploding siblings, disastrous sexual encounters and the Hibs' worst season ever... *Trainspotting* is a jarring, fragmented ride through the dark underbelly of Edinburgh, the festival city. There is not an advocate, a festival performer or a fur coat in sight as, with bitter passion and rancid humour, Welsh lays bare the lives of this ill-starred bunch of addicts, alcoholics and no-hopers. Written in the uncompromising language of the street, *Trainspotting* is [...] stark, brave, and wholly original...'

And Jeff Torrington, on the front cover, writes: '... A wickedly witty, yet irredeemably sad book... takes us on a Hell tour of those psychic ghettoes which are the stamping grounds for junkies, boozers, no-hopers and losers...'

There is no mention of heroin, and only passing reference to addicts and junkies. Early reviewers also emphasised how the fiction is set within social malfunction, of which widespread, out-of-control drug (any drug) abuse is a symptom. Heroin and HIV/AIDS are certainly part of the story, but they don't dominate in the way that later commentaries suggest.

Harry Gibson's play was on the stage in the next year's Glasgow Mayfest, and Danny Boyle's film was premiered within two and a half years of the book arriving on the shelves. This astonishingly rapid expansion of *Trainspotting* as a brand can only be explained by the sheer vitality of Welsh's writing and the topicality of the subject areas, together with the collaborative creative energy of Welsh, Gibson and Boyle. The play does without the redemptive ending, and in that sense is a more honest depiction of the junkie story. The film magnifies the redemptive ending into a much larger proportion of the film than it is in the book. Both the play and the film take the story away from Leith, and no harm is done to their basic premise: young man gets into heroin, experiences the highs and lows, has some laughs, sees the dangers, leaves it all behind. It's a universal story.

Together these three art-forms carrying the same enigmatic, elusive title, different and inseparable became a commercial and cultural fireball and a byword for a savvy, insolent transgression, strongly associated with the Cool Britannia of the late 1990s. Together they played a considerable part in changing public discourse around heroin and junkies. *Trainspotting* is now a cultural reference point that combines heroin and social history which talks about 'the *Trainspotting* generation'. And, with Welsh, Gibson and Boyle creating updates and sequels there is a *Trainspotting* cult of which Leith is HQ.

This book takes Welsh's book *Trainspotting*, father of the whole thing, back to basics in 1980s Leith. It has grown out of my tours around town. Well-informed locals, tourists, aficionados and academics have fed and tested my knowledge and insights. While some of my sources are documentary, others are fresh Leith voices, with lived experience of their subject.

To ground the whole thing on location and in history, Section I opens up the enigma that was Leith Central Station, and three real-life contemporaries of Welsh tell of their encounters with heroin in Leith. Section II analyses the piecemeal composition of *Trainspotting* the book, working through inconsistencies and confusions and revealing clever structures and tensions. In Section III *Trainspotting*'s principal characters guide us round the Leith of their day, putting their story into their context. Section IV gives a brief history of heroin and HIV/AIDS and an account of how they collided in Leith, and in Section V we go in search of literary bearings for Welsh's *Trainspotting*. Sections VI and VII put the play and the film respectively into their contexts and get under their skins to see how they work.

Tim Bell
Leith, July 2018

Acknowledgements

Over the 15 years spent writing this book, many people have generously shared with me their knowledge and insights of *Trainspotting* and its surrounding issues. In the following pages, some of the extended conversations I have had with people who have supported the project are not directly referenced. Conversely, some chance remarks have been more or less quoted verbatim or greatly expanded. Some people have wished to remain anonymous, for a variety of legal, professional and personal reasons. Thank you all – you know who you are.

All those years ago two people gave me a secure start, which has led to the whole thing growing legs and wings to the point where it is finally published: special thanks go to John Paul McGroarty and Mary Moriarty.

Thanks are due to Thomas Ross, formerly of Luath Press, and present editor Alice Latchford. Years ago I played club hockey with Gavin MacDougall, Director, and we had no idea then that it would come to this! Thank you, Gavin, for your support and encouragement, in various forms, over several years.

Finally, to Irvine Welsh, who couldn't know what he was starting way back in 1993, thanks for the 'scabby wee book' as he later called *Trainspotting*. For me it has been the perfect platform to combine my interests in community, culture, and words on a page. It's better than scabby, Irvine. It's ground-breaking.

SECTION I
By Leith Central Station
They Sat Down and Wept

CHAPTER I

Leith Central Station

YOU CAN GO to exactly the spot where the photographer stood to take the shot on page 29 of Leith Central Station and the Foot of Leith Walk. The horse-drawn tram dates it to no later than 1904, that is within a year of the opening of the station. You are standing in the heart of Leith and at the heart of *Trainspotting*. The Heart of Leith, the Foot of Leith Walk, and Leith Central Station all their have distinctive meanings but they can easily be pretty well synonymous.

Irvine Welsh uses this location to pin together his story *Trainspotting*. The small figure on the far pavement at the lower right edge of the shot stands at the taxi rank where Renton fulminates in the first episode: 'Supposed to be a fuckin taxi rank. Nivir fuckin git one in the summer... Taxi drivers. Money-grabbin bastards...' (p.4).[1] Leith Central Station is the most emphatically identified location in the entire book. Directly opposite the taxi rank, out of sight up the opening at the end of the terrace beyond the third awning, Renton and Begbie go up the ramp that ran along the gable end into the derelict station at first floor level, for the ghostly figure to suggest that they are there to spot trains. One of the most moving tours I ever did was with a recovering alcoholic. On what remains of the ramp I talked him through the literary situation, and I had to leave him alone with his thoughts for quite a while as he looked across the street and considered the implications for himself of being brought back to where he began.

When I came to live in Leith in 1980 an old man told me that 'the Fit ay the Walk' was the heart of the town. There were no changes from this photograph then, but now you will see that the ridged glass roof to the left of the station clock tower and the railway bridge a few hundred yards up Leith Walk have been removed. I was puzzled. I found a dispiriting 1960s shopping centre called New Kirkgate behind and to the right of where the photographer in the 1900s stood, with an unprepossessing residentialised walkway on the other side of it, heading away to the north. I had seen the same many times before, in towns around Britain. There was endless traffic on the junction in front of me, and the station behind the faded facade under

the clock tower that dominates the photograph was obviously derelict and useless. But with a little local knowledge and a longer view, I gradually discerned what the old man meant.

Kirkgate – that's Church Street in modern English, and the name tells you the street has been there for many centuries – ran to the edge of the crowded medieval town at the 16th century defensive town wall at St Anthony's Gate, which was over the right shoulder of the photographer. The broad boulevard in front of the camera was built as a military defence and line of communication in the 17th century Cromwellian war. When the army left, it became a fine high route to Edinburgh, provided they kept horses and carts off; hence the name Leith Walk. In the days before the tyrannical motorcar, this broad confluence was a natural focal point in the town. It was the start or end point for many a march and rally for well over a century. The centrality was already in the parlance: Central Hall was there before Central Station. In 1907 they deliberately placed the statue of Queen Victoria, which comes into *Trainspotting*, in the heart of the town; it's just off the shot to the left. Now the Heart of Leith is reduced to this broad pavement where the camera stood, 30 yards by 50 yards, not much to call the heart of a town. It's a favourite spot for canvassers. There's some seating. It catches the best of any sunshine that's going. There's a municipal Christmas tree here every year.

Whether it was arranged or not, the potency of this image lies in the line of boys and men, all with their caps on, stretching from the heart of the throbbing old town, across this social arena and fulcrum of the town's comings and goings, to Leith's magnificent entry to the wider world. This brings us to Leith Central Station, so central to *Trainspotting*. To have a full appreciation of the metaphor Welsh works in lifting an obscure, enigmatic word from a page towards the back of the book onto its title page, we need an understanding of its massive, useless, elusive, vainglorious and dysfunctional purpose and presence at the heart of Leith.

* * * * * * *

Leith Central Station was a bastard. In 1889 the North British Railway Co. (NBR), wishing to thwart rival Caledonian Railway Co.'s (CR) proposal to run a loop to Leith docks, and, having invested heavily in the new Forth Bridge and needing to increase its capacity through Princes Street gardens, undertook to build a dedicated passenger line and station in Leith in order to have its way on both counts. Corporate hubris and the absence of any strategic planning was one parent.

A single-track line with a ticket office and a shed on the platform would have been enough. The town had neither the density of population nor a sufficient hinterland, the nearby port notwithstanding, to justify one of the biggest stations in Scotland at almost three acres, and the largest to be built in Britain in the 20th century. Leith Burgh Council didn't want a level crossing at Easter Road, so at vast expense the company built a bridge and brought the trains in at first floor level; hence the ramp at the Leith Walk end. The Council wanted a clock tower; the company provided the one we see today. The station had several sidings, four platforms, generously proportioned waiting rooms and a large concourse. No-one knows why they had the wonderful roof made by Sir William Arrol, who had the Forth Bridge, Tower Bridge, London, and North Bridge, Edinburgh, to his credit. He wasn't cheap. The sheer size and extravagance of Leith Central Station is the unknown parent.

The people of Leith had no reason to concern themselves with any shortfalls of their glorious new access to the outside world. The enormous area, free of internal division and interruption of any sort, together with the great height of the roof which permitted excellent natural light throughout, created very special effects indeed. And the name: was it not something to be conjured with? Edinburgh and London didn't have a Central station. Glasgow and New York both did. And Leith! An ordinary suburban station it could never be. This place was a cathedral of visions of distant places and triumphant homecomings, an emporium of travel.

Mr John Doig owned The Central Bar at numbers 7 and 9 Leith Walk, immediately to the left of the nearest awning in the photograph. There were two small lounges at the rear of the main bar, from which there was easy direct access up to the platforms. The interior was attended to in fine style and, for the price of a drink at the bar, you can still appreciate it, unaltered, in all its glory. Look at the paintings amongst the highly elaborate tiles, wood-work, plasterwork, coloured glass and mirrors: the Prince of Wales (shortly to be king) playing golf; yachting at Cowes Regatta; hunting with pointers; and hare coursing. Evidently Mr Doig was a royalist. The fabric is now protected, as is the whole frontage from the foot of Leith Walk round the corner into Duke Street, with the clock tower on the corner. Welsh often drank here, and it is the pub that best fits the description in 'Courting Disaster' as the location for the second après-court celebration from where Renton goes to Johnny Swan 'for... ONE FUCKIN HIT tae get us ower this long hard day' (p.177).

Not to be thwarted in the end, Caledonian Railway Co., within a few months of the opening of NBR's Leith Central, opened its own line to the east docks by a circuitous route, crossing Leith Walk by the bridge a few hundred yards up Leith Walk in the distance in the Edwardian photograph. Leith Central Station became operational on 1 July 1903 with no formal opening. The *Edinburgh Evening Dispatch* sniffed that the huge station for a single train was like a two-storey kennel for a Skye terrier. The bread and butter business was the 'penny hop' to Edinburgh, but when the Leith and Edin-burgh tram systems were unified in the early 1920s a big hole was knocked into the customer base. However, during the 1920s and 1930s, they ran a good service to Waverley and round the southern Edinburgh suburban line. And, as Renton correctly observes as he pisses in the dereliction half a cen-tury later: 'Some size ay a station this wis. Git a train tae anywhere fae here, at one time, or so they sais...' (p.308). The Leith Member of Parliament, George Mathers, would proudly board his train to London here; first stop Edinburgh Waverley. They ran football specials, beer safely on board, to Wembley, London, for international matches. And you could go to Glasgow in the west or Aberdeen or Inverness in the north.

But the services gradually declined. By the end of the 1930s the station not much more than half a mile away, the Caley at Lindsay Road, offered 37 daily trains to Edinburgh while there were only 27 from Leith Central. Many of the trains leaving the Central were single carriages behind the engine, widely known as The Ghost Train. One engine driver recalled Leith Central Station shortly before the war: '...this great edifice was like a sanctuary, a retreat from the hustle and bustle of places like Waverley Station. Sitting on my engine at Leith Central I have contemplated its spacious emptiness, not a soul in sight, only the quiet murmur of steam and warm fireglow...'[2] Unglamourous and under-used, nevertheless interest and even fame came to it. It became a useful overnight shed for main line trains: enthusiasts – the trainspotters of their day – delighted in reporting that notable engines such as *Cock o' the North* and *Quicksilver* were at times only yards away from unknowing shoppers and pedestrians in Leith Walk. Alan, an apprentice boy in a wood yard near Easter Road, often took a moment to admire Gresley's *Mallard* as she glided past.

The concourse was spacious and empty enough to permit the Boys' Brigade to hold their weekly drilling and parading practices there. It was much bigger than any church hall. The boys marched up the ramp off Leith Walk, and they had the place to themselves in the evenings. Sometimes there was a train at the platform, but there were no arrivals or departures, and no passengers. Lighting was not included in the permission, so sometimes it was pretty dark before they finished. For Nina, accustomed to overcrowded housing, all those toilets in the station were a thing of wonder. She didn't have to ask if she could go! In the late 1940s Annie, living in Prince Regent Street, loved to go to the Cabin Café right on the corner under the clock tower, to meet her friends on Sunday evenings, where they would have juice and a cup of coffee. She was faintly aware that it was a railway station, but it never occurred to her to catch a train there. If she wanted a train, the Caley at Lindsay Road was far more convenient.

In 1947 the railways were nationalised, and British Rail (BR) acted on the commercial reality that its private enterprise forerunners had not, that this line and station were not viable. On Saturday 5 April 1952, the last passenger train pulled out of Leith Central Station. In the local press there was no advance notice given on the day before or on the day itself, and there was no report or comment the following Monday. Only a local photographer turned up to record the occasion. From this point Leith Central Station faded even further from collective awareness in Leith.

After a decade or so of standing empty, it became useful again in an unexpected way. In the 1960s steam gave way to diesel. BR found itself having to maintain both steam and diesel engines for several years during the changeover, and adopted Leith Central as a maintenance depot for the new diesels while the sheds at Haymarket continued to service the steam engines and were adapted for diesel. It was known to BR as Depot 64H. It was used as Scotland's first diesel driving training school. All this went on entirely within the building, behind closed doors, as it were, and without any great comings and goings from the surrounding streets. When BR had got rid of steam engines and adapted the Haymarket sheds, in 1972 Depot 64H was surplus to requirements.

Up to now the line had remained open as far as the Hibernian fc Easter Road stadium for occasional football specials. But now the line was closed completely. Just as lighter, cleaner, reversible diesel engines had been tested and were readily available, the Conservative governments of the 1960s, with their ideological objection to nationalised industries, had taken an axe to branch lines throughout the country. Any remaining chance of Leith Central enjoying a revival died.

Apathy and neglect set in. Anywhere else in the country such a large prime site in the centre of a town would have been a target for developers. In Leith there was no such pressure, and no options or plans were discussed. Leith Central Station, in all its magnificence, became an icon of economic downturn, high unemployment and, with the demolition of streets all around it, the Leith diaspora.

A flat local economy and high unemployment took hold. Councillor Alex Burton's pleas to do something constructive with the station fell on deaf ears. br let out some office space as a Job Centre at the top of the staircase from the Leith Walk / Duke Street corner. The alterations were carelessly done. The new false ceiling masked the access hatch to the clock tower. The usual contractor turned up to restore the clock to gmt in October 1978 but couldn't gain access. They had to fish out the building's drawings and the job was done in December. The main entrance to the station remained bricked up from an earlier closure, and access to the Job Centre was moved to a smaller doorway a few yards down Duke Street. An opening that was intended for purposeful comings and goings was taken up by people hanging around, the way they do when they have nothing to do and nowhere to go. br's commitment to redevelop the station area for warehousing and, ultimately, offices never materialised.

Meantime, the platforms and sidings, under their vast roof, fell into disrepair. For anyone looking for a hidden place for sex, drinking, fighting, drug-taking, sleeping rough, or an open toilet, it was perfect. There was plenty of room for all, and no need for private parties to intrude on each other. Access was easy. Inside there was a creepy air of the *Mary Celeste*. The platforms were intact, with the railings at their ends helpfully there to prevent anyone falling in front of a train. The cubicle-like café and bar were there, the ticket booths could be broken into, the toilets stood with the doors hanging off and no plumbing.

The kids found it a wonderland. It became a rite of passage to go into the station, and some kudos was attached to bringing an air rifle with which to shoot the plentiful pigeons. And best of all, there was a ghost. It was legless, so it bounced or floated two or three feet over the ground. It wore a Celtic fc top so, naturally, it had big red eyes and horns. In its previous life it came to a game at Easter Road but its legs were crushed by a train. Some daring youngsters got onto the top of the roof, and the neighbours watched in horror. There were plenty of entrance points, the easiest being at the top of the ramp off Leith Walk, where there was no serious attempt at security.

Nothing happened. Eventually the Council acquired the site. Various plans were drawn up. It was big enough for a small sports stadium, whether covered or open. There could be a five-a-side football pitch behind the Leith Walk frontage, next to tennis courts, and a running track in the area where the sidings had been. The ramp from Leith Walk would lead nicely into the upper level of the complex. This 1980 proposal came to nothing. The feisty Revd Councillor Mrs Elizabeth Wardlaw deplored the Council's 'lack of foresight and determination to find funds and expertise... for the social, commercial and recreational development [of Leith Central Station] not only for... Leith, but the whole city of Edinburgh.' She rejected a fellow council-lor's description of it as a Dickensian dump; she called for the potential of its 'vast unobstructed area and massive walls to be imaginatively developed'.[3]

Frank Dunlop, the energetic and high profile Director of the Edinburgh International Festival came to see it. Various people proclaimed its excellent potential as a transport museum, an exhibition centre, or a concert venue and arts complex. You could have a Guggenheim there. In late 1988 it was decided. The roof and the platform level would be removed and the south-ern perimeter walls reduced. There would be a municipal Waterworld in place of the concourse area, and a Scotmid superstore in place of the plat-forms. The sidings would become a car park. Annie, who had left Leith and brought up a family in Edinburgh, was astonished to be told it was going to be demolished; she hadn't realised it was still standing.

Welsh pitched his episode 'Trainspotting at Leith Central Station' in the few weeks between the decision and arrival of the demolition squads: '... the auld Central Station... now a barren, desolate hangar, soon to be... replaced by a swimming centre' (p.308).

Precisely a century after Caledonian Railway Company gave notice of its wish to run a passenger line to Leith, Leith Central Station was demol-ished. The contractor placed an ad in *The Scotsman* in February 1989:

HISTORY IN THE MAKING

You can buy a part of Edinburgh Heritage...

dressed stone for sale...

Sandy Mullay was invited to write an obituary in the *Edinburgh Evening News*. He couldn't resist the last line: 'The station now departing was one nobody wanted...'[4] A bastard to the end!

* * * * * * *

If you call yourself a creative writer you should be able to work something up from this metaphor-rich location. The episode 'Trainspotting at Leith Central Station' was published as a freestanding short story before it was given its place in *Trainspotting*. Welsh asked a friend, Dave Todd, to create an image of the vision and theme of the piece; the result was a train full of partying yuppies passing through a derelict Leith Central Station that is full of skeletons – a ghost train in reverse, Edinburgh's prosperity mocking Leith's austerity. Who were the skeletons? The crowds that never came to this vast place and who never will? Leithers? Leithers now in Edinburgh, Muirhouse, South Africa, Australia, Canada? Who is spotting whom? In an interview with *The Big Issue* in 1993, in which the image appeared, Welsh explained: 'I wanted to do a book about Edinburgh and attack the perception of it as this bourgeois city where everything cultural happens, a playground for the Guardian/Hampstead middle classes. There's another reality that runs parallel with that...'[5] He has also said that he was writing in a working class voice that happened to have a Leith accent. In a strong way, *Trainspotting* is a Leith/Edinburgh story. Todd's image was intended by Welsh and Todd to be used on the front cover of *Trainspotting*, but the publisher commissioned the photograph of the two figures with grinning skull masks in front of some trains and the departures board at Waverley station that became so familiar.

Renton's journey from Waverley station in the eponymous episode is the most focussed geographical journey in the whole book. Every step can be retraced, and details along the way can be observed and considered, much like Stephen Dedalus' journey in James Joyce's *Ulysses*. Welsh has brought his characters to Leith Central Station, on foot, for the journey and the location itself to speak loud and clear.

Coming home from London for Christmas, Renton leaves Waverley station by the Calton Road exit, as many Leithers do who are pleased to stretch their legs after a long train journey. He walks confidently past other people's problems up to Leith Street and down towards the Playhouse, with the surrounding restaurants. It is indeed 'downhill all the way', in common parlance a cheerful, well-worn double entendre meaning either that things can only get easier or that things will only get worse. But there's nothing casual about it. Look for a bit more bite. As we shall see, in Welsh's late 1980s Edinburgh's rubbish flows downstream to Leith, Leith disposes of Edinburgh's sewage, Leith takes Edinburgh's junkies and the sex trade, Leith is demolished while Edinburgh stands tall, Leith weathers economic storms while Edinburgh preens itself as a city of culture, protected by the castle walls of privileged status. In the fiction, at the top of Leith Walk 'middle class cunts' in Edinburgh have an evening's entertainment at the Playhouse and table reservations at nearby restaurants, while at the Foot of the Walk Begbie and Renton piss in their own situation in derelict ruins in the dark. It's downhill to Leith, alright.

The timing of the setting of the episode is historically precise: it is Christmas 1988. Instead of something special, there would be a supermarket. Supermarkets are all the same. This one would do for the Junction Street shops what the managed Kirkgate shopping centre did for the shops along the old Kirkgate. Even though this was going to be a Co-op (and Leith was a Co-op town), it would sweep away locally owned businesses and destroy the micro economy and diversity of interest in the area. As for the swimming centre, there was already a perfectly good pool a few hundred yards away in Junction Place. Welsh seems to sense, correctly, as many people did, that it was a vanity project (although it was popular, the pools leaked, it was massively energy-inefficient, it was unsustainably labour intensive through poor design, and it lasted a mere 20 years; the pool in Junction Place is still going well). Now it had come to this, the final insult. This was the last surgical knife in the almost moribund body of Leith as it was being laid out to become north Edinburgh's ghetto or, worse still, a suburb of Edinburgh.

While they are pissing the conversation is of distant collective memories and of what is being lost. We seem to have already met Begbie's father in 'There is a Light That Never Goes Out' and it's no real surprise that it turns out he is the 'auld drunkard' who approaches them. Is he the ghost of a generation of unemployed Leith men? Is he the ghost of the Leith diaspora? Is he the ghost of a man who has thrown his life away to alcohol? Maybe all three. Begbie is a child of all this. Violence, alcohol abuse and general depravity are strongly linked to persistent social instability and poverty. Merely to observe that the Begbies, father and son, are morally reprehensible is missing the point; they are used here as representative victims of the retreat of the economic tide and failed public policies.

Renton, who starts out from Waverley station in Edinburgh as a reasonably confident young man, and despite his feeling that he is safer because he is coming 'hame', deteriorates to a 'pathetic arsehole' in Leith's pervasive bad atmosphere. It is tempting to think of the character Second Prize as a metaphor for Leith. His nickname is explained in 'Station to Station' and it seems unlikely that it was contrived for the purposes of this metaphor, but both the name and his condition work towards it. Renton tries to help him, but it's 'useless'. The last person we meet is the unnamed guy in Duke Street who is meekly resigned to ill treatment; is he too a representation of Leith? And is Begbie's malign belligerence and indifference to others no more than a personification of everything that had gone wrong in Leith, to the permanent damage of the community and real people within it? Things are not well in Leith.

CHAPTER 2

Leith Junkies

LET'S RE-IMAGINE the Edwardian photograph. Now we see a line of 1980s Leith junkies, stretched out between home and the doorway to faraway places where problems are left behind. Their access, whether the station or heroin, is there, just a step over the road, a presence that's impossible to miss, with easy access despite the closed doors, and a dark, dirty and disordered interior, deplored by most people. Home for them is neither secure nor satisfying; demolitions and dispersals characterise their environment, and few have had the opportunity to embark on rewarding and purposeful careers. They have been brought up hearing Mrs Thatcher's rhetoric on the right to choose, that everyone has consumer options – not that they have had many. The skeletons in Leith Central Station in Dave Todd's image are now junkies, dead or alive, and HIV+ people, dead or alive.

Within the eponymous episode Renton's journey to Leith Central Station is just as much a review of his encounter with heroin as a return to Leith. He notes passing his old gaff in Montgomery Street, he nods at Albert Street, not mentioned elsewhere in the book but well known locally as Dealers' Alley back in his junkie days. Begbie's company in Tommy Younger's explicitly invites a review of Renton's career in junk since the suppository scene in 'The First Day of the Edinburgh Festival' gave him a good opportunity to quit. Begbie seems to know what happened way back in 'Cock Problems' – Renton gave Tommy his first shot. And going up the ramp to the terminal station brings Renton directly across Leith Walk from the first location to be identified, back to where he started, the taxi rank where on the second page of the book he and Sick Boy fume about taxi drivers who are unaware of and unresponsive to their junkie needs.

It is 'the festive season', the end of the year, a punctuation point in everyone's life, when we review the past and look forward to the year ahead. Intimations of mortality need not be morbid, but, for a young man, Renton is well acquainted with death. He is the only survivor of the three boys in his family. Wee baby Dawn died, and the last we heard of her mother, Lesley, she was in intensive care in a Glasgow hospital following a suicide attempt. Dennis Ross didn't make it. Renton has just been to Matty's funeral, and Tommy is in trouble. He knows it is Leith Central Station's last Christmas – could it be his too?

Begbie's reference to Tommy in the pub links this episode to 'Winter in West Granton' not only in the storyline but also thematically. There is no mention of the season in which the episode is set; it's a spiritual winter. West Granton Crescent too was a massively oversized, dysfunctional, dead end place and full of metaphorical skeletons. It should never have been built, and it was due for demolition (it was demolished about 20 years later). This stretches the junkie implications across the two episodes. When Renton is with Tommy he appreciates the reducing likelihood of successfully quitting with each failed attempt. If Renton doesn't get out of Leith Central Station quickly the whole edifice will be brought down on top of him. He, like it, will have all his unrealised potential ingloriously and unceremoniously ended. Many people will be pleased to see the almost invisible derelict trouble spot go. Renton is uncomfortably close to being viewed in the same light, his existence barely noticed, his departure unlamented, a forgotten piece of history, at best a statistic. He, like the station, will be remembered, if remembered at all, as a bringer of danger and squalor, a waster and a loser.

To adapt Psalm 103 verses 15, 16 'As for [a junkie], his days are like [Leith Central Station]; he flourishes like a flower of the field; for the wind passes over it, and it is gone, and its place knows it no more.'

* * * * * * *

Just as we can imagine that some of the men in the Edwardian photograph died in the First World War, so some of the 1980s junkies died, whether by overdose or with HIV/AIDS or some associated complication. However, Fred, Audrey and Donnie, who are all within a very few years contemporaries of Welsh, knew the Foot of Leith Walk in their junkie days and survived at least 20 years, have agreed to let me recount their stories. Their names are changed.

Fred's story

Fred doesn't like coming to Leith these days. He could see someone who might offer him something he would have to refuse. He lives in Edinburgh city centre.

Fred knows exactly when and where he acquired HIV. In London, in 1983, he shot up – only three or four times, he says – with a couple of older

hippies who had a baby. They would fill up the syringe and share it. To check
the needle was in a vein, they pulled into the chamber a little blood which,
of course, was transferred to the next one. They were not remotely aware
of any potential danger. This was the only time he injected. He left London
and took to chasing the dragon. A few years later he had a phone call from
London – he should get himself checked because one of his London friends
had become HIV+. But by then he had already been diagnosed positive. He
has been to many funerals over the years where he has strongly sensed other
people feeling: 'this should be for you, Fred'. Now, well after a Thirty Years
Later party, he has developed a talent for photography, a hobby he pursues
in many different countries.

He didn't like growing up in Pilton. He had a poor attendance record at
Ainslie Park School (Welsh attended there, about five years ahead of Fred)
and was sent to the residential Dr Guthrie's List D school in the south of
Edinburgh. There were lots of bored boys there, and he had his first experiment with drugs with them – glue-sniffing. He was sent to a more discipli-
narian establishment in Ayrshire, to which he responded quite well. Home
again at the age of 16 he got a job with one of the last of St Cuthbert's horse-
drawn milk carts in Stockbridge, where he became aware of the drug-taking
hippie community centred round The Antiquary pub on St Stephen Street,
known to everyone as 'The Auntie Mary'. Back on the schemes he saw his
own age group getting into drug-taking and stealing and he made a deliber-
ate attempt to get away from it all. He was rejected at the Army recruitment
centre because of his police record; on overhearing his mother say he would
try to join the American army, the recruiting sergeant advised them to go
somewhere they knew people and get someone to confirm that they had
known him for two years. He joined the army from Manchester, where his
uncle's neighbours obliged. In nine months he went from being a Sid Vicious
lookalike, with red-tipped points in his spiked hair, to standing to attention
in a bearskin.

Then at the age of 19, he was posted to the Falklands for active combat
duty. Nothing had prepared him for brushing this close to death. He saw
what bullets could do to a body. He thought hand-to-hand fighting was
a thing of the past, but he was ordered to fix his bayonet, with which he
killed an Argentinean who was manning a machine gun. He cleared the
dead, friend and foe, from battlefields. The bodies froze quickly in the cold.
He found some hash in the pockets of a dead Argentinean. He smoked it in a
trench with a ringside view of the aerial attack on Mount Longdon: stoned,
'it was the best show I ever saw'. Guarding captured Argentineans, he fell
into conversation with one of them. Recollecting the conversation later, he

came to the conclusion that he was fighting a politicians' war: Thatcher, with unemployment problems and Galtieri with problems of too many people disappearing, both found the theatre a welcome distraction. His only consolation now is that he played a part in toppling Galtieri. Shortly after this his leg was broken as his unit came under an infantry mortar attack.

Looking back on it, being sent to the hospital ship was the defining turning point of his life. He recalls the moment when he had a tap on his waistband. Looking down he saw a double amputee, and this was the moment he first thought about his future after the war. Although not badly injured himself, someone told him to call out for Omnopon, an easy-to-issue opiate painkiller. The nurses and medics were not set up to deal with needy, manipulative, deceitful patients. He acquired a habit in the six weeks on board before the ship berthed at Montevideo and he was flown home. There were excellent facilities at Woolwich Hospital for alcoholism, and none at all for drug addiction. It was on several day leaves from the hospital that he acquired HIV, shooting up with the hippies. He told the padré that he had a problem with drugs, and shortly afterwards he was asked if he wanted to leave the army. Without being given time to consider his options or take advice, he left, signing away his pension rights and such treatment as may have been on offer for Post-Traumatic Stress Disorder (PTSD). He heard later that three of his mates hanged themselves, presumably unable to handle the effects the war had on them.

Fred went to Liverpool, to be with the girl he had had a child with before the war. Living with her, their son, and her parents, he couldn't settle and he caused problems. Quite rightly, he says, he was put out. He was homeless for around a year – not so difficult for an ex-soldier. One day he stole the Liverpool Lord Mayor's chair from the city chambers. As he was lugging it out of the door onto the street the security guard challenged him. 'I'm taking it for repairs' he said. The security guard asked him to tell his boss to give him more information. The next day's *Liverpool Echo* reported that an Irishman had stolen the chair. Fred bought a few grams of heroin with the proceeds. The chair was recovered, unharmed, a little later. He was sent down for 18 months in Walton prison for burgling a solicitor's office. In the safe they found some photographs of a swingers' party, and his mates wanted to try a bit of blackmail, but Fred was only in it for easy money. At the court appearance he looked for help from the army – in the event the officer expressed the view that he had let down the regiment. He remembers sitting in a cell in Walton prison with two others, reading in a newspaper that one in three people with what it called the new 'Gay Plague' would die within a year. One of the others in that cell died of AIDS in 2010.

He was discharged to Edinburgh, where he saw the drug scene had changed from being reasonably relaxed and friendly to becoming violent and dangerous. He knew people – for legal reasons, he refuses to discuss whether he was one of them – who went to Glasgow to pick up consignments of heroin, running the risk of being charged with dealing if caught, and attracting a sentence of seven or eight years in prison. Telling the police who he was running for would attract a different sort of punishment. He used to buy his own stuff at The Gang Hut, which he remembers as somewhere near Albert Street. It had a heavily reinforced door – you knocked and asked through the letterbox 'anything happening?' Money went in first, then out came the wrap of heroin. Secondary dealing was done in nearby pubs – Fred remembers The Central Bar at the Foot of Leith Walk – by people who weren't set up with the security of a flat. He sold on one of his own purchases, spinning it out with some contaminants (cutting it), which he regretted, and he says he didn't repeat it. Later he got to know the people in The Gang Hut, and spent days in there, with everybody briefed on how to flush incriminating items down the toilet in the event of a police bust.

Diagnosed HIV+ by now, Fred wasn't expecting to live more than a year. His biggest fear was contracting Kaposi's sarcoma, a cancer causing foul black lesions on the skin. But he was persuaded to be positive about his condition, and he says he was the first heterosexual to join a self-help group for what was then known as GRIDS (Gay-Related Immune Deficiency Syndrome). After his initial embarrassment, he began to like the gay men and he felt comfortable in their presence. And they were indeed very positive. They were good to him – they threw some wonderful parties, and they got him involved in searching for suitable premises for a hospice. They had a buddy scheme, and it was his buddy who got him out of his habit.

With more junkies being diagnosed, Fred recalls a group of them screwing up a blind trial of new medication. Dr Brettle from the City hospital confirmed to the trial group that not even he knew who out of the group was allocated the trial drug, and who the placebo. 'Naw, that's no fair' they said after Dr Brettle had left, and they tipped all their tablets onto a table, mixed them up, and each went home with the correct number in a hopelessly confused sample. 'Never trust a junkie,' says Fred. Now, he says ruefully, he is state sponsored junkie. For the very painful peripheral neuropathy in his feet, a familiar symptom in advanced HIV, he is prescribed an opiate. When it was initially prescribed the level was calculated as an act of mercy for a dying man. A good many years later, he is slowly, slowly reducing his daily intake.

With help, Fred produced a form of autobiography, telling of his unsettled upbringing, the trauma of The Falklands War, his heroin habit and
contracting HIV/AIDS. Many people have suggested that Irvine Welsh knew
about it and took from it the idea of a Falklands veteran amputee for the
Trainspotting episode 'A Scottish Soldier'. From Edinburgh, Fred took it to
Glasgow and London. With it he travelled to several countries, meeting the
woman who became his wife and bringing her home. Fred says 'I know I'm
not always reliable and responsible. She makes sure I eat properly, and I take
my medication. She pulls me through the bad times. If it wasn't for her, my
life would be very chaotic. In fact, if it wasn't for her, I would be dead. But,
with her, I've managed to get some good out of having AIDS. I've travelled
round the world, and been to lots of countries. I like my life now'. He lives
life on the edge in a way not many people do. In the second decade of the
new millennium, there's no doubting the lust for life of this ex-junkie and
long term HIV survivor.

Audrey's story

Meet Audrey. She grew up in a tall tower block in Muirhouse, not far from
where Welsh lived at one time. 'Pittin aw they folk fae Leith intae blocks ay
flats like that wis crazy.' She'll say one thing for *Trainspotting* the film: it
catches the way they used to sit around in the shooting galleries. She says
her social worker jokingly said they must have used her house as the set for
the drug taking scenes. The police called on Audrey in 2010 as part of their
unfinished enquiries into the 1983 murder of her friend Sheila Anderson.
Audrey had nothing new to tell them. She has never co-operated with the
police since, back in the early 1980s, they knocked her about in the Leith
police cells when she refused to tell them who her heroin suppliers were.

Having left school, in the early 1970s she often went upstairs in The
Gunner pub on Pennywell Road to join her pals using a variety of downers,
and speed, and some were smoking hash. It was good fun. Going into Leith
was her downfall. In the Kirkgate she met a boy who took her to a heroin
party. Her first shot was an overdose, but even as she came round she knew
she loved this stuff. She couldn't be waiting ten or 15 minutes for a tablet
to work – she needed the hit, the rush, that warm glow travelling up from
toe to head. Very soon she couldn't shake off a runny nose, vomiting, and
diarrhoea. She had a habit, and she knew it.

The drug scene was small and quite friendly. Audrey loved it. She knew
most of the others, and they would help each other find what they wanted.
Heroin was increasingly readily available, quite good quality, but not cheap.

Audrey easily took to prostitution; she couldn't possibly earn more by other means. She says she must have walked hundreds of miles on Commercial Street, Coburg Street, and Salamander Street, over the years. On the drug scene girls would say to her: 'I'll never sell my body.' 'Aye,' she says, 'but it wisnae many weeks before there they, too, were on the game.'

The women on the street were in differing circumstances. Audrey never had a boyfriend or a pimp, but there were plenty of girls who did.

'Why don't you send HIM out to earn?' she would ask them.

'No, he's on probation... they've got warrants out for his arrest... I don't want him getting into bother in case he gets the jail...'. Audrey was never impressed by any of this. Others worked only occasionally, for family money – a school uniform, a holiday, a big telephone bill. Audrey was one of an increasing number paying for their habit, and she kept every penny to herself. In the most responsible, sensible decision of her life, in her own estimation, she refused to have children, even though with a child she would be given her own accommodation. She knew that the mothers, with £5 in the house on a morning, would say 'Will I get the bairns' breakfasts, or will I have a shot? I'll have a shot, and we'll see about the breakfasts later.' The breakfasts never came. She calculated that either her bairns would be taken off her, or her mother would be expected to have them, and neither would be fair on anyone. She was pregnant three times, and she had three terminations. She asked to be sterilised, but at the hospital they said, 'No, you'll want a baby later in life.' She never did, and there are no regrets on that score. She also takes pride in never claiming state benefits: 'I nivir peyed intae the pot, it widnae be right tae sign on.'

She was very professional. Twenty-minute blowjobs or hand reliefs at £10 each were the best earners. On a good night she could earn £200. The young guys wanted to talk, and kiss and cuddle – too time consuming. She didn't go on the ships much, though when she did the Germans and the Americans were the best payers. Russians wanted to take a lot of time, then pay in cigarettes, liquor, or possibly hash or heroin. As her habit developed, she needed to secure her next hit quickly. She couldn't be spending hours on the ship, risking not being paid at all, and getting back into town too late at night when all her suppliers had gone home.

She didn't go into the pubs, either. She didn't drink, but, more to the point, she couldn't earn in a pub. Besides, she wasn't welcome – she went into Nobles Bar on Constitution Street for the first time to find that her mugshot was in a rogues' gallery behind the bar and she was asked to leave. A couple of times she visited uptown saunas, expecting to see beautiful high class hookers, and was astonished to find they were every bit as rough as her, track marks and all. Back on the street she encouraged the others to put their prices up. 'We've got something they'll pay for.' The others were fearful of spoiling their market, so Audrey went more expensive on her own: 'See that Audrey, who does she think she is?'

She was on the street every night, whatever the weather, Christmas Eve and Christmas Night included and even, towards the end of her career, over the New Year as well. She disliked the summer evenings the most when she had to ply her trade in full view of the passing buses and cars. She was often abused, ripped off, and beaten up. She was fully aware that what happened to Sheila Anderson could perfectly easily happen to her, but Sheila's murder made not the slightest difference to her habits or her exposure to risk. She needed the heroin and for that she needed the money. The Vice Squad once said to her 'We'll have to charge you, Audrey. Just a warning this time, but why don't you go to the Rutland Hotel, or the North British Hotel, you could earn some real money there.'

By now her health had deteriorated badly. This pretty girl was toothless and haggard – 'yon junkie wey.' She was shooting up as often as ten times a day. The veins in her arms were flat, and she was reduced to finding a vein in her foot or her groin. The laddies in the area used to steal needles and syringes from the nearby Western General Hospital, but clean equipment was very hard to come by and they kept old equipment working as best they could with Blu Tack and sticky tape. They had no real appreciation of the dangers.

In 1982 a friend who was getting good supplies of heroin from Glasgow asked her to deal for him from her flat. She had her door reinforced, and there was a man on door duty at all times. Business was good. The market was expanding explosively, with lots and lots of younger people she didn't know, and they just kept coming. She says she cut her stuff with relatively harmless glucose, but she was well aware of stuff that was cut with soap powder or talcum powder. Brown heroin from India was often cut with OXO. With anything up to £2,000 worth of heroin in her flat, made up into £5 and £10 bags, she could never defend herself against the charge that she was dealing, for which she could expect a prison sentence of six or seven years, maybe more.

Once, sitting in her flat with someone whose speciality was stolen credit cards, the police made a very sudden uninvited entrance. As it happened, she had just sold her last packet. While the police ransacked the place, she was detained at the police HQ, Fettes, where she was joined a little later by her neighbour and regular customer. In her absence he had put £5 through her door, as usual, and the police returned a wrap of Audrey's customary paper. On discovering that it contained salt, he came back to complain, whereupon the police arrested him. On the occasion of another bust she managed to hide a small packet in the roof of her mouth.

But she landed up in prison by an entirely different route. She was wrongly accused of shoplifting in St James' Centre ('if I had been a better thief I would never have become a prostitute'), but when the police ran her name through their files they discovered an unpaid fine of £35. After seeing the inside of three different places of detention in the course of a week, she decided this had to stop. She was frightened. Cold turkey was doable. Now was the time. She went to her parents' flat and took virtually nothing but water for a month.

In the summer of 1985 Audrey skin popped an analgesic tablet which went septic and gave her an enormous abscess on her arm. She had it lanced at the Western General Hospital and was sent on a bus to the Royal Infirmary. She remembers the bus was full of workers from Ferranti's who gave a wide berth to this desperate looking woman with a putrid smell emanating from her. At the Infirmary she was asked about her drug-taking habits, and she told the truth. They said they would test her for HLTV. This surprised her. What little she knew concerned only gay men, not prostitutes or junkies.

In the week until the results were known she wised up a little, and the doctor was more upset to tell her than she was to be told that she was positive. She accepted an early death as the price to be paid for 'being such a naughty girl'. She was transferred immediately to the Infectious Diseases department at the City Hospital. Her room was fumigated and the ambulance men wore masks, aprons, and gloves. If this is how the professionals treat me, she thought, how will they treat me outside? But her welcome at the City by Dr Brettle, whom she came to respect deeply, was unexpected. 'Happy birthday, you're HLTV,' he sang. It was done in such an upbeat way that Audrey's only objection was that he was a day early for her 30th birthday. He gave her hope. She thinks she was one of the first – possibly the first – to be prescribed methadone by Dr Brettle.

Heroin abuse was one problem; HLTV, as it was still called, a completely new, unknown disease, was another. On discharge she was given a list of seven instructions, of which she remembers four: no tattoos; no anal sex; don't share toothbrushes; use condoms. There was no Scottish AIDS Monitor, no Waverley Care or Milestone House, no Body Positive, no SOLAS, no agencies or support. People were dying quickly of HLTV-3, within months.

She was sent home to die. But it worked out differently. The methadone stabilised her, and she went to the Church of Scotland rehab centre at Haddington, 25 miles east of Edinburgh, where in 1987 she had the best year of her life.

The price of being stabilised was addiction to methadone. On returning to live in Edinburgh Audrey went for her daily dose of 150 mls to Boots at Shandwick Place. She became depressed and it was struggle sometimes to make the effort to go. She could have easily relapsed. She went on the game a few times for a bit of extra money. The drug scene had changed a lot and she wasn't really tempted to rejoin it. She asked her GP for help – the nurse he allocated her referred her to a social worker, the best woman she ever met, who in 1991 got her a nice wee flat in central Edinburgh which she still has. With help she reduced the daily dose of methadone by tiny amounts over many, many months. She says Dr Brettle told her in 1995 that she was the only one he knew who had successfully come off methadone.

Audrey has no idea whether she acquired HIV through sex or by injecting – but probably, she thinks, it was in 1983. She looks back on her life with some regrets. She is sorry she caused so much pain and embarrassment to her parents, even though she remembers her mum saying to her the only person she ever really hurt was herself. She has been to far too many funerals over the years, and she is afflicted by survivor's guilt. She thinks of a couple, related to her by marriage, who were happy, working regularly and buying a house. He tried heroin once, acquired HIV and passed it on to her. They died within two years of each other. She can list reels of names of contemporaries who should be alive and enjoying their grandchildren. She has Hepatitis C and she guesses this is what will kill her.

And she is fragile – once a junkie always a junkie she says. It doesn't take much of a setback to bring about some form of breakdown. When this happens – it hasn't happened recently – she goes to her GP, who is something of a specialist with long term HIV/AIDS survivors, who quickly and sympathetically offers something to stabilise her again.

Audrey summarised her interview with me: 'I ken I've fucked up my life. But it was great. I loved it. I ken I'm the lucky one. For my last few years I want to be healthy and happy.'

Donnie's story

Donnie is dead now. There were high wind warnings on the Forth Road Bridge on the day I went to meet him. He lived a few miles north of the bridge, in Fife, by himself in a large Council scheme, quite pleasant, on a hillside with a good view over the Firth of Forth, the Lothians, and the Pentland Hills in the distance. He kept himself and his flat nicely, but it was obviously he wasn't well. He had been HIV+ for several years, and he was pretty sure by now that it had developed into full blown AIDS. He wasn't going to seek any more help or medical intervention; he was resigned to death. He was friendly to me, and he seemed to wish my project well, but I strongly sensed he wasn't opening up about all he could tell me. Overall, his mood was rueful, but in flashes he was bitter and cynical.

Donnie was the youngest of his family by ten years and became a choir boy to try to please his parents, but he never felt that he got on very well with his family. What got him into the drugs scene? Naivety, opportunity and peer pressure. He failed to get into college, and he had his first shot of heroin with older people, who had been to India on the hippie trail. In the late 1970s Burntisland was his best source of heroin, there was plenty coming through the docks, Indian/Pakistani stuff. At first he was a weekend user. By then he had a professional job that involved travelling round Fife, and he bought insulin needles and syringes from the chemists which extended the excitement into his working week. Getting the syringes from different chemists without arousing suspicions was a minor triumph every time, and it became part of the build-up. He was spending more money than he could afford. He was caught stealing barbiturates from a chemist shop in Aberdour for which he did two years on probation. Other people saw he had a problem before he did himself. In retrospect he could see that he held onto his job only with the help of colleagues who, wisely or not, helped to mask the problem. He said his personality was artistic and creative, and he was never hungry for heroin; for him it was an irresistible mystery, an enticement. This sounds like a classic delusion to downplay and understate a level of addiction.

He remembered the clampdown on anything that made Edinburgh look untidy ahead of the Commonwealth Games in 1986, which had the effect of making Leith into a magnet. He remembered the thrill of catching a train – he came to recognise the Dundee and Fife crowd heading the same way – over the bridge to Edinburgh, getting off at Waverley station and jumping on a bus down Leith Walk, and the feeling that now he was in the hunt. In Leith he heard a lot of Geordie, Aberdeen and Glasgow accents, adding to the sense that he was part of an exciting scene. The girls on Coburg Street were at first good people to ask who had some heroin on sale. He would make a phone call, or go and knock on a door. But soon it became apparent that the girls had been pimped out not only for sexual services but for heroin sales as well, and their prices weren't competitive. This made it more complicated, more of a challenge, but no less exciting. Enquiries would have to be made, he would have to outwit the others seeking a score without making enemies, for they were all in this together.

He usually tried to shoot up on the premises of his supplier. It was safer that way, he couldn't be arrested for being drugged up, but he could be charged as a dealer if the police found unused heroin on him. When it finally came to shooting up, it was a strange anti-climax – the fun was over, and now he faced the lonely uncomfortable road back to Fife and whatever passed for normality.

Before long Donnie had some bad experiences. He overdosed in some-one's flat and 'ah got ma heid kicked in'. He went through cold turkey, which he found frightening. He went to London to try and hit the big time, not realising how much a backwards, downwards and outwards move it was. He stole a couple of bikes and saw the inside of the notorious Worm-wood Scrubs prison while on remand.

At this point the narrative petered out. Donnie didn't want to say any more. This was the first interview I did for this book, and it was the last I did without recording equipment. Unforgivably, I left my notes behind, and I had to drop him a line asking him to send them on. Nothing arrived for several weeks, and I gave up on them. It served me right, I thought. Then they arrived in the post. Donnie had scribbled some more details, including terminology, some of it pretty hard to decipher:

A Full Blue: an overdose by pure excess.

A'm goin hame tae Scotland: a heroin and coke overdose on the verandah.

An Oxbridge Blue or A Snowball: a massive coke and heroin overdose.

Turning the neighbourhood blue: being caught red-handed.[6]

In 1983, he wrote, he shoplifted some 'bonny red dungarees' from Jen-ner's, a posh department store in Princes Street. Proceeding at speed in a westerly direction past the Mount Royal Hotel, he was brought down 'like a snowman ready to melt'. 'Don't you run, you wee bastard.' He spent the night in 'the most solid Victorian High Street cells' before appearing in the Sheriff Court the next day, where he was fined £50.

And that, as Renton might sympathise, was when 50 bar was 50 bar (p.232), all the more painful after a night in the cells.

Composition, Threads, Tensions, Structures

CHAPTER 3

First Generation Episodes

IRVINE WELSH SPENT most of his childhood in Muirhouse, the council hous-ing scheme three miles west of Leith town centre, built in the 1960s to accom-modate families displaced by the Leith slum clearances (more on this in the next section). Like most families there, his family kept strong connections in the town they had left. He knew the Foot of the Walk, and he too had an encounter with heroin. But he wasn't a Leith junkie. From the late 1970s he spent a good deal of time away from home, mostly in London. According to his friend Sandy Mcnair, in the early 1980s there was a nasty combination of standard post-adolescent angst and the death of his father, when oblivi-on seemed like an attractive option. He had several dead-end jobs and got into trouble more than once, resulting in court appearances. However, he also worked for a London borough council, he studied at Essex University and he travelled to the USA. By the late 1980s he was back in Leith with his new wife, in a comfortable flat, working in the Housing Department of the Edinburgh council and studying part time for an MBA. It seems that he wrote approximately two thirds of the episodes of *Trainspotting* as a purposeful exercise in his rehabilitation process.

On his return from London, like many of his contemporaries from the schemes, Welsh was shocked to see how many schoolmates and neighbours were dying, and dying quickly, from heroin overdoses or the dreaded HIV/AIDS. Many people in Leith and the schemes who are now around the age of 60 can show their primary school class photographs, the smiling teacher and the bright shiny faces looking at the camera, and can point out two or three, or more, who died in this period. Welsh was quite prolific as a letter writer, and, according to John Neil Munro, was in the habit of keeping a diary. It seems clear that much of his writing was creative, and that the ori-gins of several episodes of *Trainspotting* lie here. The second part of 'Mem-ories of Matty' was published as 'After The Burning', before there were plans to compile *Trainspotting*. It revolves around Spud's remark: 'Ah've been tae too many funerals for a gadge ma age, likesay. Wonder whae's next?' (p.298).

The 'too many funerals' have not appeared in *Trainspotting*, but it had become a sad catchphrase among Welsh's contemporaries that they were going to too many. We need not doubt that Spud is speaking for Welsh and for many others. In the fiction, after 12 hours drinking 'the more reflective of them realised, all their insights pooled and processed, did little to illuminate the cruel puzzle of it all. They were no wiser now than at the start' (p.299). Welsh has said that in some respects *Trainspotting* is an attempt of his to work through the cruel puzzle.

When Welsh began to select the material that found its way into *Trainspotting*, he could choose from about 50 pieces, maybe more. Some of the remainder were published in *The Acid House* (1994) and *Reheated Cabbage* (2009). Set variously in London, Amsterdam, Leith, Muirhouse and elsewhere, we meet Euan, whose voice is indistinguishable from Renton's voice in *Trainspotting*, and who worked on the Harwich – Hook of Holland ferry. The impression that Welsh has given two names to the same character is reinforced on reading *Skagboys* (2012) (prequel to *Trainspotting*) where we read of Renton working and shooting up on the ferry, just like Euan. In *The Acid House* and *Reheated Cabbage* we also meet Begbie, Spud, Gavin Temperley, Alison, and Seeker, who is referred to but doesn't make an appearance in *Trainspotting* in order to make way for Johnny Swan. After these outtakes Welsh had around 100,000 words saved on Amstrad technology which he recovered long after it had become obsolete and which formed the basis for *Skagboys*.

Welsh identified 29 pieces for inclusion in what became *Trainspotting*. This number includes the cameos that are the 'Junk Dilemmas'. We are calling this group the first generation of episodes. Episodes that had been previously published appear in CAPITALS below. They are, in order of appearance in *Trainspotting*:

Junk Dilemmas no 63
THE FIRST DAY OF THE EDINBURGH FESTIVAL
Growing up...
Victory on New Years' Day
IT GOES WITHOUT SAYING
Junk Dilemmas no 64
HER MAN
The Glass
A Disappointment
Cock Problems

TRADITIONAL SUNDAY BREAKFAST
Junk Dilemmas no 65
GRIEVING AND MOURNING IN PORT SUNSHINE
Inter Shitty
Na Na and other Nazis
Junk Dilemmas no 66
Deid Dugs
Bang to Rites
Junk Dilemmas no 67
London Crawling
There is a Light That Never Goes Out
THE ELUSIVE MR HUNT
Easy Money for the Professionals
A Present
MEMORIES OF MATTY pt 2
Straight Dilemmas no 1
TRAINSPOTTING AT LEITH CENTRAL STATION
WINTER IN WEST GRANTON
A Scottish Soldier

It's a pretty disparate collection of voices and preoccupations and styles, yet we can pick out some patterns. 'Victory on New Year's Day' and 'Memories of Matty pt 2' are a matching pair. In the first they are going on to Matty's party after the game; in the second they are going to his funeral. The singing is out of the same stable, and the line-up of characters is pretty much unchanged. Notable by his presence is Stevie, who, aside from a reference in 'London Crawling', is notable by his absence elsewhere in the book.

In the group 'Growing Up in Public', 'Grieving and Mourning In Port Sunshine', and 'Bang to Rites' we meet both of Renton's parent's families and his brother Billy. We learn a lot: between them, this ordinary working class family straddles the Protestant/Catholic divide and the British/Irish clash. Nina is present in the first and the last in the narrative order, and a death is the central point of all three short stories.

'The First Day of the Edinburgh Festival', 'Cock Problems', 'Trainspotting at Leith Central Station' and 'Winter in West Granton' are in a group. Begbie's company in the pub in 'Trainspotting at Leith Central Station' takes us back to the suppository scene in 'The First Day of the Edinburgh Festival', and Begbie is aware of what happened in 'Cock Problems' when he urges Renton to visit Tommy. In 'Winter in West Granton' Tommy is referring to his first experience of heroin in 'Cock Problems'. 'The First Day of the Edinburgh Festival' and 'It Goes Without Saying', to which we can add the five 'Junk Dilemmas', are the only pieces in which the characters are actively involved in the heroin scene. Including 'Straight Dilemmas No. 1' and 'Winter in West Granton', which describe different outcomes of the junkie story, we have a collection of ten episodes dealing with the heroin scene.

'Deid Dugs' and 'The Elusive Mr Hunt' feature Sick Boy causing damage and offence while disguising his identity. In 'It Goes Without Saying' he is a needy junkie like the others; an oddity. Elsewhere, appearances and references to him are infrequent and fleeting.

Welsh was good at picking up scraps, building them up into short stories, giving them his own twist and working in his own characters. As they were not written for inclusion in what became *Trainspotting*, they don't advance the main storyline of the book, such as it is, and they could take place pretty well anywhere: 'Her Man'; 'A Disappointment'; 'Deid Dugs'; 'Easy Money for the Professionals'; 'A Present'; 'The Elusive Mr Hunt'; and 'A Scottish Soldier'. They provide a context for the historical community setting of the book, and they add body and colour. They are easily memorable and capable of being retold, with embellishments, according to the audience and the circumstances.

'Traditional Sunday Breakfast' was probably a writing exercise for Welsh in its own context. There are strong suggestions that the football match in question was the semi-final encounter between Hibs and Celtic on 16 April 1989. Celtic needed no help from establishment-sympathetic referees, as the angry text suggests; Hibs were well beaten, yet another disappointment in too many long years of disappointments for Welsh's beloved club. Collective amnesia was an attractive option, and it looks like this short story was Welsh's contribution to that end. In the book it is a good bit of slapstick and it introduces Davie as a character.

Six disparate episodes are fairly nuanced and complex short stories: 'The Glass'; 'Inter Shitty'; 'Na Na and Other Nazis'; 'London Crawling'; 'There is a Light that Never Goes Out'; and 'Trainspotting at Leith Central Station'. In the first three we meet a perpetrator of violence (Begbie) and a victim of violence (Spud). In the other three there is a mood of anomie, alienation, dereliction and demolition.

There are two recurring themes in these 29 short stories. Violence in various forms is a significant issue in around one third. We have domestic and behind-closed-doors violence: Begbie on June, for instance, and Billy on Sharon, and it spills out into the public arena in 'Her Man'. Billy clearly is no stranger to physical *force majeure*, neither with Mark as they were growing up nor with his mates, as Jackie discovers in 'Grieving and Mourning in Port Sunshine'. Billy dies a violent death within the institution of the army, and violence is not far away from Uncle Charlie at the funeral. The violence on the part of the Orange Order in the Persevere pub is quasi-institutional. Violence is provoked by way of hooliganism in 'The Glass', and there are random, vicious, small scale acts of violence in or near three railway stations: in narrative order Waverley, King's Cross, and Leith Central. There is violence, or the very close threat of it, in pursuit of criminality in 'Easy Money for the Professionals'.

Almost as prominent as violence is the heroin scene. We are taken into two shooting galleries, in one of which a baby dies in the squalor. The 'Junk Dilemmas' drag us deep into the horrors of addiction. The identity of the voice is not always clear. Most of them are given a sharp introduction in the last line of the preceding episode, making clear the junkie's need for oblivion in a hard and complicated world, and well aware of the dangers even as he shoots up. Their very heading: 'Junk Dilemmas' is an ironic contradiction of their content – the recurring theme is that when it comes to junk there is no dilemma.

From 'The First Day of the Edinburgh Festival', 'It Goes Without Saying', and 'Junk Dilemmas no. 64' we gather that Seeker is Renton's supplier of choice, with Raymie as an alternative. Johnny Swan has 'vanished' in 'The First Day of the Edinburgh Festival', but he turns up as a retired user/dealer in 'A Scottish Soldier'. 'Cock Problems' describes and discusses the use of heroin, and addiction, and launches Tommy's story towards his plight in the varicose veins flats in 'Winter in West Granton'. The description of being free of heroin and addiction in 'Straight Dilemmas no. 1' is both measured and tentative. The scene in 'Winter in West Granton' picks up the HIV concerns that have only been aired previously in 'It Goes Without Saying'. The reference to Derek Jarman (p.317), an historical figure with HIV who was lengthening his days with a careful lifestyle and good eating, is more meaningful than mention of Davie Mitchell, who we have only met once, in 'Traditional Sunday Breakfast'. We have not seen Davie and Tommy together despite Renton's assertion in 'Winter in West Granton' that Davie is one of Tommy's best mates.

Renton is not involved in 'A Scottish Soldier', so this episode adds nothing to whatever narrative thrust exists. However, it earns its place in the book by providing such a vivid picture of just how squalid is the junkie scene. The anthology is brought to some sort of collective ending in the previous five episodes, all involving Renton. In order, the themes of the episodes are: early death, and no progress in understanding 'the cruel puzzle of it all'; a start made on doing without junk and a cautious evaluation so far; pissing in the dark, and heading in the wrong direction for home in bad company; a new realisation of the sordidness of the heroin scene; and a sober warning of how lucky he is to have avoided death so far. So far, so junkie. If this remained the ending(s), *Trainspotting* wouldn't be much different from the endings of *Requiem for a Dream* (Hubert Selby Jr, 1978), *Wir Kinderen vom Bahnhof Zoo* (Hermann and Rieck, 1979) or *Candy* (Davies, 1998).

Welsh was introduced to Robin Robertson, then an editor at Secker & Warburg, with whom he pressed the existing work into a shape and added a second generation of episodes to broaden the scope, add some structures and tensions, and bring it all to a new ending.

CHAPTER 4

Second Generation

Trainspotting Structure Diagram

PREVIOUSLY PUBLISHED
First Generation
Second Generation

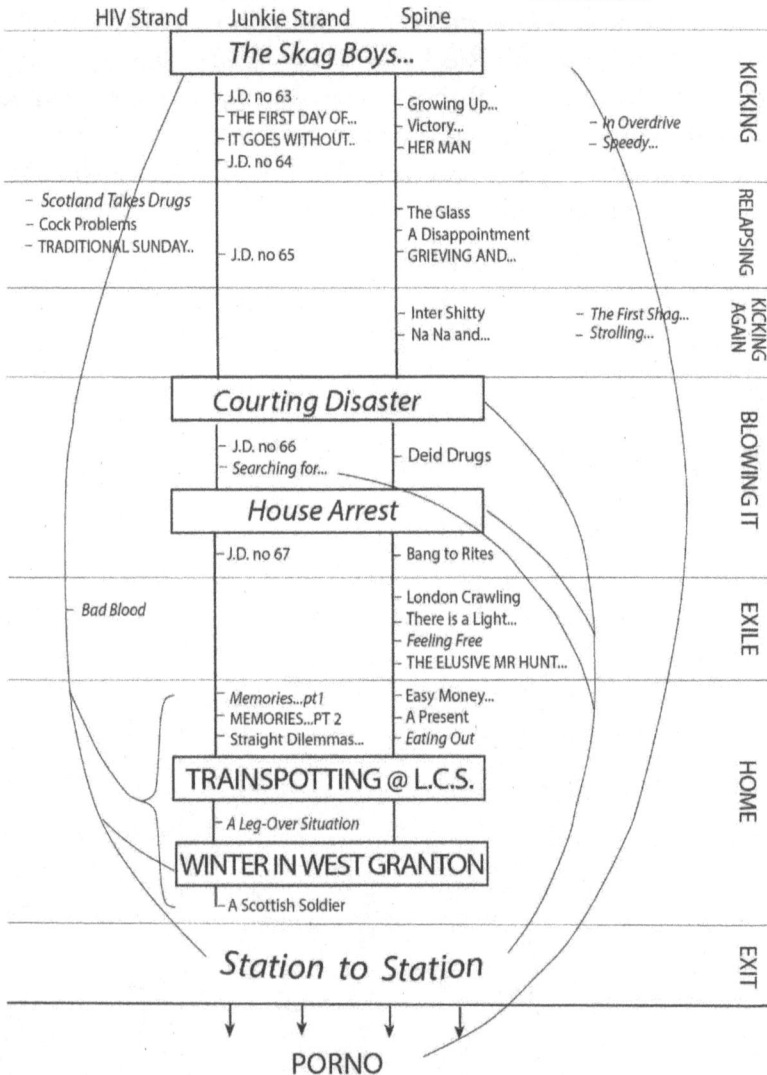

	HIV Strand	Junkie Strand	Spine		

The Skag Boys...

- J.D. no 63
- THE FIRST DAY OF...
- IT GOES WITHOUT..
- J.D. no 64

- Growing Up...
- Victory...
- HER MAN

- *In Overdrive*
- *Speedy...*

KICKING

- *Scotland Takes Drugs*
- Cock Problems
- TRADITIONAL SUNDAY..

- J.D. no 65

- The Glass
- A Disappointment
- GRIEVING AND...

RELAPSING

- Inter Shitty
- Na Na and...

- *The First Shag...*
- *Strolling...*

KICKING AGAIN

Courting Disaster

- J.D. no 66
- *Searching for...*

- Deid Drugs

BLOWING IT

House Arrest

- J.D. no 67

- Bang to Rites

- *Bad Blood*

- London Crawling
- There is a Light...
- *Feeling Free*
- THE ELUSIVE MR HUNT...

EXILE

- *Memories...pt1*
- MEMORIES...PT 2
- Straight Dilemmas...

- Easy Money...
- A Present
- *Eating Out*

TRAINSPOTTING @ L.C.S.

- *A Leg-Over Situation*

HOME

WINTER IN WEST GRANTON

- *A Scottish Soldier*

Station to Station

EXIT

PORNO

The stepping stones, introduced late in the writing process, help bring the chaotic narrative order into a pattern of strands.

WITH THE BASIC direction secure, in order to work in the second generation episodes to give some structure and coherence, Welsh now launched and separated out four strands.

Before we're off the first page of *Trainspotting* we know there is a heroin problem. In the taxi we gather our characters are not at ease in their own familiar community; indeed, at their destination, Tollcross, it becomes clear they are defensively watchful and at odds with the authorities. In the squalor of the shooting gallery the music of the day is discussed, the sadness of corrupted friendships is exposed, and sex is degraded. Behind the neediness, the relief, and the dangers of shooting up lurks the spectre of HIV/AIDS. In the first episode the context for and the main themes of the book are set out in all their immediacy and urgency.

The second generation opening episode, 'The Skag Boys, Jean-Claude Van Damme and Mother Superior', launches all strands within the book. Most of the first generation episodes fit within what we are now calling the spine of the book, from which three other strands are developed. For the most part, this is a heroin-free zone. Firstly, it establishes location, which becomes a running theme. In the first identified location, the 'Fit ay the Walk' Welsh restates his earlier intention to write a story contrasting Leith with Edinburgh, although this time it is more abstract: without saying where they are, Renton curses the festival goers who monopolise the taxis (p.4). All we know is that, wherever they are, it's downtown somewhere.

It also adds a new element to 'Trainspotting at Leith Central Station'. The taxi rank was directly opposite the ramp up which Renton and Begbie go for 'a pish', and where Begbie's father utters the eponymous word. So in the episode that was written first, Renton is brought back to where he begins in the second to be written. In his journey up Leith Walk in 'The Skag Boys...', indulgently taking a taxi to a shooting gallery, he is fearful and desperate. On the reverse journey, walking home after a train journey, he starts out in confidence. He deals easily with problems and threats, and looks back on his junkie past as he passes Montgomery Street and Albert Street. He is even in a position to help an old friend. Renton is much better. But still Leith has nothing to offer. The episode we read first in the narrative order is required to bring all this out of the one we read second.

But the episode 'Trainspotting at Leith Central Station' is no longer the end nor the main focus of the book. With 'Courting Disaster' and 'House Arrest' aimed at 'Station to Station' and faraway London, Welsh ensures that the Foot of Leith Walk sees some action in both, making them clearly stepping stone episodes. The second pub in the après-court celebrations is at the Foot of the Walk (p.172); we are taking it that it is the Central Bar. Some time later, on his first public appearance after doing cold turkey, Renton 'run[s] intae Mally' at the Foot of the Walk (p.203). The Foot of the Walk is the first location to be identified, is the most emphatically identified in the episode with the eponymous utterance, and comes into the two key link episodes.

'The Skag Boys...' launches the junkie strand before we get off the first page. Johnny Swan, his unpleasant character having been sketched out in 'A Scottish Soldier', has been chosen as the story's dealer, so Raymie and Seeker have to be written out. Welsh hits on the clever idea of Sick Boy's theory that Raymie and Spud may be the same person because they are never seen together (p.8). Together with the first generation 'The First Day of the Edinburgh Festival' and 'It goes Without Saying' we now have a collection of junkie stories, (we can hardly say they fit together well enough to make a sequence), along with the 'Junk Dilemmas'. It all comes to a climax in the second generation 'Courting Disaster' and 'House Arrest'. Matty's funeral contains a multi-faceted reflection on the junk scene as well as serving to bring together the four main protagonists (without Sick Boy, whose absence has been referred to in the previously written 'Memories of Matty pt 2'). The newly created 'A Leg-Over Situation' bookends the shooting gallery in 'The Skag Boys...'. Johnny Swan, with his sexual fantasies in Thailand still intact, reviews various things and people since the first episode; Renton realises how sordid and dangerous the junkie scene is and he checks out with his closing words: 'It's time ah wisnae here' (p.314).

The third strand to be launched in 'The Skag Boys...' is the HIV strand, only alluded to in the first generation of episodes. After the dangerous 'trust game' of sharing needles, there is an anxious discussion about who is infected. This strand needs characters to carry it: wee Goagsie is introduced, and Tommy and Davie Mitchell arrive simultaneously in 'Scotland Takes Drugs In Psychic Defence'. Thereafter it takes different directions and comes to different endings, in 'Bad Blood', 'Memories of Matty', and 'Winter in West Granton'. In the last we see of Davie, he hopes to be a long term survivor. Alan Venters, who knowingly passes on the virus, and Tommy, who becomes HIV+ by shooting up, bear the wrath and fury of mainstream society in their different fates: one murdered in his hospice bed and the other left to die in filth and squalor. Matty dies with HIV but that's not why his death is unlamented outside his family.

We have put the episode 'The Elusive Mr Hunt' into the first generation because it is a Sick Boy story, written before Welsh develops Sick Boy's character that he needs for the sequel, *Porno* (Vintage, 2003). Now Kelly is introduced in the 'The Skag Boys...', and Welsh goes on to write two additional episodes involving her, to make a group of three. Two second generation episodes make something of the feminist implications of this abuse, of which Kelly bears the brunt. In 'Feeling Free' Kelly is verbally abused again, but this time there is female solidarity. 'Feeling Free' contains the only reference to Renton without any connection to heroin – it looks like an autobiographical detail relating to the time of writing. So, twice abused, in 'Eating Out' Kelly wreaks revenge on behalf of her sex, and how! Kelly, with academic ambition, regarding her evening shift in the restaurant in 'Eating Out' as fieldwork for her essay on the subjectivity of morality would not be far from Welsh's own daily experiences. These two episodes don't advance the main storyline, but they do contain some feminist assertions with Welsh's characteristic upbeat insolence, which helps fill out the book.

Dianne is introduced in 'The First Shag In Ages'. She is younger and in the next generation as far as drugs and music are concerned, which is both a counterpoint to Renton and a necessary forward step. She is the future, literally; she plays a bigger part in *Porno*. After being such an attractive addition to the storyline in 'The First Shag In Ages' she is mentioned only once elsewhere in *Trainspotting* – in the next episode: 'Strolling Through The Meadows'.

The freestanding short story 'Speedy Recruitment', in which Spud and Renton masterfully sabotage their job interviews, is an outlier. It is written by a confident author in a sophisticated format with two voices as well as the omniscient narrator. It scores heavily in establishing Spud and Renton as firm friends, which is important in Welsh's future plans.

The second generation episodes contain information that goes some way towards marshalling the otherwise chaotic and patchy first generation. For example, without the information that Billy has 'signed up tae go back intae the fuckin army' (p.123) and that's he's going to Belfast, contained in 'The First Shag In Ages', and without learning in 'Courting Disaster' that 'he'd got his lemon, Sharon, up the stick' (p.171), his funeral and the context for it would come from nowhere. Similarly, we hardly know Matty. Spud's observation in 'Strolling Through The Meadows' that they can't be happy around Matty (p.156) helps to set the background for his funeral. The second generation of episodes also contain information that fills out some background about the central figure. In 'The First Shag In Ages' we learn that Renton has been to Aberdeen university, blowing his grant on prostitutes and drugs; before that he was a chippy, with Ralphy Gillsland; he is a vegetarian; and he declines to disclose to Dianne's parents that he is presently engaged in quite a sophisticated scamming of government benefit schemes. In 'House Arrest' and in 'Searching for the Inner Man' we learn about his profoundly disabled wee brother Davie, who has died. All this fills out the young man we are getting to know, but it has little to do with *Trainspotting*. Actually, they are scraps of background which are expanded in the prequel, *Skagboys* (Jonathan Cape, 2012), where we realise that they are well worked out and integrated parts of his character and background.

We should not expect the first generation of episodes to remain intact as originally drafted after they have been requisitioned for use in an integrated volume that was conceived later. Thus 'Cock Problems' must be counted as something of a hybrid between the generations. It seems clear that at least the bones of the main incident – Tommy fatefully asks Renton for a shot – were in place when 'Trainspotting at Leith Central Station' and 'Winter in West Granton' were written. Probably the background of the stories of auld Baxter the landlord, and of Begbie, Lizzie, and Morag Henderson were also pretty much drafted. However, as we shall see, the (distinctly Kierkegaardian) philosophising, the awareness of 'cunts wi degrees and diplomas at the Royal Ed[inburgh psychiatric hospital]' (p.89), the advice to make that his first and last time, and reference to a full house of other drugs in the last thing Renton says to Tommy, all come from the second generation. There is also a problem with 'Traditional Sunday Breakfast'. The references to drugs and alcohol (p.92) should put it into the second generation. But it was published separately, before *Trainspotting*.

And there is a clear-cut example of late editing of an already written piece in 'Bang to Rites'. Omit the paragraph beginning 'It's weird by the graveside...' (p.211) and the three short sentences two pages later which explain why Tommy, Spud and Mitch are absent from the wake, and you have the stand alone first generation piece. We are left saying that these episodes contain elements of both generations of writing, and they represent a phase in the transition from a collection of short stories to the whole book.

The list of Sick Boy's friends – Spud, Second Prize, Begbie, Matty and Tommy (p.30) – in 'In Overdrive' does not read like Sick Boy's friends, some of whom have very small association with Sick Boy indeed. Rather, it reads as a roll call of characters that Welsh needs to squeeze into one sentence to help him through the storyline he is now developing.

By this stage in the authoring process, heroin was going out of fashion, to be replaced by MDMA (Ecstasy), and retro-virals were proving to have some efficiency in delaying the worst effects of HIV/AIDS. Life after junk and life with HIV were both emerging as possibilities; this was the changing situation around Welsh, and, at least in part, he was experiencing it personally.

But Welsh is not only filling out what became *Trainspotting*; it is quite clear that he is preparing the ground for the sequel, *Porno*, set ten years after 'Station to Station'. In *Porno* Sick Boy is the central character, and Welsh needs to establish the foursome of Renton, Sick Boy, Begbie and Spud as a friendship group that reassembles, after a fashion, in *Porno*. So in the second generation of episodes he needs to expand the character of Sick Boy and Spud, and somehow run the foursome together, disparate as they are. So far we have only seen Sick Boy going in for recreational hooliganism, principally in 'Deid Dugs' and 'The Elusive Mr Hunt', but for *Porno* he needs to be sexually voracious, exploitative, utterly cynical, and, as it turns out, ambitious beyond his abilities. *Porno* needs more depth in Spud's character than the gormless sometime dope-head we see in 'Na Na and Other Nazis', 'Easy Money for the Professionals' and 'Memories of Matty pt 2', all of which he ends by being confused. This is discussed more fully in the character profiles.

With all the strands explicitly launched in the opening 'The Skag Boys...', Welsh has the subtlety to launch a theme that runs throughout the book. Johnny Swan's dictum which so impresses Renton: 'Nae friends in this game. Jist associates...' (p.6 and p.11) is more than a narrow job description for himself within the junk scene; this is played out in all three strands. The junk scene and being a junkie is friendless. Being HIV+ is to be rejected. The action in the most emphatically identified location of all, Leith Central Station, takes place in darkness and out of general view. Leith is alone. Victims of violence suffer alone. And at the very end Renton is on his own, homeless and friendless – positively this time – on the ferry to Amsterdam.

Episode and section headings

Welsh has made it explicit that he gave the title of his first episode 'The Skag Boys, Jean-Claude van Damme and Mother Superior' as a tribute to John Byrne's stage play *The Slab Boys*, first produced at the Traverse, Edinburgh in 1978, a good 20 years after the period in which it is set. It centres on young men, much like Welsh's characters, who are stuck in a boring job in Paisley, near Glasgow. They describe their aspirations and are brought down to earth: 'You'll learn, flower... you're young yet. You can afford to sift through the dross... till you come to the real rubbish at the bottom.'[7] The laughs and the sadness are never far apart, a model Welsh seemed determined to emulate.

It is possible that the title for the episode 'A Leg-Over Situation' was inspired by a memorable moment in British live radio broadcasting. In August 1991 the England cricket team was playing the West Indies in a Test match at The Oval, London, when an English batsman, of whom several allegations about his sexual exploits had been made, was given out in unusual circumstances as his inner thigh knocked the bails off the stumps: '...he couldn't quite get his leg over', as the commentator accurately described it before realising the double entendre. The commentary box, and the listening public with it, collapsed into helpless laughter. There is no evidence whatsoever that Welsh knew about it, but it is quite possible that he did, and it would be typical of him, with his customary alertness, to catch the expression and use it as the title of the piece he was writing – although the content makes the title work towards a very different end from anything connected to the radio moment. The date of the radio incident certainly marries with the proposition that this episode was written late.

The search for a pattern or meaning in the section headings is probably futile; it's impossible to fit such disparate episodes thematically under single headings. A stand-out example is 'Searching for the Inner Man', which paves the way for the ultimate release and redemption, buried deep in the section 'Blowing It'. 'London Crawling' followed by four episodes that are firmly set in Leith and Edinburgh, are in the section 'Exile'. 'Home' is dominated by episodes in which nothing goes well for Renton, and he progressively leaves. There have been some suggestions that the section headings use football parlance, but 'Kicking It', 'Kicking Again' and 'Home' are the only two with much association with the beautiful game. 'Kicking It', 'Kicking Again', 'Relapsing' and 'Blowing It' could be taken to come from junkie language. Section headings seem to want to imply a narrative progression which barely exists.

Trainspotting and History

The analysis that the episodes of *Trainspotting* were written in two generations resolves a matter that has vexed far too many commentators: how to discern a settled narrative and thematic order within *Trainspotting*, which, they say, since it contains so many topical references, should fit within history. Being sharp-eyed and taking the words at face value doesn't always help. Spotting that in the first episode the taxis at the Fit at the Walk are all up town at festival time, many people insist that the second episode must be set one year later, because of its title and based on Renton's reflection: 'Ah remembered that somebody sais that it wis the first day ay the Festival. Well, they certainly got the weather for it' (p.27).

This is a misreading. Renton's reflection is a variant of a little story with which Welsh would be familiar, of which this is another: Two Scottish soldiers sweltering in the North African desert during the war. The Leith man asks his pal:

'Is this the second Saturday in June?'

'Aye. How?' (why do you ask?)

'It's Leith Gala Day.'

'Aw. Nice sunny day they've got for it, mind.' It serves as a gently ironic reminder that whatever goes on in the rest of the world, one is left to deal with one's own situation. It fits well in a book about heroin: realities get mixed up. It is in this sense that Renton's reflection relates to the last line of the episode: 'it really is time tae clean up...' (p.27) thus securing the thrust of the episode by referring to his opening intention to stop using heroin. It certainly doesn't determine the fictional time setting.

One published commentator, trying to squeeze the contents of *Trainspotting* into chronologically correct historical and logical narrative order, insists that Welsh has made a mistake in 'Scotland Takes Drugs in Psychic Defence' by referring to Iggy Pop's *Neon Forest*, released in 1990. He maintains Tommy and Davie must have gone to Iggy Pop's gig in Glasgow on 15 December, 1988 because it had not been decided to demolish Leith Central Station until late 1988, and there is a good deal of narrative that consumes real time between the two relevant episodes. There is no mistake and no anachronism. 'Scotland Takes Drugs in Psychic Defence' was written after the 1991 gig and it appears in *Trainspotting* in front of pieces that were written, and are set, earlier.

This does give rise to an anachronism that runs throughout the book. The clearest example comes in the second generation 'In Overdrive': when, because of the new retro-virals it was possible for the 'buftie' to maintain that HIV 'was no death sentence', which could be no earlier than late 1990, it was no longer possible even for an arrogant young man like Sick Boy to maintain that 'there's no way you can get HIV... through shagging a lassie' (p.31). The high profile and hard hitting 'Don't Die of Ignorance' campaign had been running since early 1987.

Fiction is under no obligation to stick to historical sequences, however closely it may be inspired by or even attached to historical events. While Welsh keeps pretty closely to historical and geographical detail within most of the episodes and dealing with most issues, it is important to recognise that *Trainspotting* does not contain a reliable historical timeline in the matter of HIV/AIDS.

CHAPTER 5

The Bastard Twins

'BAD BLOOD' AND 'Station to Station' are so distinctive in the book and similar to each other that we can call them bastard twins. They both contradict the prevailing ethics of the book; they are both directly influenced by outside sources; and they are the only two episodes that come to well worked upbeat endings. 'Bad Blood' brings the HIV strand to an ending that was emerging as a possibility at the time of writing, and 'Station to Station' wraps up the whole book.

We can be clear that 'Bad Blood' was written no earlier than January 1991, since Milestone House, the hospice where the climax of the action takes place, was opened then, with its yellow brick approaches, the same year that Bret Easton Ellis's *American Psycho* (Picador, 1991) was published. We know that Welsh read it, and Davie Mitchell's treatment of Alan Venters and his wee son is an echo of Patrick Bateman's casual sadism. Having implicitly condemned violence throughout *Trainspotting*, we find ourselves invited to sympathetically identify with and even approve of a murder. We slip into it easily; along with many in mainstream society, we share Davie's fury and resentment at Alan Venters' behaviour to the point of believing that being murdered in his hospice bed after the torture of seeing the (faked) abuse of his son is no more than Venters deserves. By 1991 the prospect of living long term with HIV was emerging as a real possibility, and Davie's optimism at the end is designed to contrast with the fates of Matty and Tommy; Matty and Tommy are the 1980s story, and Davie is the future.

More of the whole book is invested in 'Station to Station', the title obviously inspired by David Bowie and his sound track contribution to the film *Christiane F.* (Edel 1980) and his album with this title. This is not another open ended episode with which we have become familiar; Welsh's task was to get Renton from wherever he was after the endings of the various strands onto a ferry to Amsterdam with a whole new future in prospect. Again, he crashes the narrative gears and swerves out of literary lane. Having deplored drug dealing, personified in the cynical and unpleasant Johnny Swan, now it's fine for Renton to be a bigger dealer than Johnny Swan ever was, and we don't care about the predicament of the smaller dealers and the addicts at the end of the trail, even though our hero was so recently one of them.

In a gesture towards holding the whole book together, Welsh works in details from the first generation of episodes: the Benidorm lighter, Spud's Republic of Ireland strip, remarks about Begbie and shell suits and Pitbull terriers, among others. The explanation that 'labdicks', meaning 'police', is taken from 'Lothians and Borders Constabulary' (p.333) feels clunky; there have been several uses of the term in the book, and one suspects that Welsh has been told that his readers haven't got it, and this is his last opportunity to explain his little joke. Welsh takes a final opportunity to bring in an HIV+ prostitute (p.326), which fills out the historical authenticity of the book as a whole. We learn that Sick Boy's mother is Italian, which seems to explain why he occasionally breaks into simple Italian and refers to himself as 'Simone'. But Welsh disobeys the rule not to introduce new unnecessary detail at the last gasp. He records a dispute with people we don't know at a place that hasn't been mentioned, The Fiddlers (p.330). This looks like a tribute to Welsh's drinking partner Sandy Macnair, with whom Welsh spent some time in pubs in West Port and Grassmarket, where The Fiddler's Arms is situated. On the second to last page there is reference to an incident in The Vine (p.343); there is a Vine pub on North Junction Street, Leith, but it has never been mentioned before. These two references feel like a final look back over the shoulder to Edinburgh and Leith as Renton heads off to the great unknown.

The journey to Amsterdam is an implicit expansion of the metaphor that was born in the last line of the first generation episode, 'Trainspotting at Leith Central Station': '...[on Duke Street] neither ay us looking back once' (p.309). Leith is a place to leave behind. There are no prospects there. Only no-hopers remain, the talent gets out. In the dead heart of Leith, in the dark, with no plans, Renton was going nowhere. The soundtrack connecting Duke Street to the ferry to Amsterdam is the Leith-born singing twins Craig and Charlie Reid as The Proclaimers' *Letter from America* (released 1987), which lyrically conveys concerned well-wishing from one who recognises there is nothing left in Scotland to keep the young ones. To paraphrase The Proclaimers: 'Kirkgate no more, scamming no more, Leith no more...'

And there are problems with the plot. Why on earth would Seeker (so, having been discarded as the dealer for the main part of the book, a dealer we know about but haven't met comes in handy here) part with a consider-able quantity of uncut Colombian brown, 'a once-in-a-lifetime hit'? (p.328). From what we gather, Seeker is well capable of cutting gear and taking the profit himself (p.57). Even Gilbert, who has never met him, reckons he is desperate and daft (p.340).

Further, it is an unpromising line up of characters to pull off what most of them appreciate is a pretty dangerous criminal act which could earn them all several years in prison. We hardly know Second Prize. Although he has appeared before, we find out more about him now than anywhere else in the book. His dedication to alcohol, not heroin, and his almost-permanent state of inebriation make him not only a social bore but also a major security risk to the whole enterprise. He seems to be present only because he puts up the money (p.342) – a criminal injuries compensation board payment, which we don't know anything about but we do know such payouts don't come easily. This is an implausible detail. Welsh was hard pressed to find someone we have come across who could put his hands on the sort of money that the plot of this short story needs.

Spud and Renton are bombed out, and are similarly useless and dangerous in any operational sense. Begbie's criminal tendencies commend him for the project, although he has never had anything to do with heroin. His style is violence and physical acquisition, not planning and negotiation. Really, he should know that drug dealing is specialist business. Sick Boy's cynical opportunism qualify him for inclusion, indeed the sale is made though contacts of his; but here, too, his low level thieving could attract unwelcome attention. This dysfunctional group has been brought together neither by character nor by preceding plot. This episode is not far away from fantasy, or comedy.

And there are more surprises. 'Station to Station' changes the locus and the themes of all that has gone before it. Up to this point the book has been firmly located in Leith, with excursions to Edinburgh, Glasgow and London. The centrality of the Foot of Leith Walk is emphatic. The final episode carries the story to London and beyond. Back in Leith, the backdrop is a familiar, if fractured, community; now these young men are going it alone, small timers off their territory and out of their depth. So far the main recurring themes have been violence, heroin, and alcohol. The themes of the final episode are criminality and money.

Furthermore, the whole structure of the book is changed by Renton's review of his mates and his new situation in the last two or three pages: he has a perspective on everything that has happened. The story so far has proceeded jerkily, many episodes not recognising what has gone before, and with no summaries. Renton's final reflections contribute to making the whole collection of short stories into a novel while also illustrating my claim that a good deal of it was written before there was an intention to write a novel.

As the ending to *Trainspotting*, 'Station to Station' is a key episode in two different arguments. The first is that it saves *Trainspotting* from celebrating drugs, as all that unapologetic exuberance and carelessness about the pain and damage Renton did to himself and others during the course of the book seems to suggest. The hero just saying 'no' to heroin at last shows a bit of character, and that he is sorry, really. It vindicates 'society's' opinion that all he ever had to do was walk away from it, and make a clean break. Just like that. The second argument is that Renton, miraculously turning away from drugs like this, is not a real character; the last scene reduces the previous addictions and all those 'junk dilemmas' to pastiche. This isn't grown up fiction, it's a fairy story.

Alternatively, in putting Renton on the ferry to Amsterdam with a lot of money in his pocket and in the bank, Welsh has made the ending of his book into a Western. In Westerns, the good guy gets away with the swag, and you can forget about the losers. The only significant departure from the Western genre is that Renton is not heading into a sunset at the end of a story, but eastwards to Amsterdam in a new dawn and a new day. Renton is now cast as the lucky one, the one who got away. Is it a serious depiction of the proposition that breaking out of poverty brings with it the possibility of options and autonomy? Does it go as far as acknowledging that there may be something in the Thatcherite motto 'Greed is Good'?

And let's be clear: this is no junkie narrative. Although the junkie time-lines have been chaotic throughout the book, on the whole the characters have had intervals of undisclosed proportions between being smacked up and being able to take part in their wider surroundings. In 'Station to Station' we are asked to believe that Renton can be 'smacked out of [his] eyeballs' (p.328) before he boards the bus, can shoot up again in some desperation in the back of the bus, and yet be cool and composed enough to make off with the proceeds of the sale within what purports to be no more than 24 hours. This is not the real end of a junkie story. Junkies certainly can, and do, break their habit, but not like this. The optimism and confidence of the ending is at odds with the ending of nearly all previous episodes, and the reader has learned as the book progresses that good intentions and achievements are easily reversed.

Despite all this, there is an element of real junkie truth in the final episode. Recovering junkies do indeed have to leave behind their old lifestyle and their erstwhile companions, always in a painful way. Look at the endings in *Wir Kinder vom Bahnhof Zoo*, *Candy*, and *Requiem for a Dream*. It's a matter of survival, and whether the parting is consensual, or forced, or a matter of perceived betrayal, if the protagonist is to have any future at all, permanently departing the scene has to be done.

With all this in mind, this is a resurrection story. There is a question of whether or not the story of Jesus' resurrection from the dead is a true account of events that actually took place. If it is, it broke all the laws of nature and history – single events do not make their own laws, but fall into a pattern with similar events. At its simplest, and therefore its strongest, the story of the resurrection is a narrative form of the proposition that the human spirit lives on despite everything, that evil and death do not have the last word. Welsh makes no divine claims for 'Station to Station', but it works in a similar way: breaking the laws of nature and history, it is a narrative form of his proposition that everyone, even – especially – junkies, have a lust for life. The beauty and strength of narrative is that no-one has the last, definitive word. The end of every story is the beginning of another.

CHAPTER 6

David Bowie, Soren Kierkegaard and the Professionals

THE STRUCTURE AND ending(s) of *Trainspotting* are not without some intellectual artistry. In what may seem to be an unlikely combination, David Bowie, Soren Kierkegaard, and professional counselling are at the heart of Trainspotting. Neither Renton nor any of the others was going anywhere at the end of the first generation of episodes. It seems that Welsh himself was beginning to sense that he had used the activity of writing to work through his own problems with heroin; it was good and necessary work, and now the time had come to build on it and create new opportunities.

There can be little doubt that David Bowie was an influence and inspiration; Bowie, who had gone through his own addiction problems and re-emerged to reproduce his album *Station to Station* as the soundtrack to the Berlin film *Christiane F.* (Edel, 1980), which has a storyline somewhat similar to his own writings to date, including the survival of the protagonist. But Welsh wanted something better than survival. Ziggy Stardust and the Thin White Duke were dead and Bowie was reinventing himself yet again. Welsh pinned the final episode of the book, titled 'Station to Station' as a tribute to Bowie, as the target towards which the second generation of episodes and the book as a whole would be aimed. By whatever means, Renton is to be sprung from the immediate after-effects of addiction and have a new life in prospect. *Trainspotting* ends here. But Welsh is seeing further ahead; ten years later, as the sequel *Porno* opens, Renton has been in Amsterdam enjoying a lifestyle that the junkie of the early *Trainspotting* could never have imagined. If 'Station to Station' is the end of *Trainspotting*, it is also chapter 1 of the sequel, *Porno*.

David Bowie may have been Welsh's inspiration, but music doesn't work on the page. Welsh needed to show his workings. To make a start, in 'The First Shag In Ages', in which Renton is not using, he puts into Renton's mouth his own manifesto, a Bowie-like assertion of the importance and beauty of everyone. Describing his work in the social history collection at the municipal Peoples' Story in Edinburgh High Street he says he looks for rubbish that people have discarded, and, making sure it stays intact, puts it on display as real and familiar parts of ordinary life (pp.146,147).

This is a generality; now he needs to get closer to the junkie scene, and it seems Welsh had first-hand experience of a rehabilitation process to draw on. By far the most masterly literary stroke of *Trainspotting* comes at the price of causing considerable disruption to a plausible narrative sequence. Two episodes are centralised in *Trainspotting* for important structural purposes, 'Courting Disaster' and 'House Arrest', which are topped and tailed with philosophical statements. The first is a synopsis of something Renton has stolen and says he has been reading (an odd thing, for a junkie), contained in his speech to the sheriff (p.166). We're not expecting anything serious or thoughtful and it reads like bullshit. To point out that it's a bit theoretical, and it has no practical application, except it helps save him from a custodial sentence, is no more than stating the obvious: at the end of the episode he can't fight off the need for another hit (p.177).

Renton's resolve in 'House Arrest' is to leave Leith 'right away,[8] no jist doon tae London fir six months'(p.201) makes it clear that Welsh knew at the time of writing 'House Arrest' that 'London Crawling' was in place and he was aiming beyond it to 'Station to Station'. However, after some hard experiences and no immediate reward for going through cold turkey, he paraphrases Kierkegaard again: 'failure, success, what is it?... we aw live, then we die...' (p.208) at the end of 'House Arrest'.

Between these two episodes Renton has some professional psychological attention. In 'Searching for the Inner Man' Dr Forbes, Molly Greaves, Tom Curzon, and Hazel, between them take him through a process. Firstly, with Dr Forbes he develops a little clarity about his own identity, which necessarily involves an adult perspective and a degree of objectivity on his childhood experiences and family relationships. Then Molly Greaves intervenes in his behaviour, helping him to realise at a conscious level that certain consequences will flow from certain actions, which presents him with choices. His actions are not predetermined, and no-one is making him do anything against his will. It comes down to Tom to help him understand and process all this personally, as the man he is, where he stands, and to develop some sort of strategy for putting himself into a position where he can re-direct his life on his own terms.

But, in keeping with an emerging awareness that junkies were finding it difficult to accept help from professionals, it is Hazel, who was sexually abused by her father as a child and 'understands ego needs' (we might say 'the lust for life'), who sums it all up and puts it in a way he readily connects with: 'You just want to fuck up on drugs so that everyone'll think how deep and fucking complex you are. It's pathetic, and fucking boring' (pp.186,7). 'Searching for the Inner Man' is an ill fit in the narrative order of the book: you would expect all this after cold turkey and the last 'Junk Dilemma', not before. But it is not placed to fit within any narrative order. It is placed, thematically, in the middle of the book and between the Kierkegaardian brackets. It is played out in the last pages of 'Station to Station'.

Renton doesn't acknowledge it on the ferry to Amsterdam, but he owes a great debt to Dr Forbes, Molly Greaves, Tom Curzon, and Hazel. On being led away after the court hearing, Spud suggested prison would not be a problem (p.168) and in 'Searching for the Inner Man' Renton was inclined to agree (p.181). On the ferry to Holland, however, Renton would do well to reflect that Spud seems destined to be in the prison of his own overwhelming habits, however they have come about, whether he is inside or outside HMP Saughton. Now on the run, from the authorities and from his friends, acting out the resolve to leave Leith and Scotland he made to himself way back in 'House Arrest' (p.201), having given himself no options, this, apparently perversely, is freedom. Hitherto he has searched for freedom boxed in by choices determined by society: a life of mortgage payments, spirit crushing game shows, junk food, and the rest on his famous list on the one hand, and on the other a short, disappointing life, in which we have high hopes, then we bottle it, and then we die. His only answer so far has been a punkish defiance of 'society', amply articulated in the last two pages of 'Searching for the Inner Man', and heroin.

Now on the ferry to Holland, in full possession of a comprehensive review of his past, taking everything into account, using his own judgement and committing himself to dependency on nothing but his own resourcefulness (and helped by several thousand pounds), he realises things have to change (Dr Forbes). Forced into isolation, he makes choices that only he can make, and he makes himself fully responsible for them (Molly Greaves). He can take or leave behind whatever baggage he chooses. He is at liberty to reinvent and represent himself to himself and to the world (Tom Curzon). In the last two sentences of the book 'he could be what he wanted to be... [he was] ...terrified and excited...' (p.344). Kierkegaard at last! Kierkegaard says that we only come to life in sparks and flashes; that they combine and combust into our real selves only when we are off balance and in doubt. Without these moments we live short disappointing lives then we die.

It turns out Renton wasn't bullshitting when he said to the sheriff that he was 'interested in [Kierkegaard's] ideas concerning choice... genuine choice is made out of doubt and uncertainty... without recourse to the experience and advice of others... a liberating philosophy, because... when such societal wisdom is negated, the basis for social control over the individual becomes weakened...' (pp.165, 166). A lot of energy and direction goes into the ending of the book. And it feels like a lot of the energy is, as it were, autobiographical.

CHAPTER 7

The Music Trail

WELSH MADE A point of saying in response to questions from the early reviewers that music was a big influence on his writing, and I am astonished that subsequent critics have failed to take it seriously. As a literary construction, the book has obvious problems. Read as a musical composition, however, mixing genres like a DJ, it is strung together like a disco: set the mood in the first one or two numbers, followed by something for everyone and a rousing number to go out on.

Macnair says Welsh's musical 'holy trinity' comprised Lou Reed, David Bowie, and Iggy Pop, a fine counter-cultural trio, none of them innocent of heroin and all of whom went on to make their highly significant contributions to *Trainspotting* the film. The overarching musical structure of *Trainspotting* the book is shaped by Bowie and Reed. In the narrative order the first musical note, on a downbeat, is struck by Reed. Settling in to the shooting gallery at Johnny Swan's, Raymie selects Reed's *Heroin*. A relatively long song, in forceful lyrics and music it celebrates the glories and wonders of the heroin experience, deplores the duplicity and contradictions around the heroin scene and public policy, recognises the many deaths, says no-one can help him, and ends on an accepting, or arguably defeatist, note in which he is not aware, he doesn't care, and he doesn't know. A key moment comes when he sings he has made 'a very big decision' to try to nullify his life.

Reed said in 1971:

> I meant [*Heroin* and other songs] to sort of exorcise the darkness, or the self-destructive element in me, and hoped other people would take them the same way. But when I saw how people were responding to them, it was disturbing. Because, like, people would come up and say, 'I shot up to *Heroin*', things like that. For a while, I was even thinking that some of my songs might have contributed formatively to the consciousness of all these addictions and things going down with the kids today. But I don't think that anymore; it's really too awful a thing to consider.[9]

This seems to explain Renton's remark: 'The bad-taste bastard [Raymie] breaks the junkie's golden rule by pitten oan *Heroin...*' (p.8).

David Bowie is first referenced on the bus to Mikey Forrester in 'The First Day of the Edinburgh Festival' as the girl's personal stereo leaks *Golden Years*, from his album *Station to Station* album with its reassuring, positive message of recovery from unstated dangers and good times ahead:

Don't let me hear you say life's takin' you nowhere – Angel...
Look at those skies, life's begun, nights are warm and the days are yu-hu-hung...
(p.133)

Bowie was no ordinary performing celebrity. Certainly in his early years, mental health was an issue for him, and later he was as comfortable in the surreal as in what the rest of us call reality. Tributes and obituaries in January 2016 were full of testimonies from people whom Bowie had taught that fat people, thin people, ugly people and, yes, junkies, are beautiful people. In his Berlin years, in the 1970s, he went from addiction (mostly to cocaine) to reborn independence, emerging as a living example of refusal to comply with any damn thing; that means resisting demands to determine your very identity, including your sexual identity. He lived intensely in his present moment, with his antennae alert to glamour, dress code, expedience, music, drugs, of course, and always anticipating the next things. He taught a generation that in the personal or artistic endeavour it's better to try an idea and risk looking silly than not trying at all. Let's say that in giving the final episode the title 'Station to Station' to his speculative, connected and pretty chaotic collection of stories that became *Trainspotting*, Welsh is a child of Bowie.

'Station to Station' forms the basis for the musical soundtrack to the film *Christiane F* (Edel, 1981), in which Bowie plays himself. It is based on *Wir Kinderen vom Bahnhof Zoo*, on the real life of Christiane Felscherinow and her juvenile heroin addiction, squalor, sex and survival in Berlin; not unlike *Trainspotting*, then, both set in capital cities and both (briefly in the case of *Trainspotting*) centred on a train station. Told as a narrative episode in Welsh's book, 'Station to Station' doesn't convince: no-one shoots up, twice, and within 24 hours or so of narrative time confidently steps out to a bright future. This is impossible. Imaginatively, however, and, carried by music, nothing is impossible. A new self, strangely breaking out from a familiar self, can enter a new future. Bringing the themes of the silent music of the book to a rousing crescendo, Welsh transforms the book from a deadbeat dead-end into an up-beat, visionary, hopeful story; it's a fairy tale miraculous escape from death. In what is not a secure, fully worked out reference – nothing ever was, with Bowie – to the resurrection, Bowie later suggested that the title refers to the Stations of the Cross. He regarded the album as a call to come home, in his case from the USA to Europe. Renton also goes eastwards, to a better place. This idea is supported within the episode in the reference to The Pogues, the Irish band that sang of emigration and immigration. There was a Pogues gig in London on St Patrick's Day, 1990 (p.338), which we can take as a time of writing indicator as much as giving the thrust of the piece another musical reference.

According to Sandy Macnair there is no doubt that the name 'Sick Boy' derives directly from Iggy Pop with The Stooges' song *Death Trip* with the line 'Sick Boy, sick boy baby, now learning to be cruel'. *Trainspotting*'s Sick Boy is dealt with separately; Iggy Pop's more weighty influence on Trainspotting is contained in the single episode 'Scotland Takes Drugs In Psychic Defence'. Many drugs are mentioned in this episode, but the thrust of the musical association is to keep heroin in play at this point in the book.

Let's go on location and meet Tommy and Mitch in the Hebs (p.74) (the Hebrides pub), opposite Waverley station on Market Street, before going to Glasgow. Sammy Dow's pub, just outside the Queen Street station in Glasgow, is still going strong, but Lynch's bar and the Saracen Head (p.74) (the Sarry Heid) have clearly fallen on hard times. This is Barra-land, the street market originally on barrows. The Irish and Catholic dimensions are still strongly present, but there is a lot of demolition and dereliction in the area now. This has always been scruffy downtown. The Barrowlands ballroom, with its retro neon light frontage which Tommy sees in a blur (p.74), was built in the 1930s for 'dancin-daft' Glasgow, but for 30 years and more it has been a small-to-mid range gig venue with a wonderful acoustic, the best in the country, many claim, greatly preferred by its aficionados to the sanitised Scottish Exhibition and Conference Centre a couple of miles down the Clyde.

Iggy Pop, the showy, strutting, hellraising, heroin-addled innovator of punk rock, who personified subversion and survival, remembers replacing 'America' with 'Scatlin' in one of his Barrowlands gigs, which gives Welsh the title for this episode. It does a lot of work in the book. It wraps up Renton's raging at the pettiness of ordinary life at the taxi rank on the second page, on the bus as he goes to score at Mikey Forrester's in 'The First Day of the Edinburgh Festival' (p.17), and his more expanded justification for heroin in the night club in 'The First Shag In Ages':

> Whin yir oan junk aw ye worry aboot is scorin. Oaf the gear, ye worry aboot loads ay things. (p.133).

This is the classic rationale, the well-worn route to addiction, articulated by many a junkie. Welsh marries history and music into the internal functions of his book: Tommy has just blown it with Lizzie, which precipitates him into asking Renton for a shot later, in 'Cock Problems'. We can see it coming.

Welsh's earlier musical roots are in punk. The punk of the 1970s and going into the 1980s was an attitude, of which music was its most prominent expression. The attitude was rejection and defiance of the status quo. If it can be attached to a single 'provocation', which was also its high water mark, it was the Queen's Silver Jubilee celebrations on 7 June 1977, ostensibly a public display of warmth, affection and loyalty to the pinnacle of nationhood, wealth and privilege, while the punks saw decay, corruption, and, well, things were just b-o-r-i-n-g.

The chief elements of punk were a do-it-yourself approach, brevity, insolence, and, pinning them all together, egalitarianism. In a major cultural break, punk was an expression of those who were using the newly available drugs – out went alcohol and hash, in came the harder drugs of heroin and cocaine. Punks cross-dressed, some had dangling chains, men wore make-up, hair was grown long and was ferociously gelled into often brightly coloured spikes. Musically, punk pulled away from the rock bands on their faraway concert stages, and their five-minute virtuoso guitar riffs. Way back in ancient history now were the lovable Liverpudlian mop-tops, The Beatles. Naturally, the big bands depended on publicity and they went on tours – they were commercial and professional – but everything purported to be as rough and ready as possible, up close and personal. Punk was smelly, sweaty, noisy, rude and in-yer-face or it wasn't punk. With so many internal paradoxes, anarchy and contradictions, perhaps punk was not so much a movement as a moment that couldn't last long. But during this moment, it certainly made some waves: in a sign that the Establishment was badly rattled, there are strong suggestions that the British pop charts were rigged to prevent the Sex Pistols' track *God Save the Queen (and her fascist regime)* becoming #1 record in the week of the Jubilee.

By the time Welsh went to London in 1978 to pursue his interest in punk as one biographer almost certainly overstated it, punk was moving into its second phase. With the departure to USA in 1978 and death the following year of Sid Vicious of The Sex Pistols, the shock element had somewhat dissipated. The Clash, if you can pierce through their ranting, addressed serious issues of the day, particularly in their most successful album *London*

Calling, released in UK 1979. Rising sea levels (the Thames Barrier was built a few years later), police violence (well documented), and a 'nuclear era' – or was it 'error'? – (an ever-present anxiety in the Cold War) are the concerns of the title track. It certainly looks like Welsh has borrowed and adapted The Clash's title to give him the episode title 'London Crawling', although the content of the episode is more of a complaint than a rant. Renton turns up in London, but the place has few charms. It crawls.

More appositely, however, we could say the book as a whole is a rant on serious issues: violence, heroin addiction, HIV/AIDS, and a youthful lust for life. Welsh turned to writing. Literature, theatre and cinema generally lag behind music and artwork (think of graffiti), which are more immediate expressions of a cultural moment or movement. In parts, *Trainspotting* can be viewed as performance literature, something close to stand-up. Or think of the book as a series of punk songs. Let's try one episode. Supply your own music – it doesn't need to be sophisticated – in your head. To go on location we can stand on the grass opposite Welsh's flat at No. 2 Wellington Place.

DEID DUGS
Pit bull, shit bull, bullshit dug,
Friend ay the dealer, nae friend ay mine.
Peaceful day in the park
But there's nae peace till this bastard's deid
By my hand.
Shell suit, shell suit, stand aside
Ugly brute in my sights.
Oh ya dancer! I got him full square
OAN HIS AIRSE!
Shean shaysh tae me ye're a beautiful shot.
That'sh you an me Shean, we're beautiful men
Cos I am the Sick Boy the scourge of the schemie
An blooterer ay the brain-deid.
Dug attached tae his maister's airm
This is real, this is me.
Baseball bat inside the collar,
A twist and a shout an the bastard's deid!
Polisman says Ah'm a hero ay sorts.
Only doing my duty, sarge, have a nice day
Cos Marianne's goannae git some stick the night!

You could try at home giving the single-incident episodes similar treatment: 'Her Man'; 'Speedy Recruitment'; 'A Disappointment'; 'Feeling Free'; 'The Elusive Mr Hunt'; 'Easy Money for the Professionals'; 'A Present'; 'Eating Out'; and, perhaps the most fertile of all, 'A Scottish Soldier'. A dark, dark number could be made out of the 'Junk Dilemmas', with perhaps a reprise from 'Straight Dilemmas No. 1'.

Punk's most iconic and enduring image is of the Queen in the run up to her Silver Jubilee as monarch in 1977, smiling, with a safety pin through her lip, punk-style. Disrespectful or what? In 'Na Na and Other Nazis' Spud mooches about on a hot day. He gravitates towards the Foot of the Walk, where stands the best known statue in Leith, modest in size but unveiled with great ceremony almost a century previously in memory and honour of Queen Victoria, Empress of India. It is also, following the Boer War, a monument to the elevated virtues of patriotism and loyalty with, in a bas-relief on the plinth, particular reference to the Leith Volunteers (the 7th (Leith) Battalion, The Royal Scots). It was deliberately placed in the heart of the town. Spud clocks her presence as 'Queen Sticky-Vicky' (p.120), which at first sight is simply a bit of youthful cheek. Is this Welsh's riposte to Victoria's remark in 1842 that Leith 'is not a pretty town'? Probably not. The several references in the book to Benidorm (Spain), a popular place for cheap sunshine in the 1980s, make something different out of 'Queen Sticky-Vicky'. There was a famous nude stage act in a Benidorm night club in which Queen Sticky-Vicky produced an astonishing range of objects from her vagina: silk handkerchiefs, ping-pong balls, beer bottles, and the rest. Welsh's 'Queen Sticky-Vicky' is a literary version of the safety pin. Let's say Spud's throwaway line is *Trainspotting*'s most punk moment.

Trainspotting is more than punk fiction, but punk fiction it is. The chaos, the ranting, the energy, the passion, the brevity, the roughness, and the insolence combine to make *Trainspotting* punk literature, perhaps the best and most famous example of its kind. As punk fiction, it is not available for conventional analysis and criticism. The whole point of punk is to defy such processes.

Having established the overarching musical structure and anti-structure of the book, we can go on location to pick up some fillers. Let's go into the Dockers' Club on Academy Street, within a very few yards of Welsh's front door in Wellington Place. We go in the function room, where music is put to work in setting the scene and the mood in 'House Arrest'. It is middle of the road, middle-aged stuff, much of it dating from Renton's parents' hey-day, appalling Renton as much as it appeals to his parents. It is the playlist you would find in any Working Men's Club in that period. One commentator says that Renton parodies the genre in describing a stage in his cold turkey: 'Ah've never known such a sense of complete and utter hopelessness, punctuated by bouts ay raw anxiety' (p.201) as a parody of Chris de Burgh's popular *Lady in Red*.

Welsh may well have had in mind some pub which had exceptional opening hours near the all-night postal sorting office on Brunswick Road for the setting of the beginning of 'There is a Light That Never Goes Out', but we'll never know for sure. The title of the episode is also the title of an album and track by The Smiths, released in 1986. There is little live narrative in the first part of the episode; it comprises mainly reflection and memory. It begins in darkness and there is no mention of the arrival of daylight. The young people move on to a breakfast transport café, from where the group breaks up. It is a lyrical, moody piece. Throughout there is a yearning and sadness: there are broken relationships, harsh judgements, anger, lost opportunities for reconciliation and love, the death of a real baby, and a dysfunctionality that, for once, isn't funny – it hurts. In putting some words from the mournful eponymous song into Spud's thoughts as he talked and walked through an underpass with Nicola after a party, Welsh makes explicit his indebtedness to The Smiths.

> *...and in the darkened underpass*
> *I thought Oh God my chance has come at last*
> *but then a strange fear gripped me*
> *and I just couldn't ask...*

Welsh has carefully worked the geography of Spud's movements to make use of the very few underpasses in Edinburgh, around Sighthill and Wester Hailes, and it is plausible enough; there were plenty of youthful and junkie (and broader) connections between that part of town and Leith.

This is the essence of The Smiths' output. They intelligently expressed and affirmed ordinariness, vulnerability, unlovableness, outsider-dom; they were a 'lighthouse or lifeline... for the weak and wounded.'[10] Their ordinariness – anonymity? – is contained in their name, deliberately chosen in contradistinction to the market-branding pretentiousness of contemporary syncopated chart conscious pop groups. In 'There Is A Light that Never Goes Out' Welsh works his own characters into a tableau inspired by The Smiths.

At the Market Street entrance to Waverley station (it was a very scruffy entrance in the 1980s), only a few yards away from the Hebs pub where Tommy and Mitch meet (p.74), we'll mark the spot where Johnny Swan sets up his pitch in 'A Scottish Soldier'. This is the title of a song in which a Scottish soldier 'wanders far away...' and dreams of home as he lies dying.

It is firmly in the realm of popular culture, often wheeled out for Scots of the diaspora and for tourists, and it is impossible to think of Welsh not enjoying the dissonance between the wistful romance of the song and the harsh realities of soldiery in foreign lands. He might well have known one or two returning soldiers from the Falklands War.

Our final stop is the Meadows. Welsh is ready to pick up scraps from all sorts of music, even a 1946 song *You Make Me Feel So Young* sung by Ol' Blue-Eyes himself, Frank Sinatra, among many others, which he slightly misquotes (p.157) to give him the title for 'Strolling Through The Meadows'.

Although there has been some sort of musical progression for the purposes of the book, this tour has been as far reaching musically as geographically, without a clear route or horizons. A happy coincidence.

SECTION III

Trainspotting on Location and Character Profiles

CHAPTER 8

Leith, Edinburgh, Scotland

WELSH HAS SAID that Renton is the most autobiographical character in *Trainspotting*. Several features point to the truth of this. We are exposed to more, and a more diverse range, of the character's inner thoughts and experiences than of any other character, and certainly his geographical movements broadly match those of his creator. He knows Leith Links and the Kirkgate; he travels the length of Leith Walk twice, in very different circumstances; he seems to be familiar with the former junk zone of Albert Street, and he has a flat in Montgomery Street which we thought he had left before the beginning of the book but he lives there in one of the last episodes to be written, 'The First Shag In Ages' (p.152) – an oddity. He is a frequent traveller to London, and from 'London Crawling', 'Straight Dilemmas no 1' and 'Station to Station', we know he is familiar with England's capital city. He declines to tell Dianne's dad that he uses his 'management skills' to fraudulently claim benefit in Edinburgh, Livingston, Glasgow and two addresses in London (p.146). Welsh has said Renton is *Trainspotting*'s 'cynical intellectual'; that might be overstating it, but we'll recruit Renton and Welsh interchangeably, local boys with a wider perspective, to give us an overview of Leith and Edinburgh.

We'll meet up with them in one of the many west-facing pubs on Shore; those north of Bernard Street Bridge, downstream, have less traffic to contend with. Let's pretend it's a sunny day, even if it isn't. That's what we do in Leith. In the year 1561 the 19-year-old Mary, Queen of Scots, landed here to claim her throne. She had become Queen of Scots at a week old, on the death of her father, James V, and her French mother had packed her off to France for safekeeping. The Scottish lords were departing from the Church of Rome and Scotland was unsettled. Married to the Dauphin, quickly widowed, and now orphaned on the death of her mother, it was bold of her to come. She said was pleased to be in 'sunny Leith'. It seems that was political spin; she had to make the most of her moment of arrival. Other reports say there was a thick sea mist, a haar in the local parlance, or a Presbyterian fog as some said. Whatever, the term 'sunny Leith' has been something of a catchphrase and a local joke, with enough legs on it to last four and a half centuries. The Leith-born singing twins, The Proclaimers say it is at the root of their title *Sunshine on Leith*, which recently generated a stage and film musical of the same name, and there can be little doubt that Welsh renames the Port o' Leith pub on Constitution Street as Port Sunshine in *Porno* as a play on and continuation of the royal utterance. 'Aye, it's sunny whin it's no rainin', comes the reply.

Access to the sea was as crucial to medieval power centres as an airport and cyberspace are today. The trouble here was that the itinerant early medieval royal family found the isolated volcanic plug in the south-east of the emerging country of Scotland to be an irresistible location for a castle; but it is a good two miles from the coast. In 1128 King David in Edinburgh castle secured by royal charter the key assets of the kingdom, including control of Leith Shore. Other assets – Holyrood Abbey, Dean Village – later lost this status; but not Leith. It was too valuable. If the lie of the land had been only slightly different, the capital of Scotland would be Leith, noted for the rocky outcrops in its southern suburbs. This was the beginning of centuries of control of the river mouth from Edinburgh castle, a deeply symbiotic relationship in which Edinburgh always had the upper hand.

Two centuries later the hero of Bannockburn, King Robert the Bruce, awarded control of Leith's trade to the burgesses of Edinburgh. Medieval trade relied on control and monopoly. This power, normally confined to control over the market within the town walls, was a quite exceptional arrangement: Leith was not free to trade on its own terms. Ever-greedy royal families, with their power to demand taxes from royal burghs, repeatedly strengthened Edinburgh's hand, always at the expense of Leith. Leith became a member of the Hanseatic League, a string of ports based on the German Baltic. The idea was that while quarrelsome kings and lords engaged in warfare which they could ill afford and which kept the populations in constant poverty, the merchants themselves would take the taxes and invest in their facilities and their communities. But in Leith's case, it was the Edinburgh burgesses who collected, and they invested in no-one but themselves.

Leith Shore is perfectly proportioned for medieval shipping. The town developed on the east bank of the river, the outside of the curve, naturally the deep water channel. To give the ships a secure berth, it was shored up – hence the name. Shore was a working dock, in the heart of the town, not a through street as it is now. A medieval street pattern developed behind it, everything except a market square. The west side of the river was given over to the trades: ship building, sail-making, warehousing, and the like, and the looser street pattern remains to this day.

When the Scottish lords broke from the Church of Rome in mid-16th century the royal French widow Marie de Guise, Regent for her daughter Mary, departed Edinburgh and resorted to Leith. She called on French troops to protect her, who fortified the town with a new style of wall, the very latest in military defences and the first of its type in Britain by ten years. Her daughter, Mary, Queen of Scots, later raised some money by mortgaging her rights over Leith to Edinburgh. Leithers helped her raise money, in the hope that on eventual repayment the rights would revert to them. It never happened. Edinburgh acquired royal warrant to give itself the power to levy taxes on the port of Leith. It survived the Union of 1707.

A century later the Cromwellian army, unable to attack Edinburgh castle, did what all incoming armies do: it cut off the capital's means of communication with the outside world. Leith was occupied for a decade. The occupying General Monck was known to have much sympathy for Leith's underdog status, and one English merchant reported that Leith was 'under the greatest slavery that ever I knew'. Edinburgh became a suburb of Leith, and Leith did rather well. Two of Scotland's earliest newspapers were published here. Glassmaking flourished: drinkers of wine the world over can thank Leith for the bottle with parallel sides, sloping shoulders and a long neck. But the Edinburgh burgesses knew that armies come and armies go, rarely leaving behind the status quo ante. Their huge payment of £5,000 sterling looks very like a bribe to the Cromwellian army to keep intact their legal rights over Leith upon the departure of the troops. It was money well spent.

From Leith in 1698 set forth the ill-fated expedition to colonise for Scotland a key piece of territory in the isthmus between the Americas now known as Panama. The idea was sound – they would transfer goods, overland, between Atlantic and Pacific. The Darien Expedition, as it was known, carried everything required: shovels, axes, ropes, pigs, horses, Bibles, representing huge speculative cash investments from all sections of Scottish society. Planning and leadership were woeful, and the whole thing was a dead loss failure. The ensuing bankruptcies were a large factor in the union of the Scottish and English parliaments in 1707.

In 1779 the authorities were alarmed that their key asset was under-defended as Leith almost came under attack from the nascent American navy, and they built some barracks known as the Fort, just up the slope from an intended naval dockyard that never materialised.

As James Scott Marshall remarks, Leith was an exciting place to live. There was no end of 'irregular arrangements' to outwit the authorities and avoid taxation on commodities going on and coming off the ships; also known as smuggling. As the 18th century wore on, Leith traders could see that the early medieval control over their home port was a howling anachronism, the last such arrangement anywhere. When it was brought to an end in 1828 the burgesses proposed to set up a private company, theirs, of course, to own the port, but Leith was having none of that. The Docks Commission had at least some Leith representation, which rapidly grew in the following years. Scotland's premier east coast port was in public hands for a brief 165 years, until 1993.

* * * * * * * * * * * * * * * * *

Without any doubt, Leith's heyday was its period of municipal independence from 1833 to 1920. Most of its prosperity came from the docks, which were built out over the low tide beach. The first merchant ship through the Suez Canal was captained by a Leither, and Trinity House proudly keeps the letter from Ferdinand de Lesseps to attest to this. Railways ran alongside every dock, so countless tons of cargo could be transferred between land and sea and on the move within hours. Albert Dock was the first in Scotland to be equipped with a hydraulic crane. There was a good-going ship building industry – perhaps the most famous Leith-built ship was ss *Sirius*, the first ship to cross the Atlantic using steam only, beating Brunel's *Great Western* by a matter of hours. The largest whaling fleet in the world set forth from Leith.

This was the century of municipalities, and Leith set about its task with great good purpose. In the early 1860s the Water of Leith at Leith was officially the most foul waterway in Scotland; not surprising since Balerno and Corstorphine used it as an open sewer, and for the several tanneries upstream it was an easy means of disposal of the scraps and fat from the hides they were working on. The town council supplied piped water, and developed its own services: transport (the trams were much better than Edinburgh's), the police service, the fire service. Slums were cleared, their replacements now well into their second century and looking good, and schools were founded, well-loved in their day. Leith Shore was one of the first streets in the world, after streets in London and New York and well before Edinburgh, to be lit by electricity. They made their own street lamps, each complete with the burgh insignia. There are several survivors on Shore and around Leith.

The Corn Exchange on Constitution Street set benchmark prices for central Scotland and northern England. Just over the street was Leith's own

Assembly Rooms, and round the corner on Bernard Street was the Leith Bank. A fine Custom House was built on Commercial Street to replace the old Tolbooth. A nautical school was established, a magnificent sailors' home was built, and the hospital was founded, partly funded by a donation and the remainder raised by public subscription. The Co-operative movement found a natural home in Leith. It financed a considerable amount of well built, good value residential accommodation for rent, some of it very popular colonies (one up, one down) in contrast to the municipal tenement stair, and Leith Provident opened shops throughout the town, providing good value for more than a century. Leith is where the first ever Yuletide card was sent and received (the more famous first Christmas card in 1843 in London was inspired by the Leith card), and Leith held the first factory making playing cards. In Leith the paint for the Forth Bridge was made. Any stranger knew by the names of the pubs when he was entering Leith on the major approaches: The Halfway House, at 72 North Fort Street, coming from Newhaven; The Bonnington Toll at 284 Bonnington Road, on the old road from Edinburgh; and the Boundary Bar at 379 Leith Walk. The names of all these pubs lasted until well into the present century.

The town's motto was PERSEVERE, adopted centuries earlier to help the people through hard times. It became strongly attached to the icon of the Port of Leith, the Madonna and Child on a ship under, variously, the sun, a cloud (the Holy Spirit), and a canopy – there is no authoritative version. The Burgh Council formally adopted the combination, and there are many examples throughout the town. It remains a powerful identifier.

Leith was the home town of most of the more than two hundred people killed in the worst ever railway accident in British history. In 1915 a troop train, bound for Liverpool and onwards to the Dardanelles, collided with a stationary engine a mile or so north of the English border. It burst into flames and fell on the north bound line, and was ploughed into by the London to Glasgow express train. Although they had not even left the country, because they were in uniform and were under orders the men on board were deemed to have fallen in action. Almost no family in Leith was unaffected. News of the accident was suppressed for fear of further depressing public morale in the middle of a war that was going badly. Leith was furious that Edinburgh refused to fly the flag at half-mast. No honorific statuary for Leithers after the war; their memorial was a children's wing for the hospital, such an ambitious project that it wasn't opened until 1927. The present Leith Gala Day and Festival are direct descendants of the week of local fundraising for the hospital.

Over the centuries of adversity and almost a century of civic independence a fierce community pride developed, an important part of which was an identity that clearly distinguished Leith from Edinburgh. In 1920 the unimaginable happened. Despite a local plebiscite which voiced near unanimous opposition to amalgamate with Edinburgh, the Edinburgh Extension Act was passed in the House of Commons. Although in a larger view it was no more than a timely bit of administrative tidying up, it took no account of local feelings. Captain Wedgwood Benn MP, spoke passionately against it in the House on behalf of the community, saying that Leith was unique. It probably was.

Such was the Leith antipathy to Edinburgh upon the demise of the Leith Council that the regalia was entrusted to the Leith Harbour Board, later transferred to Forth Ports Authority, then to Trinity House and now it is in the hands of Historic Scotland. Anywhere, obviously, except Edinburgh. In its own way, similar to Scotland after the union with England in 1707, several key institutions did not fade away, and they may prove to be the foundation for a revival of community life: the Leith Battalion of the Boys' Brigade, the Leith Civic Trust, the Port of Leith High Constables, Leith Rotary Club, the Leith Benevolent Society, among others.

About the time Welsh was born, the last sea-going ship left the upper Shore, after which Bernard Street Bridge was made solid. As he was starting at Ainslie Park Secondary School, to improve operational facilities for ships, the outer lock was installed, since when the docks and the river mouth back to a kilometre or so upstream are held at a constant level of about one foot higher than mean high tide. It removed the problem of the foul smell of Edinburgh's rubbish, brought downstream and exposed at low tide. It was more than a talking point; on bad days it wafted as far as Junction Street. However, not even this problem was completely solved; for a further 20 years, unmarked tankers regularly rumbled down Ferry Road, heading for the docks and MV *Gardyloo* for offshore dumping, leaving behind the unmistakable whiff of Edinburgh's shite.

And at a stroke Leith lost touch with the tides, a force of nature which had forged its very identity.

****

We'll take a 22 bus from the Shore, up the Champs ay Leithy to Edinburgh, the street well-travelled by Renton. It's 1993, and we are going to the Book Festival in Charlotte Square, to an event at which Welsh is reading from his new book, *Trainspotting*. Before long we are running along Princes Street, with the Old Town forming the horizon to the south.

It is pretty well the same profile that the city fathers saw in the aftermath of the failed Catholic/nationalist uprising of 1745 and 1746. They knew that the power had moved, emphatically and permanently, to London. Glumly they surveyed their now useless castle perched on a hill, the empty palace at the bottom, the echoing parliament hall in between; and all surrounded by dangerously insanitary and crowded buildings clinging to steep slopes. The new merchant city of Glasgow, on the Atlantic coast and facing the New World, was where the money now changed hands and the deals were done. It wasn't inconceivable that Edinburgh could become a suburb of Leith! They had to make their own future.

And they did. The wily old political fixer, George Drummond, gave the gifted young architect James Craig his head. Over the next half century the New Town was built, of which Princes Street is the best known thoroughfare. Determined not to let the topography dominate the layout as it does the old town, it is a grid, and the naming of streets and squares is a carefully balanced choreography that celebrates the institutions of the new United Kingdom. The generous specifications for the New Town were subsidised by the proceeds of Empire: the theft of assets around the world, the trade in sugar, tobacco, and slaves, and all topped up by welcome receipts from Edinburgh's anachronistic hold over the port of Leith.

An educated and professional class, relieved of the responsibility of running a country, put its energy into what became known as the Edinburgh Enlightenment. There was a comparable moment in Berlin and Paris, but London was too busy running a worldwide empire for such things. Walter Scott recreated the castle as a tourist attraction and in 1822 he brought royalty to Scotland for the first time in almost two centuries. In his fiction he created attractive Scottish characters, so that no longer would England look upon Scotland as rebellious and disloyal. In the 19th century Queen Victoria was at the forefront of a romantic love affair with Scotland. While rural Scotland depopulated and the west of the Central Belt and Glasgow industrialised, Edinburgh settled for being an attractive provincial capital.

Two world wars in the first part of the 20th century had a unifying effect on the various countries and regions of Britain, and it seemed in the aftermath that differences between Scotland and England would melt away in the face of advancing urbanisation, industrialisation, secularisation, and ever more rapid communications and travel. But it was a lazy and misleading assumption. As the British Empire collapsed around the world, it became clearer that England's first empire was the other countries of the British Isles, and underlying tensions began to emerge. An early sign was the theft from Westminster Abbey of the Stone of Scone. This was the stone on which Scottish kings were crowned until it was taken as spoils of war to London in 1296, both to deny the legitimacy of the Scottish crown and to assert English supremacy. It was built into a wooden throne on which English and then British monarchs have been crowned ever since. At Christmas 1950 it was stolen and taken to Scotland, where it was regarded as a rather good prank. In England, however, the establishment was apoplectic. The police knew who the culprits were but there were no prosecutions for fear of inflaming and providing a vehicle for nationalism. Before long it was returned to London.

Tensions rose again in 1953 when the new queen was crowned Elizabeth II. The problem was that this was the first Queen Elizabeth of Scotland – not a small point. The blowing up in Scotland of some new pillar boxes emblazoned with EIIR was an expression of neither republican nor anti-English sentiment, but of Scottish nationalism. Nationalist sentiment was for the most part a minority sport, although there were some colourful characters and notable successes at the ballot box. The only 'state' that most people were concerned with was the newly created welfare state. It was designed to protect people from the harshness of unemployment so vividly recalled from the 1930s, and it created a state system of care 'from cradle to grave'.

It was accompanied by the government playing an active part in modifying raw capitalism by directing major industries to where there was social and political need for them. Thus the car manufacturing plants at Linwood and Bathgate[11] and the steel mills at Ravenscraig were created and supported to offset declining traditional industries. Nevertheless, nationalist sentiment was growing and a devolution referendum was held in 1979. The two major political parties (Labour and Conservative) were unable to hold any consistent vision and policy even internally. A slim majority of those who voted on the day wanted devolution, but the proposal fell because 40 per cent of the total electorate was required to vote in favour, and it was a further 20 years before devolution arrived.

At the general election a few weeks later, Mrs Thatcher romped into 10 Downing Street on the overwhelming strength of English votes (Labour won a comfortable overall majority in Scotland). She was determined to break the government industrial/welfare interventions, and the country was exposed to the full blast of market forces. The British manufacturing base fell away in the course of one brief decade, leaving traditional communities and the young disorientated and welfare-dependant. The winners were in the service and finance sectors, predominantly located in the south-east of England and London. Scotland felt robbed, disenfranchised, and abandoned.

Welsh was awake to the shifting political landscape. Whereas it was traditionally the working class and intellectuals who voted Labour, and the well-to-do and deferential who voted Conservative, he created Sick Boy who notices the new climate of opportunity brought about by the breakdown of traditional community and political loyalties under Mrs Thatcher's governments:

"…the socialists… The Tories… Fuck that… It's me, me, fucking ME… versus the world…" (p.30).

Here is Thatcherite ideology in the mouth of a fictional character, in a passage that makes *Trainspotting*, at least in part, a diary of public life in the 1980s. Sick Boy is alongside the young man in the City who in Harry Enfield's famous satirical sketch flashes his cash for the cameras gloating 'loadsamoney, loadsamoney'.

And Welsh seems to know that it couldn't last. Discussing the clientele in a London pub with the barman, Renton observes 'It'll hit the fan one day. Thir are sackloads ay repossession orders in the post' (pp.229, 230). This was written in the late 1980s. You won't find many politicians, or even economic commentators, who saw and said how London-centred, flawed and hollow the Thatcher reforms were, or foretell how it would end, as it did, in the crash of 2008.

On the political/administrative stage, in 1974 Regional Councils had been created in Scotland in order to take advantage of the economy of scale in the delivery of services. Thus the City of Edinburgh Council, accustomed to Conservative rule as part of the natural order, found Labour policies in education and social work, among other functions, operating within the city, controlled by Lothian Regional Council. It was policy of the Labour Party to use the Regions to redistribute wealth and resources, and going in to the 1982 elections Labour in Lothian proposed to increase the business rate. The Conservatives and the Chamber of Commerce, with the active help of *The Scotsman*, drew attention to the impact this would have on small businesses and corner shops – a distraction. The real target, of course, was the prosperous financial sector, then based in Edinburgh's Charlotte Square. A proportionate rate from that quarter would have been a very welcome contribution to education and social work budgets throughout the region. *The Scotsman* ran an ongoing scare story about a 'Trot plot', an absurd misrepresentation, and on election day carried an image of a red flag over the City Chambers even though it was not a City election. This was the heyday of Thatcherism, and Labour lost control of Lothian Regional Council.

Welsh has said that his work of fiction has nothing to do with 'those fuckers up in Charlotte Square'. It isn't clear whether he meant the fuckers in the finance houses in the Square (which have since relocated), or the fuckers in the literary establishment whose annual showcase we are about to attend. We get off the bus at the last stop on Princes Street and go up Charlotte Street. The marquees of the grand, prestigious Edinburgh International Book Festival are all there, thronged by the literati. We go through the entrance opposite the end of George Street and find out the venue for this event. Welsh has already read from *Trainspotting* several times, and he knows what works for him. He reads 'Traditional Sunday Breakfast': sex and slapstick. As we leave are you thrilled that the very portals of literary greatness have been breached by punks, or do you join those muttering that this is puerile rubbish and that's the last we'll be hearing from Mr Welsh?

Irvine Welsh, Mark Renton and friends

Now we need to separate Renton from his creator. To get on Renton's trail we catch up with him in Fort House, a 1960s council housing block built on the site of the 18th century military barracks, where, it seems, he was brought up (p.190). It was almost surrounded by a 12-foot high wall – for historical reasons a protected structure – which combined with the name by which it was universally known, the Fort, to give it a palpably detached and beleaguered air. It was a single block of irregularly-angled limbs. It deserved its reputation as a rough and wild place, and in the 1980s it was a haven for drug dealers. It stood for barely half a century, another poor investment and experimental disaster of the 1960s. A vivid illustration of this is that only three of its 157 flats were bought under the Right to Buy scheme.

You would expect Renton to go to Trinity Academy from here, not, as he has it in 'Cock Problems', and Spud in 'Speedy Recruitment' to Leith Academy ('Leithy' p.63). However, because of wee Davie's special needs, the family was offered a Housing Association flat beside the river (p.190), probably somewhere near Junction Bridge. We go with him as he strolls 'self-consciously doon Great Junction Street' (p.203). This is his first outing after being a prisoner in his own home in *House Arrest*. He meets Mally at the Foot of the Walk. We don't know Mally; he's not important. What is important is that Renton is brought to the Foot of the Walk in this stepping-stone episode, to bring together theme, structure and location. To the left is the Kirkgate shopping centre which he whizzes round in 'The First Day of the Edinburgh Festival'.

But we don't continue with him on his journey to the Dockers' Club, straight ahead on Duke Street and left down Academy Street. Instead we cross Leith Walk and go in to the Central Bar just as they are singing 'There's only one Mark Renton' (p.175) after Renton's 'result' in the courtroom, echoing the chant of the football terraces in support of a particularly popular player. But is there only one Mark Renton? It has already been suggested that Renton and Euan in *Stoke Newington Blues* are interchangeable; the similarities between their voices, their experience on the ferries to Holland, their familiarity with London, and their junkie habits, are striking. Now, much later, we can add to this the young Renton's story in the prequel, *Skagboys*.

But not so fast. You couldn't get a cigarette paper between the voices of Renton and Stevie. 'Victory On New Year's Day', in which Renton is just another party-goer, is told from Stevie's perspective. He has a girlfriend in London; so did Welsh. From the way Stevie is presented at Matty's wake in 'Memories of Matty pt 2', it's clear that he goes way back in the friendships. Stevie comes up again in 'London Crawling', by which time Renton, who is by no means clear of a long and problematic acquaintance with heroin, has 'fucked up wi Stevie...' (p.230), and there may be an autobiographical element in both characters. It may well be that at the time of writing these loosely related short stories Stevie, who went to London, found love and came back to Leith only occasionally, was, *in embryo*, more of an autobiographical character than Renton.

Then there's Davie Mitchell. Davie's voice and attitude in the HIV+ group could easily be Renton's: in reply to something Tom says he thinks '*Not really, you doss prick, it was a fucking lie. I shrugged*' (p.242). His experiences in the groups are not a million miles from Renton's meetings with his therapists, and we can even wonder if Davie's group leader Tom could be Renton's Tom Curzon in 'Searching for the Inner Man'. The trajectory of Davie and Renton are similar: born to working-class parents, the two young men knew each other slightly as chippies before they both went to university. Both their fathers have their prejudices, which are problems until they both demonstrate that parental love and loyalty is stronger. We note that Stevie, Davie and Renton are the only characters in *Trainspotting* to have upbeat endings.

But Davie is not as simple as Stevie. The last mention of him in the narrative order, in 'Winter In West Granton', is, roughly contemporaneously with 'Traditional Sunday Breakfast', among the first to have been composed. The purpose of expanding his character in the second generation of episodes is to provide a different storyline and outcome within the HIV strand from Tommy dying in squalor. So in the narrative order Davie is now introduced simultaneously with Tommy in the second-generation 'Scotland Takes Drugs In Psychic Defence', in which Davie's wild part matches his voice in 'Traditional Sunday Breakfast'. But this is not what is required for 'Bad Blood'. Here we see an open-eyed, decent young man who contracted HIV through a heterosexual encounter; neither junkie nor gay. At the end of the episode Davie regrets having waited so long to become a human being and looks forward to becoming a long-term survivor (p.262). The characterisation of Davie Mitchell suffers greatly in the jolt between the two generations of writing the episodes of *Trainspotting*.

So will the real Mark Renton please come off the page and make himself known? The character is assembled piecemeal. Let's first meet the family. In 'Growing Up In Public' we get a bit of background through his cousin Nina. This is an ordinary working-class family that straddles British/Irish history and the Protestant/Catholic divide. Nina likes Renton's mum, her Auntie Cathy, who 'treated her like a person rather than a child' (p.34). She knows Auntie Cathy has her problems, with a severely handicapped son who died, and Mark, who, she has heard, is 'into drugs' (p.37) and another, Billy, who has just come out of the army.

We don't need to be told that Auntie Cathy's husband, Davie, is from Glasgow ('Gles-kay-kee-lay-thit-ye-ur') as Jocky says (p.205); we know it as soon as he opens his mouth, from the way he pronounces Portobello, the town just along the coast from Leith, as 'Portobellah' (p.34). That's Portybelly, or 'Porty' as Begbie has it on behalf of the locals (p.285). We don't have to go along with Renton's sexism, but he's dead right when he says 'The Weedjie [Glaswegian] aunties are clucking around... ah can hear these horrible accents; bad enough oan a man, fuckin revolting oan a woman' (p.213). It's true – those strange inflexions and long flat vowels jar on the refined Leith ear.

Welsh inserts what was then a stereotype cultural perception in saying that his father is a Weedjie like the others (p.191). Renton denies this, and Welsh himself, in becoming Edinburgh's literary keelie, challenged perceived Glasgow domination of working-class credentials and cultural output; a bold and sophisticated autobiographical assertion.

Davie Renton and his son have a somewhat strained but ultimately loving relationship. Paternal/filial tensions apart, Renton supports his dad: on being made redundant at least he took a stall at a couple of local markets instead of 'sittin in Strathie's Bar moanin his fuckin box oaf...' (p.190). Even so, the young man has some real opinions about his father's family's Orange connections, and he can stand up for himself in a tense situation, junkie or not. At Billy's funeral his uncle Chick harshly says 'Billy was ten times the man you'll ever be...' Renton's reply: 'If ye did gie us a kickin, ye'd be daein me a favour.' (p.217).

Renton is significant in around one-third of first generation episodes, in which, for the most part, he is not far from heroin. It's not always explicit that Renton has the voice in the 'Junk Dilemmas', but it is clear that he is no stranger to the horrors of addiction. He is trying to give up in 'The First Day of the Edinburgh Festival', but in 'It Goes Without Saying' he is another needy junkie like the others. 'Cock Problems' is the last episode in which he is using before he has a sobering experience in 'Memories of Matty pt 2'. After this we catch a glimpse of him on the road to recovery in 'Straight Dilemmas no 1'. He seems to be reviewing his rehabilitation progress in 'Trainspotting at Leith Central Station' (progress is precarious), and his sadness at the losses incurred is expressed in 'Memories pt 2' and in 'Winter in West Granton'. In 'The Glass' and in 'Inter Shitty' Renton is heavily involved with Begbie, who scorns heroin and all its users, so in these episodes junk is well into the background. In 'Bang to Rites', as in 'London Crawling', we meet a fairly self-aware and self-controlled young man who can handle himself with confidence in a variety of situations.

In the second generation of episodes, in which Renton is significant in about half (the combination emphatically makes him the central figure in the book), his career in junk is filled out. Before we get off the first page, we know he has a junk problem. He is brought to face conventional society in the courtroom; he undergoes a brutal experience of cold turkey, has some therapy, and, quite explicitly, in 'A Leg-Over Situation', reviews his career in junk from the beginning and departs the scene.

And his character outside the junk scene is broadened. He is an anxious, self-conscious, vulnerable boy who is infantilised by his mother after the court scene. He worries he might be 'a blind and stupid arsehole' (p.11) when the others suggest Kelly might like to see him; he hates his nickname and is insulted when Alison says 'Ye dinnae ken much aboot women, do ye Mark?' (p.12). In 'The First Shag In Ages' he envies Sick Boy's skill in raising only one eyebrow – he has spent many a long evening practising, without good results (p.134). He is concerned about having dyed his hair but not his pubes, even asking his mother for advice (p.136). Within this same episode we jump to the confident young man we see talking with Dianne's father. When he declares his support for Hearts, Renton 'smiled, glad for the first time, for reasons other than sexual ones, to have shagged this man's daughter' (p.150).

On occasion he is possessed of a good level of insight as well as empathy. Talking with Tricia about Sick Boy he notices the bitterness in his voice: 'Why am ah giein the cunt such a bad press? ...I envy the cunt. He doesnae care. Because he doesnae care, he cannae be hurt' (p.208). This is fairly mature. In 'Searching for the Inner Man' we see a young man who is capable of some moderately advanced abstract thinking, even if in the last page or so of the episode he puts a characteristic subversive twist on it. He is a good friend of Spud in 'Speedy Recruitment', and in 'Strolling Through The Meadows' they share confidences (p.161).

The presentation of Renton in the book as a whole is a compression of what we see in the prequel and the sequel. Some details about Renton that are brought out in 'The First Shag In Ages' are expanded in *Skagboys*: his time at Aberdeen university and as a joiner's apprentice with Ralphy Gillsland. In the prequel we also find out more about his handicapped wee brother Davie, who is referred to in second-generation episodes. They are well worked-out features of Renton's history and character. The more mature aspects of his character are the prototype of the young man we meet in the sequel *Porno*; not using and making out on his own. Within *Trainspotting* it's not entirely convincing. We can piece together a recognisable character who meets the requirement for the basic premise of the book: young man, born into a traditional working-class family in a tight-knit but fragmenting community, has some laughs with his mates, experiments dangerously with junk and the attendant HIV, and leaves both home and heroin for a new life.

Beyond that, we cannot say that he is a fully developed fictional character. In *Trainspotting*, the oscillation between an angsty teenager and a self-confident young man puts the reader *in loco parentis*, as it were, indulgently overlooking and making allowances for this unpredictability and patiently waiting for some balanced maturity to emerge. One critic has commented that Renton seems younger in *Trainspotting* than in the prequel *Skagboys*. Finished almost 20 years after *Trainspotting*, the younger Renton we meet in *Skagboys* is much more confidently handled. But the comment doesn't quite catch it; it's the author, not the character, who matured in the interval.

Can we interpret Renton's geographical mobility as a manifestation of his restlessness, and indeed his homelessness? What we sense is a young man with broad horizons and wide ambitions who will never be comfortable in the perceived narrowness and predictability of community life in Leith. We sense a young man who is so steeped in his community that he is bound to be ill at ease in the bourgeois community at Aberdeen University and the social climbers in London. None of this automatically leads to alienation and dysfunctionality; on the contrary, it can make for creative tensions and fertile fields in which people grow and thrive. But it can go wrong. Renton is young, but both his brothers are dead. Wee Davie's life – his very existence, not only the experience of being a sibling of his – throws up questions about life itself. The cause for which Billy dies is in question, but whether he dies at the hands of an enemy of the state or of a criminal, Renton is the surviving brother of one who was lethally targeted, and that needs some processing. Here are two well established triggers for personal difficulties.

Any of this can make a person a likely candidate for heroin, which soothes pain and anxiety like nothing else in a cruel world. When we put it like that, we wouldn't put much of a wager on Renton ever shaking off the habit. But he does. In 'Cock Problems' he may ridicule the Royal Ed[inburgh psychiatric hospital] (p.98) but he needs and benefits from their professional attention, provided by the welfare state, which he has been scamming. As we see in 'Searching for the Inner Man', the professionals combine his personal issues with his junk problem; they are not separate. The book closes with his mates having nowhere to go but back to their own unresolved problems, while he is outward bound, released, on the move, homeless and happy.

Trainspotting is a nascent *Bildungsroman*, in which the protagonist develops his psychological and moral personality through experiment and experience. Not that Welsh planned it that way from the beginning, but we see the outcome in the sequel *Porno* and what precedes it in the prequel *Skagboys*. Let's say that *Trainspotting*'s Renton is a characterisation, and indeed the book as a whole is a manifestation, of Welsh's talent, limitations, and ambition at the time of writing.

CHAPTER 9

There was an Irishman, a Dutchman and a Scotsman

WE'LL GO BACK to the Shore, but not to a pub; this time we'll take a seat on one of the benches at the top near Henderson Street and just off the end of Sandport Bridge, where we'll find Spud complaining that 'The heat, man... is hot. That's the only way you can really describe it, ken?' (p.121). It's a delicious example of Spud's distinctive voice. I often come here on the tours, and read this passage, going three lines over the page. Literature on location. This chapter is based on Spud's journey in 'Na Na and Other Nazis'.

Welsh may remember families feeding the plentiful swans as they came right up to the bank at high tide. There is only one family of swans now, occasionally coming into view as one does for Spud, inspiring a regretful thought about Johnny Swan, who used to be a nice boy. We can see that the former shipping offices to the right (east) of the water have more than a passing suggestion of similarity with Leith's trading partners in the Baltic and the Low Countries. Immediately to our right, close to the corner with Tolbooth Wynd, now there stands an off-the-peg government building at no. 63 Shore, which for many years was the 'dole office', or the place to pick up one's unemployment benefit. Spud spots his 'fellow Fenian freedom fighter' (p.123), Monny, coming out. Spud Murphy: the name itself spells 'poor, Irish, Catholic'. After many generations of universal education it spells no such thing, of course, but a hundred years ago it did, and perceptions can linger. His mother is Colleen, his cousin is Desmond, both recognisably Irish names. We follow these two young men of distinctly Irish descent as they head to the Fit ay the Walk.

We go up Henderson Street, which when it was built in the early 1880s swept aside some desperate hovels, many occupied by their immigrant Irish forebears. What we see today was the first secure accommodation some families ever had. And there over the pub on the corner with Yardheads, set in stone, with shamrocks and a harp, is a clear reference to Ireland. The

Irish dimension in *Trainspotting* is a significant element in the book, and it deserves to be properly understood.

* * * * * * * *

Following a failed bid for independence in 1798, which was inspired by the American Declaration of Independence and the French Revolution, Ireland was brought into the heart of the British Empire. Poor and rural, it could not cope with exposure to the full rigours of the marketplace within the Empire. In the early years of the 19th century the peasants watched in fury as much needed grain was collected in village squares and taken under armed guard to the coast for export. Millions died from starvation and disease, and millions emigrated around the world. The Great Hunger of the 1840s, when the potato crops failed disastrously, gave rise to the unkind nickname 'Spud', to be given to almost any Irish emigrant. Throughout the 19th century the Irish were a mobile workforce that built much of the infrastructure in Scotland that survives to the present: canals, railways, reservoirs, bridges, and public and tenement buildings. Indeed, for some the wandering habit persisted till well into the 20th century – Spud's grandfather, 'a chancing auld cowboy' (p.125) seems very similar to the grandfather of an old woman in Leith who remembers her grandmother saying that her Irish husband cleared off every time she became pregnant.

By the mid-19th century, according to the official census, probably as many as four people in a hundred in Leith were Irish-born. For reasons that are not entirely clear, Leith developed and kept a reputation of good inter-community relations, in contrast to many other areas in Scotland. This plaque, dated 1885, is one of the few contemporary positive acknowledgements of the Irish contribution to their host country. The Irish provided a welcome boost to beleaguered Scottish Catholics, not only in their numbers but also in providing a well-educated and confident priesthood. The presbytery house in Leith, within the grounds of the newly-founded church St Mary, Star of the Sea, was the first post-Reformation house for Catholic men in Scotland. Right down to the 1960s, it never entered the heads of the children of the parish that the priests could be anything other than Irish, as they went to the church hall early on St Patrick's Days to collect their shamrock that had been specially sent over and they sang their party piece 'If you're Irish'.

Let's go into the pub below the plaque. Spud has just shown a level of ignorance about the local football team that wouldn't be easy to maintain in 1980s Leith. Let's see if we can educate him.

For most of the 19th century, Edinburgh's Cowgate was known as 'Little Ireland', and it was here that Hibernian ('Hibernia' is the Latin word for 'Ireland') Football Club was born in 1875. With the Easter Road ground neatly equidistant between Cowgate and Leith, club meetings were held either in Cowgate's St Patrick's church hall or in Leith's St Mary's church hall. The first club motto was 'Erin-go-Bragh' ('Ireland For Ever'). Poor though the immigrants were, the club played a generous and creative part in the foundation of modern Scottish club football, although in 1891 it needed some munificence and forthright intervention from Philip Farmer living at 31 Duke Street, and his brother John, to ensure its emergence into the next century and down to the present as one of the great survivors from the early days. Celtic FC was very nearly called Glasgow Hibernian, in deference to the more senior club on the east coast. Celtic went professional earlier, and its poaching of Hibernian players was thought to be divisive within the homogenous Irish community. The clubs may share Irish and Catholic origins, but no love is lost between the two now. Hibs fans like to remind Celtic fans that their club is older, although the latter now outstrips them financially and therefore in player-power. In the 20th century Hibernian FC progressively lost its direct connections with Ireland – apart, that is, from the name and the club colour, green – and has become the local Leith club and long standing city rival to Heart of Midlothian FC (HMFC). In contrast Rangers FC (Glasgow) and Hearts are the Protestant clubs, more readily connected with the Scottish establishment.

Welsh inserts many references to his beloved club into *Trainspotting*. They are accurate, if sometimes cryptic. Renton quotes the 'Famous Five' (p.86), the key figures in the Golden Age of contemporaneous living memory, in the correct order. He invokes Pat Stanton, a direct descendant of a sister of one of the club's founders and popular midfield stalwart in the early to mid-1970s (p.188) (he is 'Paddy' in the book), who also makes an appearance on a poster in Renton's bedroom in *Trainspotting* the film. Stanton attended the launch of *The Acid House* in 1995. Welsh rarely misses an opportunity to take a poke at Hearts, with a scathing reference to Wallace Mercer (p.141), wealthy chairman of HMFC who seriously proposed a merger of the two Edinburgh clubs, and a more cheerful reference to Gary Mackay (p.310).

While there is no ground for doubting the authenticity of Welsh's depiction of the Hearts fans' loutish and racist behaviour after the match (pp.49,50), it should not be thought that bigotry and hatred between Hibs and Hearts is on the same scale as that between Celtic and Rangers in

Glasgow. Capital City Service, a nasty group of football casuals associated with Hibernian FC in the 1980s (the club itself deplored it and had nothing to do with it) has no mention in *Trainspotting*, but is raised several times in some of Welsh's other writing. The Cashies, as they were known, had thuggish tendencies and criminal associations, and they were a malign influence not only at Hibs away games, particularly at Aberdeen, but also in the Muirhouse and West Pilton schemes.

Hibs had a difficult decade in the 1980s, both on the pitch and in the boardroom, but things improved markedly in 1991 when local philanthropist Sir Tom Farmer secured the financial future of the club exactly a century after direct ancestors of his had done the same. He has explained many times that he did not do this out of any passion for football – he never had time for it, he says – but because he could see the importance of the club within the Leith community. Around the same time Gordon (Geebsie) Hunter scored key goals that restored some respectability to the team. These happier days seem to be reflected in Renton's dreams (p.143) and in Spud's uncharacteristically well informed observations in the Meadows (p.157).

We'll move on up Henderson Street to the Foot of the Walk. This is where Spud met Begbie and Lexo just before we caught up with him at the top of Shore (p.120). Begbie slips him £20 – 'a double ten-spot' (p.121). Feeling better immediately, he goes into Woolworth's, the doorway nearest the statue of Queen Victoria. It was an L-shaped shop, with another doorway on Kirkgate, which gave it a serious and permanent problem with shoplifters; Welsh inserts an authentic piece of local information into his fiction.

Here in the 1960s, when specifically anti-Catholic statements were emanating from the upper echelons of the Church of Scotland, John Cormack, a rabble-rousing baiter of Catholics was rounding off his regular soap-box rants with 'One, two, three, no Popery.' He had been, but was no longer, a Leith councillor. The public and institutionalised violence in *Trainspotting* is not given any background, but no portrait of Leith in the 1980s, nor a good appreciation of the book, can be complete without some understanding of its origins.

* * * * * * *

Sectarianism arises when differences of perception and belief are concentrated on, taken out of context, and worked up into problems and causes for hatred. Scottish sectarianism is both home grown and imported from Ireland. The origins go back to the 16th century Reformation, when Ireland refused to go along with the English king Henry VIII's nationalisation of the Church of Rome. He made himself the head of the new Protestant Church of England. His daughter, Elizabeth 1, founded Trinity College, Dublin, precisely to assert Protestant supremacy and to downgrade Roman Catholicism. The Scottish reformers went a step further: wanting neither king nor pope as head of the Church, they place the founder of the church universal, even Jesus Christ Himself, at the head of the Reformed Church of Scotland. Whereas the Church of England is deeply ambivalent about its relationship with Rome, until very recent decades there was no doubt in the Church of Scotland about the relationship. The merits of theology and practice were judged on their distance from Rome – the further the better. As recently as the 1950s, Christmas Day was a working day for many in Scotland. The problem was the Popish-seeming suffix *mas*. This explains Scots' taste for a better party than the English at New Year.

In 1688 it was not tolerable to the English establishment that the crown was on the head of the Catholic James Stewart and the heir was his son. The avowed Protestant William of Orange was invited to take the throne in The Glorious Revolution. William defeated a Jacobite (from the Latin for 'James') comeback attempt at the Battle of the Boyne in Northern Ireland in 1690. The matter of putting the crown firmly on Protestant heads was finally settled at Culloden, near Inverness, in 1746 when Protestant troops of what was by then the United Kingdom of Scotland and England crushed the rebellion of James' grandson, Bonnie Prince Charlie. Although this uprising is now better known for its Scottish nationalist associations, it was also, and more significantly, an international inter-church struggle. Legislation of the period that surrounds these issues, which is still in force today, secures Protestant supremacy at the pinnacle of the British establishment and specifically denies legitimacy to the Roman Catholic Church. The Orange Order was founded, with the sole purpose of asserting and perpetuating Protestant supremacy. Orangeism became the glue between three separate issues, to make a potent combination:

LABEL	THEME OR PURPOSE
Protestant	Loosely describes any non-Catholic church.
Unionist	Supports the integrity of the United Kingdom of Great Britain and Northern Ireland as the sole political unit within the British Isles.
Loyalist	Loyal to the British royal family, which necessarily entailed inviolable Protestant supremacy (partially revoked in 2015).
Orange	Combines all the above and is specifically and explicitly anti-Catholic.

Apart from polemical tracts there is no body of theology or political theory in support of Orangeism. Of course, as its defenders will claim, there is room for an entirely benign Christian fellowship in a Protestant context, but in its foundations and at its core it is little more than glorified and institution-alised triumphalism and bigotry.

Following the signing of the Good Friday Agreement in Belfast in 1998, the public and ostentatious manifestations of Orangeism have been fading fast, but up till then local Orange Lodges in Ireland and the west of Scot-land traditionally organised marches, as near possible to the anniversary of victory in 1690, which were often routed past Catholic churches to cause maximum offence. The racist British National Party (BNP) which, despite its name is overwhelmingly English, was not given such ready permission to march, and it often turned up on Orange marches to enjoy a day out with likeminded bigots. The cameo scene at the Persevere pub (pp.126-129) is an authentic snapshot of the Leith/Edinburgh Orange marches of the 1980s: the mixture of accents and preoccupations; the arrogance and provocation; and the ingrained violence. The Persevere is the nearest pub to the rallying point on the Links round the corner. Some drinking was dutifully under-taken in The Duke's Head on Duke Street, then in the hands of ex-Rangers player and Orangeman Jimmy Millar.

From the Fit ay the Walk Monny leaves 'tae meet this lemon up the toon' (p.123). We go with Spud towards his Na Na at the bottom of Easter Road. We'll go along Duke Street.

The Edinburgh Orange march came this way from the rallying point on the Links to the Foot of Leith Walk and from there straight up to Edinburgh. Actually, Leith was not home to an Orange Lodge, or even a battalion. John Cormack and the Duke's Head pub notwithstanding, this was not easy terri-tory for the Orangemen and they seemed to sense that they weren't at home. They probably weren't aware that Philip Farmer lived at the very address where The Duke's Head is now. The Marksman, a few doors along, was a Hibs pub which organised buses to away games, on one of which Davie Mitchell meets Tommy, Renton and other Leith heid-bangers (p.92). At least one flat on Duke Street used to throw open the window as they were pass-ing and play the Irish bands U2 or Planxty as loud as possible. One day the minister's wife nipped smartly across the street between marching units to howls of 'Fenian bastard!' The minister's wife!

John Patrick Mulvey, standing as a Labour candidate in the 1982 Lothian Regional Council election, was not the only one with an apparently Irish/Catholic name to receive threatening phone calls which were traced to a pub in Coburg Street, Leith with well-known Orange connections. All this was taking place during a protracted period of intolerance and violence, focussed on Northern Ireland but regularly spilling over into the Republic and mainland Britain. Welsh's generation grew up in this tense, dangerous confusion. Do Spud and his people have something to answer for? With a glance along Gordon Street, because it feels like his Na Na's flat (p.123) is somewhere there, we'll take a seat in the Persevere pub and review British/ Irish history that led to the complex and violent incident that is set here in the fiction.

* * * * * * *

In the wake of bringing Ireland into the heart of the United Kingdom, during the 19th century, a group of Irish intellectuals gathered in Paris, a safe and vibrant place, to prepare the ground for a better bid for independence. They devised a tri-colour flag: three panels, green for the Catholics, orange for the Protestants, and a white panel for peace between them. Their vision was clear: Ireland was diverse, united, and harmonious. Back home, the middle class set about rescuing the Irish language and culture from the influences of mainland Britain. An opportunity to strike for independence came in 1916, while London was looking the other way, in the thick of the Great War. In what became known as the Easter Rising, the Post Office in central Dublin was captured and the tri-colour was hoist. The planned uprising throughout the country never happened. James Connolly, Edinburgh-born linguist, internationalist, lecturer (he shared a platform with George Bernard Shaw), traveller, activist and, as Gav observes, a 'fuckin great rebel... socialist and... Hibby' (pp.47, 48) along with six others, signed a Proclamation claiming and declaring independence. He and 13 others faced a firing squad within a month. As a military operation the Rising was a dead loss failure. As a piece of theatre, we have not yet had the final curtain call.

The General Election of 1918 produced an overwhelming vote in Ireland for independence, but there was a well-armed and well connected Protestant minority in and around Belfast. Protestants, many from Scotland, had been planted and cultivated there over several generations. After much bloodshed and many dirty tricks, in 1921 this small island was divided along 17th century religious/political lines, with the Catholic majority area – by far the larger part – becoming self-governing (it was not yet a republic), and a fully British Protestant enclave in what became known as Northern Ireland, or Ulster. The Irish nationalists had worked up what they believed to be a viable vision for a new, modern country: emancipated, educated, socialist, religiously disparate, democratic, peaceful, and united. The hopes and passions behind the dream should not be understated, and nor should the sense of anger, oppression and betrayal as the dream died.

The Irish Republican Army (IRA), strongly associated with the political party Sinn Fein, agreed to a ceasefire in order to draw an end to the bloodshed. But the aim of a united and free island remained unfinished business. This is the meaning behind Spud calling his friend Ricky Monaghan his 'fellow Fenian freedom fighter' (p.123).

During the half-century after Partition, it was made clear that Northern Ireland was a Protestant province that was governed by and in the interests of Protestants. Several militant Protestants organisations with Orangeism running through their veins adopted the medieval symbol of the dominant Ulster O'Neil clan, The Red Hand, and attached to it the motto NO SURRENDER. This cry dates back to 1690 when the Apprentice Boys of Londonderry bravely raised the alarm at the approach of the Catholic Jacobite army. Many people deplored this misappropriation for partisan use of what had hitherto been an all-embracing cross-community symbol. In the new Northern Ireland Catholics were overwhelmingly the poorest, the least educated, the least provided for and the most ignored. The most cautious of proposed reforms produced a hard line Protestant backlash. But the 1960s was a decade of protest and change. Northern Ireland developed a civil rights movement based on the Martin Luther King model.

In 1969 the Apprentice Boys violently clashed with a peaceful demonstration, and mainland Britain was aghast to see on television screens scenes of a weekend of mayhem and a far from neutral police force. The British army was sent in to protect the Catholics, but it was all too quickly and easily portrayed as a hostile occupying force and a return to the bad old days. Operation Banner turned out to be the longest ever single deployment of the British army (it was finally wound up in 2007), in which there were 763 military casualties and several thousand civilian casualties. Crucially, the IRA changed its strategy: out went the peaceful protest, in came armed guerrilla warfare similar to Vietnam and Cuba. The Provisional IRA (the Provos) was born.

For the next 30 years, Northern Ireland was home to sickening, never ending rounds of inter-community outrages and tit for tat revenges, which often spilled over into the mainland with London taking the brunt of the atrocities. In 1981 the IRA began a series of hunger strikes. Dramatically, the first to die was Bobby Sands (p.127), who had been elected as a Member of the British Parliament from his prison cell. In October 1984, the Provos exploded a bomb at around 2.45 am in the Brighton hotel where the governing Conservative party was having its annual conference. It killed five people, including Members of Parliament, and very nearly killed Mrs Thatcher herself. It was an astonishing, daring strike at the heart of government that was partially successful and was very close indeed to being highly successful. The Provisional IRA issued a statement:

> Mrs Thatcher will now realise that Britain cannot occupy our country and torture our prisoners and shoot our people in their own streets and get away with it. Today we were unlucky, but remember we only have to be lucky once. You will have to be lucky always. Give Ireland peace and there will be no more war.

It was the IRA answer in kind to the Unionist NO SURRENDER. The collective heart sank ever lower. If there was no sympathy for the IRA and its tactics within public opinion, neither was there much enthusiasm for the risks and sacrifices of army personnel who had the thankless task of trying to keep apart two traditional enemies who couldn't and wouldn't be separated.

The fictitious Billy Renton (by clear inference, his first name derives from William of Orange) is one of many who, in history, died in bandit country near Crossmaglen (p.210). Bearing in mind that this was a civil emergency, not a declared war, is he a hero who dies for his country, or 'a spare prick in a uniform'? (p.210) Renton's sympathies lie with the Republican cause, in line with many around the world, but he can't condone the tactics (p.221).

And he sees it not as a war between the people but as a politicians' war: at Billy's graveside 'some ruling class cunt... says that his killers will be ruthlessly hunted down... Aw the wey tae the fuckin Houses ay Parliament' (p.211). The Partition of Ireland almost a century ago was the biggest single piece of misgovernment in the British Isles in the 20th century.

As ever, Welsh carries some of the issues in play through the music. In the 1960s and 1970s, going into the 1980s, in the folk clubs the Irish story and dimension was carried with a certain amount of wistfulness and rebellion, all in a youthful and harmless enough way. For Glasgow-born and Leith-bred singer and songwriter Dick Gaughan, scion of fiercely Republican Irish lineage, this was all too tame. Leith's most famous musical son of that generation, he was passionate in supporting the miners in their struggles with the Thatcher government and no less so in expressing the rage and pain of Ireland. *Trainspotting* steers a route between these two: less confrontational than Gaughan but more subversive than the folk clubs. In 'Victory On New Year's Day', after the obligatory Scottish Harry Lauder song, all the singing is Irish: they belt out the battle cry *We're off to Dublin in the green – fuck the queen*' (p.45) and they croon the ballad *The Lonely Banna Strand* which tells of a failed rendezvous in the 1916 Rising, and the lament *James Connolly*. Similarly, at the wake after Tommy's funeral the singing is raucous and Irish, although there is no Irish connection in the fiction. There is tension when Renton whistles *The Foggy Dew*, a tune of Irish rebel origins with many different word versions, at the funeral of his brother and within earshot of Billy's army pals (p.212).

From our comfortable seat in the Persevere pub we won't go with Spud and Dode to the hospital, which would be the Royal Infirmary, then on Lauriston Place. Instead we go up Easter Road for half a mile or so to see the Hibs stadium. Just before we get there we pass a little cemetery where lies Peter Hughes, a heroin addict who died in 1992 aged 30 years. He was laid in the shadow of the Famous Five stand. His younger brother, the popular John 'Yogi' Hughes, later played for the Hibs first team and subsequently became the manager. In the fiction it is to a New Year derby game against Hearts, imaginatively three or four years before the death of Peter Hughes, that Spud and Second Prize, don't manage to turn up, 'their match tickets good for nothing except future roach material' (p.49). Yogi Hughes has said he wants to be a role model of a different sort.

Spud

We have enjoyed Spud's company on this tour round Leith, using him as some sort of archetypal Catholic Leither with Irish ancestry. But what of Spud, the character we find in *Trainspotting*? This is the one everyone loves to love, the gormless, hapless, well intentioned and basically decent Spud. He spends a lot of time bombed out, on one substance or another and, according to Renton, it is inexplicable that he does not acquire HIV through sharing needles (pp.55, 56). He never hurts anyone, and he deplores violence and anything unpleasant. He knows a lot about Frank Zappa, but he is ignorant about recent Hibs history and the differences between Celtic and Rangers. There is a pattern of him finishing first generation episodes not understanding ('Na Na and Other Nazis'), not being quite sure ('There Is A Light That Never Goes Out'), and, with others, none the wiser ('Memories of Matty pt 2').

It seems he is from a pretty disorganised family; he has an 'auld cowboy' for a grandfather, an unpleasant former prostitute for a granny, and his mother, Colleen, is one of her children by several different men. Colleen is 'the billy (bully) of the washhouse', (p.170) but she is easily beaten down by Begbie's vituperative insults after the court scene. There is no mention of his father. Spud hardly knows his own cousin, Des Feeney, and the others have to remind him who he is (p.266).

He is not sexually voracious or predatory. Thinking he had got lucky with the sexually prolific Laura McEwan, it went horribly wrong (p.268), and he couldn't screw up the courage to put his arm around Nicola in the underpass (p.267). In 'Na Na and Other Nazis' he sticks by his mixed-race uncle in a hostile situation for them both. Nothing goes right for Spud, but he doesn't lose his good, generous nature. Welsh has called him 'the lovable loser'.

But is he so innocent? At his court appearance the sheriff says he is a 'habitual thief' (p.166). Spud, honest lad that he is, agrees. In the case of shoplifting, the victim is at some removal from the theft itself, and the sheriff delivers the standard judgement, that people work hard to produce and buy the things he steals. (p.166). Tommy has already told us about Spud's stolen flat warming present (p.72), and Spud himself has made no secret that 'aw ma uncles are oan the chorie' (p.126). However much he deplores Begbie terrorising the youngster who supplied the information and the keys for the heist in 'Easy Money for the Professionals', and however sickening the violence meted out to the unfortunate Richard Hauser of Des Moines, Iowa, USA (p.155), Spud does not omit to take his share of the spoils in both cases. And right at the end Renton acknowledges that Spud has 'a tendency to liberate the contents of people's pockets, purses and homes' (p.343). When personal, irreplaceable items, often of little cash value, were stolen by pickpockets, bag-snatchers, and opportunist burglars in a wave of petty, opportunist thefts to feed heroin habits in Edinburgh (and elsewhere) in the mid to late 1980s, the outrage, condemnation, bitterness, and demands for very stiff penalties was vociferous and widespread. None of this is attached to Spud.

So why do we love him? Is it only because his creator does not take us into the consequences of his actions? It is widely said that Welsh based Spud on a punk, poet and author of short pieces with whom he was friendly during the late 1980s and to whom he remained loyal well after he became famous. If there is anything in this, it raises the question of whether Welsh's personal feelings towards his model overcame artistic integrity.

This profile of Spud does not take into account the comic character we come across in 'Speedy Recruitment', nor what we learn of him in 'Strolling

Through The Meadows'. They are second generation episodes, written with *Porno* in mind as much as how they fit into *Trainspotting*. In 'Speedy Recruitment', revved up on speed, Spud's heavy accent and subversive intent clash with the formalities of the occasion, with hilarious effect. 'Strolling Through The Meadows' is different. Still recognisably Spud, it is a rather changed young man we meet. He makes some sharp observations about his companions: 'Begbie raped us aw that night' (p.155), describing the brutality of the attack on the Sherman Tank; 'Ye cannae love yirsel if ye want tae hurt things like that' (p.159), condemning Renton throwing stones at the squirrel; and 'they posh wifies think people like us ur vermin, likesay, does that make it right thit they should kill us...' (p.160), putting a perspective on the two women they have just greatly offended. He is uncharacteristically well informed about Hibs FC and the slogan Let's Do It For The Fans. He elicits from Renton a key moment in Renton's journey away from heroin: 'Ah dinnae ken what ah'm daein wi ma life...' (pp.160,161).

His verbal tics do not obscure clear thinking. He is not confused and ineffectual. He has opinions, he engages with the others on equal terms, and we see more personality. Heroin is not part of either of these two episodes, and in the narrative order they intrude into Spud's uneven though overall progressive descent into the world of the junkie, culminating in him being a useless, miserable passenger in 'Station to Station'. So do 'Speedy Recruitment' and 'Strolling Through The Meadows' add to Spud's authentic character, or do they make him a caricature, or a composite that doesn't fit together, useful only for adaptation into various situations as required by the book?

Ah dinnae want tae say nowt against the laddie, likesay. But the questions huv tae be asked. Ken?

CHAPTER 10

Maistly Rubble Nou...

FOR ALMOST 20 years there was a popular parlour game in Leith: 'Who is Welsh's model for Frank Begbie?' There were several candidates. In 2011 Sandy Macnair ruined everything by providing the answer: Begbie is a composite of a 'Glaswegian nutter' who shared a flat with Welsh in London and 'an Edinburgh nutter who succeeded in drinking himself to death in his mid-30s...'[12] Welsh used to watch him hiding a stash of alcohol before going into his hostel near Leith Links.

To start this tour we stand outside no. 2 Wellington Place, from where, presumably, Welsh saw all this. Welsh went to this fellow's funeral, and he incorporated into 'Bang to Rites' some clichés commonly uttered at a premature death that he heard there. Seafield crematorium is at the other end of The Links, and there are several hotels on the south side vying for the wakes – it looks like Welsh also incorporated some of this into Tommy's funeral. We are going in search of Frank Begbie to be our guide through the post-war Leith in which he grew up. I think I know where to find him.

Almost directly opposite Welsh's old flat is Leith Victoria Boxing Club, the oldest in Scotland, of working-class origins, and boasting a proud history from Tancy Lee (British Flyweight Champion 1915, British Featherweight Champion 1917, and Scotland's first outright winner of a Lonsdale Belt) to Alex Arthur, (Gold Medallist at the Kuala Lumpur Commonwealth Games in 1998, where he was one of three club members), with plenty of belts, titles and international representations in between. A recent refurbishment should ensure further nurturing of Leith's enthusiasm and talent for the Noble Art.

The building directly across the narrow Laurie Street at the end of Wellington Place is the Dockers' Club. It is in the fine working class tradition of community self-help through socialising and organising. The function room is a classic of its type: a stage in the corner, a small dancing area in front, and long tables arranged not for private parties but for community. They say Welsh's parents were members here, which fits with Renton's parents' appearance here in 'House Arrest', and some say Welsh has a memory of the bingo nights there. There has been a good number of occasions here in which Welsh has been involved; in April 2014 he unveiled the mural in the courtyard, which is a fond look back at the Leith that was being demolished during living memory, more particularly during Welsh's childhood. Many of the human figures have a ghostly appearance. Welsh was given an honorary membership of the club (the first ever) and a key to the front door (they didn't tell him the security drill). The club has always been good and generous to many Leith initiatives, including my Trainspotting Tour. I have sat here many times reading through and discussing Renton's difficult evening here as he makes his first public appearance after doing cold turkey in 'House Arrest'.

Leith Links is long-beloved turf. It is the oldest stretch of open land in Scotland that is protected by Act of Parliament, and the first written rules of golf in the world were drawn up for playing here in 1744. Badly hooked shots from the first tee of the 18th-century course would break windows in Wellington Place. St Andrews' boast to be 'The Home of Golf' is not a claim to the historical origins of the game. The 18th-century golfers drank copious quantities of claret in the Leith howffs, which is the origin of the Claret Jug, the most coveted trophy in world golf as the prize for The Open wherever in Britain it is played. Leith is home to an extraordinary collection of golfing firsts: in chronological order, the first recorded game; the first club; the first port of export of golf equipment; the first written rules; the first competition for a prize; the first international challenge match; the first club house; and the first professionals' tournament. Golf is Leith's gift to the world.

With the possible exception of Glasgow Fair, the annual Leith Races, held on the beach at low tide three or four good drives to the north of the golfers, were the biggest single gathering of ordinary people in pre-industrial Scotland. In 1795, a time of great turbulence in Europe, the Royal Leith Volunteers received their colours on Leith Links, somewhere in front of Welsh's flat. We are heading for the howff that was named for them some time later, The Volunteer Arms on Leith Walk.

But first we head north, past the fine houses of Leith's 19th-century wealthy John's Place, and turn left along Queen Charlotte Street to the police station at the junction with Constitution Street. There is a well known tongue twister: 'The Leith police dismisseth us/It pleaseth us to say/The Leith police dismisseth us/They thought we sought to stay/The Leith police dismisseth us/We both sighed sighs apiece/And the sighs that we sighed/As we said our goodbyes/Was the size of the Leith police.' This has the languid air of having been penned by someone who didn't know just how rough it could be in there.

In the 1950s a Leith teenage girl was walking down Constitution Street when a stranger, a man, walked alongside her and tried to engage her in conversation. A policeman standing outside the station called them over. 'Has this man been pestering you?' 'No,' she answered truthfully. 'It looked as though you didn't want his attentions.' 'I didn't mind him.' 'Alright hen, you run along now.' As she left she heard the thuds and the gasps as the first punches went into his ribs. Did they have something on him from previous knowledge? Were they having a quiet shift which needed some action? Were they issuing a lively just-in-case reminder that nobody should mess with nice Leith girls?

Some time well into the 1960s, a doctor who was on night duty at Leith hospital tells me, the police brought in a man who needed a bit of patching up. 'He was obviously a nasty piece of work. He had been knocking his wife about and the police had taken the law of justice and retribution into their own hands and overdone it a wee bit on this occasion.' No questions, no reports. It takes no stretch of the imagination to see the 'old drunkard' (p.263) who we take to be Begbie's father in 'There Is A Light That Never Goes Out' as this man. The 'slippery step' story was often used in court by the police to explain to the sheriff injuries that had obviously been incurred the night before: 'Yes, your Honour, there are some slippery steps in the station. We must get that seen to.' Leith was a rough, tough place in the 30 years after the war. It was often referred to euphemistically as 'Edinburgh 6', fore-runner of the present post-code.

Leith pubs were certainly rough. Especially on the Shore, some were little other than knocking shops with drinks available. This is a port, after all. King's Wark was known as Leith's Jungle; every port has a Jungle, the sailors' first pub ashore. The police turned up at closing time as the prostitutes sorted out their customers. Their purpose was to see fair play on behalf of the girls. There are plenty of models for Spud's uncle Dode, the product of a local girl and, in his case, a West Indian sailor (a seaman's semen, as Welsh puts it: p.125) who was passing through.

Going south on Constitution Street, we turn off to the right at Coatfield Lane. Here we can see the stump of some slums that were demolished after World War Two. Councillor John Crichton recalled for me visiting a family here in the 1950s. There was an umbrella over the pram in the room, keeping the steady drips of water off the baby. A great deal of the housing in the town had hardly been maintained, far less improved, over the previous

half-century that had been dominated by war and depression. Gumley &
Davidson were the factors (agents) for many absentee landlords who were
sharp enough collecting the rent and deaf to requests for repairs. Many families had one bedroom and a bed recess off the room for the parents. 'Single
ends' were common: one toilet and often one tap with running water for up
to four families. There were many unsafe landings and stairways and leaking
roofs.

The poverty in the post-war slums of Leith produced circumstantial
and inter-personal tensions that made violence a matter of everyday gossip
among the women. Who had been thrown down the stairs, who had a black
eye and wouldn't be out for a few days, who had a broken arm? Women and
children were mostly the victims, but read what happened to some of Spud's
Na Na's menfolk for a fuller picture (pp.125,126). Just how endemic it was
is conveyed in Nina's Aunt Alice's tribute to her late husband in 'Growing
Up In Public': 'He nivir lifted his hands tae me...' (p.39).

Leith voices in the city chamber were easily drowned out or ignored
by the majority of Progressives (Scottish Conservatives) from Edinburgh.
Crichton, much respected councillor and later chair of Lothian Regional
Council, who emerges as something of a hero of this story, was clear that
the Leith Chamber of Commerce had the ear of the Progressives in the council chamber, and certainly compulsory purchases and wholesale demolitions
suited their ideology and their wallets much better than repair and resto-
ration of their properties. In the 30 years following the war great swathes of
Leith town centre were demolished. The town lost 20,000 families. It left a
small, elderly, often poor and unsupported population looking out over gap
sites. Edinburgh deserved its reputation for being all too ready to demolish
and not quite so quick to rebuild. Crichton was instrumental in setting up a
soup kitchen at South Leith church.

Let's move into the Kirkgate. You've seen it before; it could be in south
London, or Chicago, or anywhere, it's one of those charmless, anonymous
walkways with low slung residential blocks either side. To the north we
can see that the slight rise near to the junction with Tolbooth Wynd is now
achieved by broad steps, breaking up what was a natural pathway between
the town and Shore, and is dominated by the brutal multi-storey block at
the top called Linksview House, a ridiculous name since it is the blind gable
end of the block that looks over to the Links. To the south, there is a bit of
hustle and bustle in the shopping centre.

Without any question, Kirkgate was the heart of the community. In the
1950s it boasted a string of family businesses along its length. The only two

surviving buildings are the imposing Trinity House and the late medieval church directly opposite, which, after the Second World War, was one of the richest parishes in Scotland with one of the largest membership rolls to match. The ever-popular Gaiety Theatre was next door. It was a walking, talking street. Stories abound of how much fun it was. Sailors came, Lascars in single file carrying big bags. They say the police never went alone. Before the days of freezers, late on Saturday nights people would get 'parcels' of perishable goods at a clearance price.

One woman who lived in Edinburgh's Southside who had family in Leith would come on a Saturday afternoon. Her mother said if she just wanted to go shopping she could go to the department stores in Princes Street. Leith was in a time warp, she says now, fondly recalling the rough and ready vitality of the street. A Borders man, a soldier who had been barracked at The Fort and married to a relative of hers, was one of Leith's many colourful characters, in his case getting up to some dodgy buying and selling at the Foot of Leith Walk. There are many recorded voices and written anecdotes (but not many images) in the collective archive of the Kirkgate.

In the early 1960s the investigative BBC television programme *Panorama* conducted a study of poverty in Scotland. As they expected, most of it was to be found in the west of the Central Belt, in and around Glasgow. However, the programme discovered a small pocket of acute poverty in Leith, which was masked in most statistical assemblages by Edinburgh's prosperity. A woman was interviewed in what looks like Junction Street, sadly but stoically saying that her husband had tuberculosis in a damp house. Edinburgh, preening itself up the hill as a provincial capital and cosmopolitan city of festivals, was mortified. Leith was a problem, not an asset. More demolitions would quickly improve the statistics, and Kirkgate was targeted.

Germans on my tours say that if a Kirkgate in their country had survived the war it would have been sensitively refurbished; if Leith Kirkgate had been refurbished it would now be a bijou and a tourist trap. But it can't be said that this demolition was particularly an anti-Leith move on the part of Edinburgh – after all, in the same mood they knocked down the fine but rundown St James Square in Edinburgh and gave us St James Centre shopping mall, which, at the time of writing, is being demolished.

John Crichton subscribed to the demolition of Kirkgate with a heavy heart, knowing that this would bring serious and permanent damage to Leith town and community. He said many times afterwards that the project looked much better on paper than it did on the ground. There were discussions about replacing the various sports facilities that had disappeared in the

town, and the so-called community centre beside the new shopping centre
was the outcome. But it never was much more than a series of sports halls,
and Crichton's pleas for money to put on an extra floor were overridden.
All the shops were bundled into the shopping centre at the south end, tenants of a management company. Family businesses need to own their own
properties; the last family business left long ago, and we have nothing but
branches of chain stores. Giving shop keepers no incentive to stay in Leith
further distorted the micro-economy.

If you think it's dull, you should have seen it before its make over ten
years ago. Let's go for a cup of tea in what is now the much more pleasant
community centre, catching the morning sun and overlooking a rare bit of
green, the kirkyard on the other side of the narrow Kirkgate. There's Frank,
sitting on his own, looking older than his years, nodding briefly to other folk
and occasionally having a bit of rough banter with the kitchen staff. He did
a few stretches for small-time robberies, and he was involved in one venture
with drug-dealing, but he didn't have the sophistications or personal controls to handle the complexities. Prison rehabilitation has been successful to
the point where he doesn't really cause any more bother, but he's a whipped
man, subdued rather than healthy and happy. He's not very articulate, but
he recognises this story of Leith as he grew up. Now he's a ghostly figure,
rather like his father.

A man now in his 70s – older than Frank – recalls for me being a post
boy in the last days of the old Kirkgate. He came across a woman greetin
on her doorstep. 'Ah wish ye hud nivir come yesterday, son.' 'How?' She
waved a letter. 'They're sending me to Niddrie. How kin they dae that?
Aw ma faimly's here.' This high-handed break-up of tight knit communities
was common at the time. Nothing much swung Leith's way in the Swinging
Sixties.

They say the other demolitions were bad enough, but that the loss of
Kirkgate tore the heart from the town. The lengthy interval between demolition and rebuilding the residential accommodation down the length of
the street meant that families had the children settled in their new areas and
were not in a position to return to the town centre, so the new accommodation was taken by non-Leithers. Whether intended or not, this was highly
destructive of what had been a robust community. I often stand in the Kirkgate on the tour, the only point at which I don't read a passage from *Trainspotting*, discussing how heroin finds the gaps in community and personal
lives, and how there were plenty of gaps in Leith.

Welsh and his parents were part of this generation. Although fading fast after the war, the Leith spirit was still present. Despite the difficulties, it was strong and supportive. If a pauchle of fish, landed that morning, went upstairs to a neighbour, a plate of scones would come the other way. In the tenement blocks every household took its turn washing the communal stair. And it wasn't just a joke that when the no. 7 bus passed Pilrig, and the Edinburgh passengers had got off, Leithers relaxed and talked to each other. In the mid-1960s the woman sitting next to a girl going to visit her mother's cousin in Leith said 'Ah dinnae ken you, hen.' Before the bus was in Junction Street the woman had her fully cross-referenced and she was welcomed to Leith.

Some people thrive in this intimacy: the philanthropic millionaire Sir Tom Farmer, for one, who, not wealthy as he grew up in the Leith of the 1940s and 50s but protected from the worst of poverty, has always praised the virtues of Leith's strong community. Others – Irvine Welsh, perhaps – find exactly the same thing oppressive, and leave at the first opportunity. Making allowance for the fact that Renton is particularly sensitive about his status after cold turkey, there seems to be something larger behind his 'irritation at huvin ma every word policed by morons...' (p.205). There can be little doubt about his feelings for the Leith community even though he is not entirely comfortable being in London when he says in 'London Crawling': 'Ye can be freer here... because it isnae Leith' (p.228).

Again, in keeping with narrow business interests more than with the interests of the community at large, in what was surely the most destructive single policy of all, Leith was not given Development Area status in the late 1960s. Development Areas offered generous relocation and start-up grants for incoming businesses and industries. While the nearby towns of Penicuik and Broxburn prospered, Leith found itself at the wrong end of a vacuum cleaner. In the first half of the 1970s the prestigious Crawfords bakery, Edinburgh Crystal (a Leith firm), half a dozen bottling plants and bonded warehouses, several engineering firms and dozens of smaller businesses – all good employers – took the lure. This spelled the end of traditional work patterns; Naz's mention of the 'trades' (p.102) in 'Grieving and Mourning In Port Sunshine' is a reference to the first fortnight in July in which many businesses closed down, co-ordinated for efficiency.

Leith had lost its place as the premier port on Scotland's east coast to Grangemouth in the 1950s, 30 miles upstream – so much more convenient for central Scotland. The rate of loss accelerated in the 1960s and 1970s when Grangemouth, with a busy railway line running into the docks, developed container berths and smooth dual carriageways for articulated container lorries leading directly to the nearby motorway; unlike the port of Leith, boxed in by city streets and only one under-used railway line remaining. With the accompanying mechanisation of stevedores' work, the hundreds of workers in the port of Leith rapidly dwindled to dozens. The *Training Ship Dolphin* was towed away, and the Nautical College closed.

In the late 1970s a mid-ranking police officer newly posted to Leith gave himself a day to familiarise himself with his new beat. Knowing it only by out-of-date reputation, he was expecting plenty of life and colour. He was aghast to see how drab, empty, and down-at-heel it was. Revd Jack Kellet, minister at South Leith church, used an image in a radio interview: Edinburgh had castle-like security up the hill, with its establishment functions such as banking, the university, the courts, the festivals, and all, leaving Leith exposed to all the elements, vagaries, and economic storms. The Historiographer Royal for Scotland, Professor Gordon Donaldson, is quoted as saying that Leith was as ill-served by Edinburgh in the 20th century as it had in any previous century. Robert Garioch, one of Scotland's famous Seven Poets, put himself in the boots of a latter day Robert Louis Stevenson whose father had business interests in Leith and who roamed Leith (probably in search of women) less than a hundred years earlier:

Leith wes a place for merchants, a century <u>sinsyne</u>,	<u>*ago*</u>
wi <u>wiell-appyntit</u> pubs whaur they could talk business,	<u>*well-appointed*</u>
carved wudden alcoves, tables, ye ken the kind of thing,	
and I <u>mind</u> the time whan they still had that character aboot them,	<u>*remember*</u>
whisky, and port and <u>buirdly</u> men wi confident heids.	<u>*sturdy*</u>
Leith <u>crined</u> in Embro's grup; Scotland in England's;	<u>*shrivelled*</u>
Britain in...? <u>Aweill</u>, Leith's <u>maistly</u> rubble nou.[13]	<u>*Ah, well... mostly*</u>

The annual Edinburgh Festival took place in a faraway country. Edinburgh people had no business in Leith and visitors to Edinburgh, including university students, were told not to go, and they didn't go. Whereas under the oppression of previous centuries, when the community could form a strong identity in adversity, and in the 19th century when they enjoyed civic pride, there can be no resistance to demolitions, dispersals, isolation and being ignored. Sue Mowat, in her scholarly history of the port of Leith, wrote that Leith has been written out of Scottish history. For this generation of

Leithers, there was more to it than that. *Ubi solitudinem faciunt pacem apellant.*[14]

Shortly before the Labour government gave way to Mrs Thatcher and the Tories in 1979, John Crichton with, as he used to say, his Bible in one hand and his Labour Party card in the other, showed a shocked Bruce Millan, Secretary of State for Scotland, round Leith. Millan allocated £5m to kick-start what became The Leith Project, a consortium of agencies tasked with bringing to an end the depredations of the previous three and a half decades.

Things didn't improve quickly. This was the heyday of Thatcherism bringing full exposure to the harsh winds of market forces. Not even the Leith Project could prevent more losses. In 1983 the last Leith-built ship went down the slip at Henry Robb's shipyard, amid fury and resentment that such a big employer and a long tradition had been brought to this. Shortly afterwards, the deeply loved Leith Hospital was deemed to be surplus to requirements in north Edinburgh and was closed. 'They can't do that', said the Labour MP for Leith, Ron Brown: 'it's our hospital.' He was wrong on both counts. And, notably, the Project did not keep open Leith Central Station which could have been such a distinctive and creative feature of the regeneration. As the most densely populated area in Scotland (and third most dense in the UK) the wedge of streets between Leith Walk and Easter Road contained abnormally high levels of unemployment, poverty, and poor housing. It still wasn't easy being a Leither.

As Edinburgh tidied up for the Commonwealth Games of 1984, Leith became the dustbin for on-street trouble in general, and the public face of the heroin scene in particular. Junkies congregated round the anchor and chain, a decorative reminder of Leith's maritime past, in the small broad area of the Kirkgate shopping centre. They were noisy, and went in for surreptitious handshakes as they exchanged heroin, and the police seemed happy to leave them there: 'We ken who you are and we ken where you are'. In a scene similar to the so-called ice-cream wars in Glasgow that ended so violently, it was pretty common knowledge that some juice vans ran heroin wraps. To the horror of their teachers, many junior children seemed to be familiar with where the dealers lived on their stair and in their neighbourhood. Some of them were pretty obvious, with their reinforced doors. One teacher recalls how a child who was claiming free school dinners was whisked away during term time to Spain for a family holiday. On return he showed her pictures of ostentatious wealth; there was little doubt in the teacher's mind that the child's father was a drug dealer. Whatever the economic situation, the social damage had been done.

Let's hook up with the fictional Frank Begbie. He has no time for junkies, of course, his drug of choice was alcohol. He agrees to walk with us to an old haunt of his, the Volunteer Arms. Although he's embarrassed to be seen walking with strangers by people he knows, he's also pleased to have a wee bit of attention. We pause at the top of Kirkgate. 'Ah used tae meet aw sorts ay folk here, back in the day' he says. We walk a few paces to the left, to the statue of Queen Victoria on the plinth of which The Leith Volunteers (5th Battalion Royal Scots) are honoured in a bas-relief, armed and standing to attention before a resplendent Britannia, for their service in the Boer War. 'Glorified, state sponsored violence' someone mutters. Frank doesn't catch it.

He says he often went up the ramp into the old station to see who was there and what was going on, and he used it as an open toilet. One dark night he came across his father in there, when he was with Renton – a bit embarrassing. He did some serious drinking at the Central Bar, and he remembers his one-legged grandfather was there when they celebrated Renton's 'result' in court (p.175). Another favourite was The Volley, at 184 Leith Walk, now renamed, which opened for breakfast and sold the cheapest beer in Edinburgh. He dimly recalls in the Volley coming across someone he knew as a boy in Granton, and there was the real possibility of a good fight but it came to nothing. He's pleased the story entered local folklore, however, and with pride he points out the cartoon on the wall outside, a caricature of some Weedgie in a film reenacting that moment, updating the name of the pub and the fact that the pool table is replaced with gaming machines. 'Ah nivir had a tache, but' he says. 'Ah couldnae be airsed wi one ay thaim.'

A Walk on the Dark Side: Begbie and Sick Boy

Begbie's character is fully worked out within the first generation of episodes. As he doesn't touch heroin, he does not need to be reshaped for *Porno*, so references to him and appearances he makes in the second generation 'Courting Disaster' and 'House Arrest' are consistent.

We first see Begbie through Stevie's eyes in 'Victory On New Years' Day', where he is 'at ease with himself' (p.43) but he comes across as loud, domineering and malevolent. We are introduced more fully in 'The Glass', in which Renton has the voice but it is mostly about Begbie. It contains an in places humorously good analysis of a damaged man and the difficulties of being in a relationship with him. He starts violence in 'The Glass', he looks for it in 'A Disappointment', and he comes within an ace of it in 'Easy Money for the Professionals'. Two episodes close with a show of violence in public: 'Inter Shitty' and 'Trainspotting at Leith Central Station'. In 'Strolling Through The Meadows' Spud recalls an incident in which Begbie's attitude to violence is on display: 'We fill in some Sherman Tank... Whae gies a fuck aboot that cunt?' (p.154). It was so sickening that he (Spud) almost forgot to remove the victim's wallet.

The second time Begbie has the voice, in 'Inter Shitty', he confirms the warning we had at the end of 'Her Man', in which he and Second Prize agree that physical restraint 'is different whin yir in a relationship...' (p.62). His treatment of June and his attitude towards their unborn child and other children of his tell us this is a very dangerous man behind closed doors, and there is no doubt that June and any children will never be safe with him – they should be offered a shelter. He repeatedly refers to women as 'it': '... so ah'm oan toap ay it, ken, cowpin it, likes... n it's fuckin screamin likes...' (p.336); 'Ah'd fuckin shag it' (p.266) he says of Anne Diamond, on seeing her the telly. And his epitaph on the now dead Julie Mathieson: 'fuckin waste ay a good bit ay fanny' (p.79). A misogynist, a criminal, and a violent man, in public and behind closed doors.

And a sociopath. He is unbearable on the train in 'Inter Shitty'. In the pub, and more so in the café in 'There is a Light That Never Goes Out' he causes offence with almost everything he says. His behaviour with Renton's mother in the pub after the court case is cringingly, offensively inappropriate. Yet she and her husband see him as one who works hard and plays hard (p.198). It seems to be to do with the fact that Begbie is dedicated to the traditional drug of choice – alcohol – and scorns heroin and all its users. He is old school, not in touch with popular culture in the way the others are. His nickname, Franco, is the sort of adaptation of Frank that you might expect from someone wishing to create an aura of power. Spud makes an association with the Spanish dictator Generalissimo Franco (p.156). 'The Beggar', by which he is also known, enhances his otherness. At several points in the book we are told that others collude in maintaining his aura. When he flashes the cash as he gives Spud two tenners at the Fit ay the Walk (p.120) it's consistent with his self-aggrandising tendencies.

Both Renton and Spud call Begbie a 'psycho'. We should be careful about our terms here. It is a legitimate part of fiction that words can be used for their effect rather than in a dictionary definition. 'Psychopath' is widely misunderstood and misused. In popular usage it can be a shortcut term for a bogeyman, an anti-hero, one who is mad, beyond redemption, and about whom we need not care. Psychiatrists avoid it unless a complex clinical diagnosis of a psychosis is available. The analysis in this book is of Begbie as an angry, aggressive, violent, emotionally immature man.

His language is unvaryingly foul. We know that Begbie has no prospects of moving out of his status as a social outcast until he can express himself without resorting to crudities and profanities. They are, after all, an expression of his mind-set and outlook. He gives no-one, friend or stranger, any reason to like or respect him. Polite society will always reject him. He hates the world, and it is reciprocated.

There are a couple of caveats to this view of Begbie as a consistently drawn character. The first comes in Tommy Younger's bar, now renamed, at 300 Leith Walk, a couple of blocks up from the Volley. Unexpectedly, Begbie encourages Renton to visit Tommy (p.308). Is this fleeting show of empathy a stroke of genius on Welsh's part, the moment that shows Begbie does have a kind side? Or does it pull him out of character? The other caveat, as discussed elsewhere, is the big question mark over his involvement with a bunch of junkies as they take the skag to London. It seems that Welsh's other requirements in 'Station to Station' overrode the requirement for consistency of character.

Sometimes on my tour I ask (rhetorically, of the women): would you rather be beaten up by Begbie or pimped out by Sick Boy? Of course, there is no sensible answer. The purpose of asking is to raise awareness that Welsh has put two highly unpleasant characters on the page, or three if you count Johnny Swan in 'A Leg-Over Situation' and 'A Scottish Soldier'. Four, if Alan Venters in 'Her Man' and 'Bad Blood' qualifies. But we are only considering well developed characters here, so we have already narrowed our competition for the Most Unsympathetic Character of the book award down to two finalists: Begbie and Sick Boy. We backtrack to Leith Links and stand outside no. 2 Wellington Place.

* * * * * * * * * * * *

There is lots to suggest that Welsh has Sick Boy shooting out of his own front room in 'Deid Dugs', so we can stand in the line of fire, between the cherry trees. Sick Boy is not using, so time can drag a little and here we find him having some fun on an otherwise dull day. He has a distinctive voice, helped by his recurring fantasy conversation with Sir Sean Connery as James Bond. His plan works out beautifully; not only does he kill a despised Pitbull terrier, he also dupes the police (well, he doesn't entirely convince the older one) as he disguises his part in the incident.

This episode can be twinned with 'The Elusive Mr Hunt', although he doesn't have the voice in Rutherford's Bar. This time mimicking the convoluted vowels of Malcolm Rifkind, an Edinburgh Conservative Member of Parliament and sometime Secretary of State for Scotland and Foreign Secretary, again his base intentions and actions go undiscovered. We can say in these two episodes he goes in for recreational hooliganism. Markedly at odds with this character, in 'It Goes Without Saying' Sick Boy is a needy junkie just like the others, although he does stand apart a little in that he is (allegedly) a father. These three episodes apart, there are only passing references to and fleeting appearances of Sick Boy in the first generation of episodes.

This is not the Sick Boy that Welsh wants to finish with and take on into *Porno*. Sick Boy's character is developed and his trajectory into the sequel is launched within the second generation of episodes. It was in an instinctively insightful moment that Welsh made Sick Boy a son of the Banana Flats, so-called because of the curve at the southern end. Brutally Brutalist – despite problems which quickly became apparent, the block is now listed and protected, as a fine example of its kind - when it was first opened in 1965 it was widely thought of as the Brave New World.

In the second generation we learn that he was raised in the Banana Flats, and that his mother is Italian, which seems to explain why he sometimes breaks into simple Italian and refers to himself as 'Simone'. For the reader of Trainspotting this is patchy and incomplete, but Welsh certainly had all this in the wider contextualising of his character. In the sequel Porno and more so in the prequel Skagboys, we meet his no-good Scottish father who treats his Italian wife and their family, Simon and his sisters, so badly. Therein lies some sort of context for Sick Boy's cynicism. From all of this we can say that Sick Boy was an embryonic character in the early stages of writing what became Trainspotting, and that Trainspotting is a first draft and a launch pad for the character who is developed further in works that appeared later.

So we'll cut across the Kirkgate to Cable's Wynd House (only the postie calls it that), the Banana Flats, notoriously home to many a drug dealer in the 1980s. The kids make the most of scant play areas outside. This is where I usually stop to meet the sexually voracious, arrogant, self-centred, exploitative, manipulative, entirely cynical character who stays in the memory. His creator can hardly do more to put us on notice for what to expect than giving him this memorable line: 'Ah'd rather see ma sister in a brothel than ma brother in a Hearts scarf...' (p.30). This is the label on the tin, to be taken seriously and literally. The whole of Sick Boy's character that is taken forward into Porno and cast backwards into Skagboys emanates from his personal manifesto contained in 'In Overdrive'.

We walk up Henderson Street to the Foot of the Walk for a full view of Sick Boy as Welsh is grooming him for *Porno*. We are taking it that The Central Bar is the second location for the après-court celebrations in 'Courting Disaster'. Sick Boy has played second fiddle to Begbie's offensiveness in Deacon's (Deacon Brodie's) pub opposite the court house, and comes into his own here. Effortlessly and publicly offering to pimp out wee Maria Anderson to Planet Ay The Apes, he repeats his credo from way back in 'In Overdrive': '... ah'm looking eftir numero uno... His eyes wir crystal clear and treacherous, untainted by conscience or compassion' (p.174). This is him putting his manifesto into action. When he turns up ten years later in *Porno* he has failed at every enterprise he has tried but has lost none of his cynicism or exploitative tendencies.

We only meet Sick Boy in Leith town centre, in Edinburgh, or London. He goes to France and Corsica, places beyond the wildest dreams of the others. He puts imaginary distance between himself and them with his recurring fantasy conversation with Sir Sean Connery as James Bond. (In *Porno* Sir Sean is replaced by Alex McLeish, then manager at Hibs, with whom Sick Boy has macho man-management conversations.) His 'friends' endure personal put downs and sexual rivalry. We certainly don't see him as 'Leith Bannanay Flats's lovable cavalier', nor as 'some sort ay *Oor Wullie*' (p.198) of Renton's parents' imagination. He has learned the value of being discreet, or secretive. Notice that we have no better source than himself for stories of his sexual conquests. Neither do we see how he gets out of addiction.

Welsh makes two brackets to open and close Sick Boy's appearance in *Trainspotting*. On the second page of the book Renton says: 'This cunt has a wey ay makin ye feel a real petty, trivial bastard... [but] ...The cunt is irresistible oan this form' (p.4). The closing bracket comes in the final episode when he cadges a drink on the bus to London: 'One can, then, ya tight cunt!.. Second Prize reluctantly hands a can over...' (p.332). He hasn't changed a bit! He is in play for a little longer on the bus and in London, but despite his manipulations and sophistications, he is well out of his depth when it comes to dealing with Gilbert. He is almost missing from the second half of *Trainspotting*; he disappears after 'House Arrest', and apart from playing the crude joke on Kelly in 'The Elusive Mr Hunt' he doesn't reappear till the last episode. If we like unpleasant, unsympathetic characters to fill a role in fiction, we're almost pleased to see him back, the bastard.

It is tempting to marry Sick Boy's over-stated ambition with the Banana Flats in which he grew up, and with the false promises of the Thatcher project, so ridiculed in the 'choose life' rant of the book (and later magnified in the film). None of the three lives up to its glossy initial presentation. And, squeezing everything in while we're at it, we could add the early seductiveness of heroin with its subsequent problems. A multi-faceted metaphor.

Directly outside The Central Bar we can catch a bus up to York Place and the bus station. Now it is as pleasant a place as a bus station is likely to be, but at the time of writing *Trainspotting* it was a noisy, greasy place. Actually at ground level, under a 1960s office block it felt subterranean in all the worst ways. Pedestrians were separated from the buses as they roared in and out by the sort of railings you see in cattle markets. A fine place, then, for Sick Boy to rip off Molly, an HIV+ prostitute, 'a victim...' (p.237) and immediately wish he had ripped her off some more when he sees how much she has in her purse. On their way to London to sell all that skag, he hooks up with the other contender for Most Unsympathetic Character of the book award, the dangerously uptight Begbie. And the winner is...

CHAPTER 11

Meanwhile in the Schemes

HISTORICALLY, THE CONNECTIONS between Leith and West Pilton and Muirhouse are strong. However, it is not possible to construct much of an on-location tour from the scant references to the area in *Trainspotting*, even though Spud and Begbie went to school at Craigroyston, and from 'A Disappointment' we know Begbie is familiar with it. Most of 'The First Day of the Edinburgh Festival' and the whole of 'Winter in West Granton' are set here, and, from the beginning of *Trainspotting* Welsh seems clearly to want us to make the connections in his reference to Seeker, who is in the 'Muirhoose-Leith mob' (p.6) as a heroin supplier. But we don't have a *Trainspotting* character to guide us.

Around the time that Welsh was born in the late 1950s the first wave of Edinburgh Corporation new post-war housing was coming to an end. Much of it was similar in style to the pretty successful pre-war Craigentinny and East Pilton: terraced houses with pitched roofs mixed with small blocks of flats, and all solidly built. In the 1950s many Leithers went to Clerwood and Clermiston on Corstorphine Hill, and Drylaw off the west end of Ferry Road. The war-time pre-fabs of West Pilton were converted and the scheme extended westwards to what became Pennywell Road. But the chairman of the Housing Department said that while the Corporation could be pleased and proud of all this, it was not possible to afford any more in the same vein.

The parlance among local government councillors and housing officials around the country was changing from 'families', 'houses' and 'flats' to 'units' and getting a target number of people onto an acre. It was the conception of what became Muirhouse. With an inadequate budget for the building process, site security there was poor, and a lot of materials went missing. Concrete was often inadequately compressed to fill the shuttering so that many window- and door-frames were wedged in with folded fag packets, the shortcomings skimmed over. Several Clerks of Work had difficulty signing off finished buildings. West Granton Crescent, a single complex block which arrived later, was an extension of the West Granton development that ran along the north of West Pilton. Within a very few years the outer facing had deteriorated and was patched up in such a way as to give rise to its universal nick-name: the Varicose Veins flats.

Granton and Muirhouse were built on land previously owned by nearby Royston House (now Caroline Park House), giving rise to the confusion of names that Begbie is aware of but can't explain (p.84). The scheme was laid out for plenty of cars, with short dual carriageways, sweeping curves, and generous parking space in front of every block. There was no provision for small shops among the housing, nor any pubs or prominent feature that would give the scheme a focus or variety. The Pennywell shopping centre was a glum place indeed from the beginning, managed by a company, which, like the Kirkgate Centre in Leith, was no incentive for local shopkeepers, who need to own their premises; many of the units were let to branches of chain stores with little interest in investing in the local community. There was no bank, an obvious opening for loan sharks. Open spaces were never the pleasant parkland of the glossy brochures, quickly becoming little better than urban deserts.

Within less than two decades the whole scheme was a slum, different only in type from the slums in Leith town centre that it replaced. The Scottish Office declared it eligible for Urban Aid Fund - the first in Scotland - and the Church of Scotland made it an Urban Priority Area. By the early 1980s it was home to poverty, disorder, alcohol and other drug abuse, and it became the epicentre of the collision between intra-venous heroin injecting and the dreadful HIV. The occupants were not qualitatively different from those who went earlier to Clermiston and Drylaw. What went wrong?

The background to all this is missing in *Trainspotting*, but Welsh chronicles it, vividly and historically plausibly, in some of his other fiction: *Glue*[15], *The Acid House*[16], and *Marabou Stork Nightmares*[17]. All was well to begin with:

> They sat up most of the night drinking, reminiscing about where they had come from before the slum-clearance flats. They all agreed that they were the best thing that had happened to the working classes... Wullie and his wife came from Leith via the West Granton pre-fabs. They had been offered Muirhouse but they went for this cause it was nearer Sandra's mother who had been ill and lived in Chesser.
>
> - We're in the older part of the scheme [Pilton], but, Wullie said semi-apologetically, it isnae as smart as this.
>
> Duncan tried not to feel superior, but that was the consensus in the area: the newer flats [Muirhouse] were the best deal (*Glue* p.26).

>For Davie Galloway it was the big windows that exemplified
>all that was good about these new slum-clearance places... That's
>the best thing aboot these places, Susan, Davie ventured, – the
>big windaes. Let the sun in, he added, before glancing over at the
>marvel of that wee box stuck on the wall above her head. – Cen-
>tral heating for the winter n aw, cannae be beaten. The flick ay a
>switch (*Glue* p.4).

Problems began to show after the first summer. The new-fangled central
heating was something to be wondered at, but the day when the first bills
landed on door mats is etched into the collective memory. Very few had bud-
geted for such a financial shock:

>The Ewarts, like other families in the area, enjoyed their airy
>flat. All their neighbours commented on the under-floor heating,
>where you could heat up the whole flat with just a click of the
>switch. Maria's dad had recently died of TB in Tollcross's damp
>tenements; now all that was a thing of the past. Duncan loved
>those big warm tiles under the carpet. You could put your feet
>under that fireside rug and it was sheer luxury. Then as winter set
>in and the first bills came through the post, the central heating
>in the scheme clicked off; synchronised to such a degree it was
>almost like they were operated by one master switch (*Glue* p.27).

Ten years later in the same flat:

>It seemed like the entire tenement building hissed and shook
>as the whistling drafts of cold air shot through, leaving it cry-
>ing, creaking, and leaking, as if it were a lobster thrust into a
>boiling pot. Those high-pressure blasts of dirty chilled wind from
>the gales outside gatecrashed relentlessly; via the cracks in the
>window frames and under the sill, through the vents and spaces,
>between the floorboards. (*Glue* p.33).

The accommodation, being so very permeable to wind, water, tempera-
ture and noise did not encourage affection or loyalty as family homes – on
the contrary, it was inadequate and unpleasant and, for some, positively
unhealthy. And the fact that most Leithers arrived in the new scheme in good
spirits and grateful at last to have an identified and responsible landlord
masked the obvious fact and delayed the realisation that it was always going
to go wrong. The demography had a dangerously imbalanced profile, con-
sisting entirely of tenants, mostly of young families, and a high proportion
of unskilled employees. However, for most of the 1960s, things were OK.
Buses to Leith were full of people working in the docks, or in Salamander

Street. There was work available too in the nearby gasworks, the wireworks, at Parsons Peebles, and at the flourishing arms industry, Ferranti's at Crewe Toll, all offering good apprenticeships.

There was nothing wrong with the primary schools. Ainslie Park secondary school offered traditional Scottish educational fare, and Telford College, not far away, taught the youngsters a trade. The two latter establishments drew in youngsters from outwith the neighbourhood, maintaining connections with the wider city. Although there was little enough in the way of infrastructure for recreation, clubs were started for the youngsters: drama clubs, cricket clubs, holiday clubs, and the rest. Families watched television of an evening from a selection of three or four channels, which were discussed the following day in the workplaces and schools – a shared community life. Nearby Granton harbour, which was still busy with trawlers and small coasters, was interesting and active, and Gypsy Brae, Silverknowes Foreshore and Cramond Island were pleasant and adventurous places to get away from the streets.

Some problems became apparent in the 1970s. The enthusiasm and energy on which the community functions were founded began to dissipate as parents and children grew older. They were unsupported by any length of history and tradition and there was no succeeding age group. With no other demand for the open spaces, they became depositories for broken glass and dog shit. The fictional Coco Bryce cuts across a large stretch of open ground which, when the scheme was new, was home to cricket and football clubs: 'He hunched up and stole quickly down the path that split the massive canine toilet which was West Pilton Park' (*The Acid House* p.154). Those who could left the area, a good many emigrating to Canada, Australia, New Zealand or South Africa, often with the help of assisted passages. Women did their shopping in Junction Street, Leith, and men and women kept up their socialising, whether bingo, pubs, or church, by maintaining their loyalty to the Leith they had left. The area was losing too much of its talent while failing to establish roots and institutions locally.

The council lost control of its own estate. Travelling folk occupied two empty stairs in West Pilton, stabling their donkeys on the ground floor and letting them graze outside, where the kids played with them. One man took the floor out of his front room to plant a tree there, and the room became an aviary. For four years a young man lived in the flat of a friend of his who had emigrated, without paying any rent. A local man who voluntarily kept the play-park nice and safe gave up, disheartened by persistent vandalism. A painting and decorating contractor, a decent local man who wanted nothing more than to do a good job as he earned a living, was driven to the point where he wouldn't bid for work in the scheme because he couldn't provide good enough security to protect his materials.

In *Marabou Stork Nightmares* Welsh tracks the everyday experience of life in the scheme for the youngsters. Roy Strang wasn't finding it easy to grow up in the 1970s in an 'ugly rabbit hutch': 'It was a systems built, 1960s maisonette block of flats, five storeys high, with long landings jokingly referred to as "streets in the sky"' but which had no shops or pubs or churches or post offices on them, nothing in fact except more rabbit hutches. Being so close to those other families, it became impossible for people, as much as they tried, to keep their lives from each other' (*Marabou Stork Nightmares* p.19). It was difficult to find an alternative to the 'sterile boredom' outside the house: 'All those dull broadsheet newspaper articles on the scheme where we lived tended to focus on how deprived it was. Maybe it was, but I'd always defined the place as less characterised by poverty than by boredom, although the relationship between the two is pretty evident' (*Marabou Stork Nightmares* p.19). '...I was charged by the polis for playing football in the street. We were kicking a ball around in a patch of grass outside the block of flats we lived in. There were no NO BALL GAMES signs up, but we should have known, even at that age, that the scheme was a concentration camp for the poor; this, like everything else, was prohibited. We were taken up tae court where my mate Brian's dad made a brilliant speech and embarrassed the judge into admonishing us.... (*Marabou Stork Nightmares* pp.21, 22) Welsh has said that this happened to him, with others, as a child, that it was his dad 'doing his nut at the judge', and that although 'we were let off without a fine, I officially had a criminal record at eight years old.' It was, he observes, 'a geographically short but culturally long distance from the historic city centre experienced by tourists...'[18]

Back in the fiction, when Roy is attacked by the family dog and goes to hospital, the story '...made the local paper and the Tory council, who hated spending the snobby ratepayers' money on anything to do with our scheme, grudgingly sent an environmental health van to round up the savage pack-beasts for extermination.'(*Marabou Stork Nightmares* p.21) 'Boney [Bonfire] nights were the best nights of the year in the scheme... we'd go doon the beach tae get wood or find other boneys in the scheme and raid them. Sometimes, though, we got raided ourselves. You would get cudgels and stanes and try to defend your bonfire against raiders. There was always fights with stanes in the scheme. The first thing I learned tae dae was tae fling a stane. That was what you did as a kid in Muirhoose, you flung stanes; flung them at radges, at windaes, at buses. It was something to do' (*MSN*.p.25). Roy becomes a troubled teenager, getting involved with the Hibs Casuals (City Centre Service, or the cashies) by way of avoiding the pain and confusion of his family life: 'In Muirhoose nae cunt can hear you scream... well, they can hear ye, they just dinnae gie a fuck'(*Marabou Stork Nightmares* p.141).

Not everything was black. The visionary Deputy Director of Education, Fraser Henderson, could see that conventional Scottish education was never going to answer the needs in Muirhouse. He head-hunted Hugh MacKenzie and gave him the space to run the newly-built Craigroyston Junior Secondary School, as it was then, ('Craigie' in *Trainspotting*) along the lines of A S Neil's Summerhill. Such freedom was not easy to fit into a state system, but the project was pursued with verve and confidence for 20 years and more, the school providing genuinely innovative courses and programmes that were emulated elsewhere. One girl hearing gales of laughter from the staff room thought 'I would like some of that', and went on to become a teacher herself. Gordon Strachan, at the time of writing the Scotland football team manager and within a couple of years the same age as Welsh, attended Craigie. Within the community it was more than a school: it was a welcoming centre of resourcefulness and creativity. There were other valiant attempts to generate and maintain community cohesion – clubs, newsletters, and so forth – but nothing could overcome the monster of unemployment.

In the first part of the 1970s practically all youngsters found work on leaving school. By the end around 60 per cent in this neighbourhood were unemployed three years after leaving school. A generation had come of age that had no knowledge of a stable well-ordered community, and had no loyalty to the larger society that had put it in Muirhouse. The welfare state, designed to avert the harsh, biting poverty of the pre-war years, had done its job well. When there is financial support available in periods of high unemployment, it is difficult to maintain the fiction that there is a job for everyone, and that there is a meaningful incentive to get out of bed in the morning. Some people were well versed in maximising the benefits that were theirs by right. *Trainspotting*'s Mark Renton is far from the only one who regarded fiddling the system as a job of work. A few youngsters, probably only ten or a dozen, who had grown up away from the neighbourhood in some form of care - a foster family, or a children's home - came back at the age of 16 with tenuous connections in the community and took to hanging around the shopping centre. They were streetwise and insolent. And the arrival of heroin, in quantities, as 1980 approached, changed everything.

By now the notorious, awful Varicose Veins flats were occupied. Actually a long single multi-level block, it was irregularly shaped with many turnings in the walkways which, with a difficult-to-follow sequence of door numbers, were confusing and were often poorly lit. I went there several times (long before this book was conceived), in connection with a boy with special needs. I'm not fearful or squeamish, but I found it dispiriting, and no place for this loving and hard-working but vulnerable family – or, come to that, for any family. In a local publication a woman later wrote a poem describing how when she was a school-kid her mum used to take and make every opportunity to get away, after school and at weekends. She used to regard the space outside, visible from her flat, as hostile territory. One older woman who lived alone there made it clear that she did not expect anyone to visit her after dark.

The rivalry that was harmless enough in the early days when the fictitious Wullie and Sandra compared West Pilton unfavourably with Muirhouse became more serious and developed into an unhealthy territorialism. It was expressed, childishly, in school: 'Sir, the people in Pilton have six fingers, don't they?' Welsh picks it up in *The Acid House*. An angry and confused young man

> cross[es] the dual carriageway, leaving posh Muirhouse and get over to scruffy Pilton. That might no be how people see things now, but that's how it's always been tae me. Muirhouse is the newer hooses. Pilton's for the scruffs. It disnae matter what problems Muirhouse has got now and how much they tart up Pilton. Pilton's Pilton, and Muirhoose is Muirhoose, always fuckin well will be. Fuckin scruffy Pilton cunts. These cunts that gave me the kicking were fae Pilton; that's these cunts' mentality. I've probably got fuckin lice just through being in the vicinity of the dirty Pilton scruffy fuckin cunts (*The Acid House* p.287).

This rivalry was the seed-bed for violent and criminal gangs, in the 1980s often connected with heroin trafficking; the City Centre Casuals, for example, who purported to be associated with Hibernian FC, but of course the club rejected any connection.

The Church of Scotland minister who arrived newly posted to West Pilton in 1983 found the area desolate, derelict and depressed. On his first weekend many people's giros didn't arrive. He couldn't help in any immediate practical way. A young man turned up at the manse with scars to show for a beating he had received. Later, he remembers, an HIV+ woman with a child came to his door, rejected by her family. Very painful and pitiful it was, but, with a young family of his own he couldn't give either of them refuge or any form of immediate help. One day he was asked by the chaplain at the Royal Edinburgh [psychiatric] Hospital to visit a woman from Stornoway who had been discharged with a young child to the Varicose Veins flats. The stair was filthy, partly obstructed by a broken fridge. She was in the only flat occupied on that stair. 'Caring Britain', he thought. 'This vulnerable person has been allocated the worst possible accommodation.'

The Roman Catholic priests were deeply respected for their non-judge-mental and non-partisan work in the community. When I asked one how he squared the issue of condoms from a project in which his church was actively involved with Catholic doctrine on the subject he replied: 'Ah, the Vatican is a long way from Muirhouse.' Ecumenical work thrived at an everyday level in a way that the clergy in more prosperous areas didn't even aspire to. But the area was isolated. Desperately needing help in the parish, the minister reflected that it was more likely that the Church would send a missionary to Africa than an assistant to West Pilton, not much more than a couple of miles from the Church of Scotland head office in central Edinburgh.

While much of the public, street-level action of the heroin scene was going on in Leith, Muirhouse and West Pilton was home to a lot of users. The reckless, opportunist thieving made people fearful of leaving their flats. Any family with a using member, or even someone with connections with junkies, just couldn't leave him or her alone. On return, something of value would be missing: maybe the curtains, or the television. One user or dealer in a stair made the whole building hazardous. The attempt by the Housing Department to put people who needed help in a stair where someone else in the stair would offer support, Leith-style, had been long since abandoned. The reverse of what was intended actually happened - one or two people who didn't put their rubbish out or take their turn washing the stair had a destructive impact on this traditional informal functioning.

Wishing to create a society of property owners, under the government's Right to Buy policy, sitting council tenants were given the opportunity to buy their homes at knock-down prices. For people who were in a position to take advantage, this was irresistible. It amounted to the biggest privatisation of all in a series of anti-public body policies of the Thatcher years. There were plenty of problems with municipal landlordism, but the morality of flogging off public property was highly questionable. To be sure, one effect has been to introduce a healthy, welcome diversity into what used to be monolithic schemes. But there always was an ugly downside. The purchase price brought scant return for public investment and assets, which was, in any case, spirited away from housing department budgets, leaving them with the hardest to let properties and unable to invest in new housing stock. It was part of a wider war between Whitehall and town hall in which local initiative, responsiveness and responsibility were overcome by centralised ideology. The Right to Buy legislation was finally repealed by the by-then devolved Scottish parliament in 2016.

On a dull, drizzly morning in the mid-1980s a small crowd gathered in West Pilton while George Kenneth Hotson Younger, 4th Viscount Younger of Leckie, Secretary of State for Scotland, cut the ribbon upon the sale of the first Council house in the area. Welsh brings out some of this in *Trainspotting*. If we can sense why he attaches the themes of his early writings to the contradictions of Leith Central Station and its demolition, we can sense that his anger is more focussed in 'Winter in West Granton'. We can expect him to know more than a little about how HIV+ people were treated, since he was an official in the municipal housing department with a brief concerned with this matter, and he took it personally. He describes how Tommy ends up in a flat in the awful West Granton Crescent with abusive graffiti daubed on the reinforced door: 'Tommy cannae get oot ay West Granton... [he] got it through the council's hotline. Fifteen thousand people on the waiting list and naebody wanted this one. It's a prison. It's no really the council's fault; the government made them sell off all the good hooses, leaving the dross for the likes ay Tommy...' And the chair he sits on originally belonged to 'some rich cunt...', and has passed through several owners before ending up with Tommy (p.315).

In the late 1980s there was a 10 per cent churn per year in the school roll at Craigie, while absenteeism went up markedly. One teacher realised that only one child in his class lived with both parents, and school parlance was adjusted to refer to 'your people at home'. In 1990, looking over his class registers for the previous decade he realised that at least one from every year had died, and that was only the ones he knew about – the real count was almost certainly higher. One man went to several weddings of his contemporaries in the 1980s and noted the large number of friends who should have been present: more absentees (prison, hospital, death) than you would expect in wartime, he reflected.

****

For all the shocking state of the housing in Leith, there were strengths in the community which were comprehensively derided, devalued and demolished along with the infrastructure, and which were left undermined and unsupported in the schemes. The work of Octavia Hill, who worked in the late

Victorian slums of London (the period and the place are recognised laboratories of such matters), was completely ignored. She demonstrated that people need to be and are willing to be engaged in their own destiny; that when overall plans are consensual and resources are made available, where there is firm leadership and kept promises, any community can improve the housing stock incrementally and strengthen its own functionality in the process. All of this could have been explored and applied in Leith town centre. None of it was. To have no say in intimate and important decisions about your accommodation and your neighbourhood is disempowering and de-motivating. The middle classes won't allow themselves to be treated like this.

At first sight, the council as landlord would seem to be an improvement on the absent, profiteering and irresponsible landlords of the Leith slums. But too much was being asked of the council. It had to assess the need for services it would itself provide; it had to act as landowner, developer, contractor, estate manager, and now landlord. And the remit was not clear. Was it to be housing fit for heroes, or decent housing at a fair rent, or a safety net for people who had fallen through all other nets and would, out of their own energies, aspire to leave as soon as they could? Was it to be an investment in property that would be good for several generations, or a cheap job to meet immediate needs? The council had to be financially responsible as well as politically responsive. The financial provisions were not generous, and public attitudes to public housing were increasingly ambivalent. However, the overall judgement has to be that the Muirhouse scheme (along with many another British housing scheme of the 1960s) was high-handed and experimental in conception, cheap and shoddy in execution, over-planned from above, poorly managed from a distance, and populated by a very narrow cross-section of society.

It became all too easy for mainstream society to find fault with every transgression in the schemes from its own values and standards, to designate the people as losers and 'the underclass', and further to isolate them. *The Scotsman* and its sister paper *Edinburgh Evening News* were unremittingly harsh and hostile. Channel Four ran a series on the area, depicting it as a sink estate. The Tory government, recently the party of pragmatism, paternalism and patriotism, lurched to free-market talk of benefit scroungers, they said if you were unemployed you should 'get on yer bike', and for Mrs Thatcher there was 'no such thing as society'. Social Work department area offices were established in West Pilton and Muirhouse, and it was striking to see the cars parked outside while their middle-class professional owners did a day's work in the scheme and went home in the evenings.

The Housing Department discovered to its cost, and at the expense of a generation of Leithers, that providing 'solutions' to 'problems' from above will always lead to alienation and community dysfunction. Responsibility for the arrival of heroin cannot be laid at the council's door, nor can the rise in unemployment in the 1970s and 1980s. But if the council is responsible for the provision of safe and affordable accommodation, as it was, then Edinburgh did not except itself from a general failure throughout Britain in the 1960s housing schemes. It's not fair even to blame the politicians for this – society gets the politicians it votes for. Ultimately, we are all responsible for ghettoising certain sections of our community, and for excessively privileging others.

As a general rule, Welsh uses authentic local history neutrally, as a backdrop for his fiction. But, as we have seen, he has attitude. He is entitled to it – he knew the area well, having grown up in it, and by the time he was writing the fiction he was working there as a professionally educated young man who had travelled in the British Isles and further afield, and he was seeing it all again through new eyes. He knew not only the history of Edinburgh's council housing schemes: Clermiston (first post-war phase), Muirhouse (second post-war phase), and Wester Hailes (third post-war phase), but also the reality of living in some of them. In *Marabou Stork Nightmares*, fictionally writing in South Africa, in a much-quoted passage he compares the schemes to the infamous township outside Johannesburg, Soweto: '…the only difference [from Soweto] was that Kaffirs were white and called schemies or draftpaks. Back in Edinburgh, we would be Kaffirs; condemned to live out our lives in townships like Muirhouse or So-Wester-Hailes-To or Niddrie, self-contained camps with fuck-all in them, miles fae the toon. Brought in tae dae the crap jobs that nae other cunt wanted tae dae, then hassled by the polis if we hung around at night in groups. Edinburgh had the same politics as Johannesburg: it had the same politics as any city. Only we were on the other side' (*Marabou Stork Nightmares* p.80).

Howls of protest and outrage in critical commentary objected that the comparison is unfair – that being black in apartheid South Africa was a permanent state of disadvantage, which is not the same as being white in a sub-standard British housing scheme. This is true. However, there are similarities. Both these categories of people are easily ghettoised, ridiculed, and exploited. In both cases they are the flotsam and jetsam of economic and social conditions, the pool of cheap labour available when required by capitalism, yet expendable, discarded and maintained at not much above poverty levels – and that grudgingly – when not required. In the case of Soweto in apartheid South Africa, ever-heavier oppression was required to maintain the status quo, which makes it different from 1980s Muirhouse where there was, at least in theory, some personal and social/economic mobility if enough sops and scraps were thrown to the schemies to secure an adequate level of public order.

The reader will judge whether, when fiction becomes polemical like this, it loses certain literary qualities. The reader will also consider whether this is one of Welsh's limitations or one of his strengths. Welsh may have been remembering that in 1950s Edinburgh there were marches along Princes Street by people who were still stuck in war-time camps that were supposed to be temporary. They carried placards likening their situation to the inmates of the German extermination camps. Now, that was unfair. But they made their point. And Welsh makes his.

CHAPTER 12

Welsh's Women

YOU DON'T NEED much imagination to figure out Sick Boy's use of the word 'mantovani' (p.29), as he cruises the sexual opportunities on the Bridges in 'In Overdrive', abbreviated to 'manto' on the next page and used occasionally elsewhere and by others. It's probably a loose reference to Annunzio Mantovani, the Anglo-Italian best known in light musical entertainment and who had some influence in pop and punk. Leith boys of Welsh's generation sometimes referred to girls as 'manto'. Jeff Torrington uses 'Mantovani' as a sexual euphemism in his *Swing, Hammer, Swing* (Vintage, 1992), set in the 1960s as the Gorbals in Glasgow was being demolished, just like Leith.

The word 'cunt', referring to female genitalia, is the most foul word in the English language. It is frequently used in *Trainspotting*, casually as well as deliberately to be crude and offensive, but it is so over-used that, perversely, it becomes a term of affection. Begbie uses both meanings as he aggressively greets Renton, 'jist up fae London', then denounces Second Prize in the next thing he says (p.307). The unrestrained use of the word throughout the book is a major difficulty in quoting from it in many situations.

Once I did a quickie tour for an American lady who only had an hour. We met at The Black Bull on Leith Street. Two hundred years ago well-to-do gentlemen came to Leith Street and St James Square, (replaced by the 1960s St James Centre and now being re-built), the then seedy east end of the New Town, looking for prostitutes. The women asked their customers to recommend them in the local newspapers, which they did: 'she has her own teeth...'; 'Mary is excellent at the Critical Moment...' I doubt very much that it is with this connection in mind that Welsh placed *Trainspotting*'s only women-only episode, 'Feeling Free', on Leith Street.

It is much more likely that he used the housing advice office at 23-27 Leith Street, a few doors up from the Black Bull, with which he would be familiar in his working life, as a place where Edinburgh's private business meets Edinburgh: the international destination. Kelly and Alison, two young women with a pre-occupying assortment of men problems, health problems, heroin problems and housing problems, come out of their appointment and walk straight into a wider world. They turn left up Leith Street, and there was the public counter of the GPO (General Post Office), now re-named, opposite on Waterloo Place, which had scaffolding on it for many years. Male crudities from the 'workies' are challenged head-on by a combination of these two, a pair of Edinburgh wifies, and a couple of travelling lesbians. This disparate grouping, spontaneously formed, immediately develops a positive intimacy and mutual supportiveness that is quite unlike any grouping of men in *Trainspotting*.

Welsh has not included women in the main thrust of the narrative and action in *Trainspotting*, but he has drawn a diverse collection of female characters. For our purposes, we make two groups, the first Renton's parents' generation and the second his contemporaries.

Molly Greaves is professional and plays a part in Renton's redemption. She appears only once, in 'Searching for the Inner Man', where she fits comfortably into her place alongside male colleagues. Spud's Na Na is, explicitly, a retired prostitute and an unpleasant one at that. She may also be an active drug dealer: the hint is contained in the 'series ay different locks' (p.123) to her door (an implausible detail in supported accommodation). Welsh works up the idea of a drug-dealing granny, which was certainly not unknown in 1980s Leith, into a short story, *Granny's Old Junk* (in *The Acid House*) in which the old woman is not dissimilar to Na Na. The reader's sympathy is all with Na Na's daughter, Colleen, Spud's mum, as she is bullied by Begbie after Spud's court appearance (p.170).

Renton's Ma is the most filled-out of the female characters in *Trainspotting*. To Nina, she is the most outgoing of her aunties, who treats her as a person rather than as a child (p34). Renton loves her too: even in the grip of addiction he reflects 'Ah love Ma... too much... So much ah don't want her tae have a son like me' (pp.56, 57). Cath Renton defends and supports Mark, lovingly taking control over his period of withdrawal following the overdose at Johnny Swan's, and Mark, in his perverse and convoluted way, goes so far as to acknowledge his debt to her and his father: 'Ah love the fuck oot ay the bastards' (p.203).

She is Catholic – that's implicit from her maiden name of Fitzpatrick (p.33) and explicit in Renton's reflection at Billy's funeral that his mother is from 'ayesur papish bastards' and his father from 'soapdodging Orange cunts'. (p.218). It seems she knows how to keep the peace in her marriage. Renton says she still blames herself for the birth of her profoundly handicapped son Davie, for her inability to manage him at home, for having him cared for in hospital, and for his eventual death having only recently secured

more suitable housing because of him (p.190). That's a very familiar portrait. There is lots to like in Cath Renton.

Cath Renton shows all the signs of having lived within a tight community all her life, in some respects entirely comfortably. She is an enthusiastic member of the Dockers' Club, and all that that implies – regular Saturday nights, sitting with the same friends, dancing the same dances, singing
the same songs, drinking the same drinks. She is the one who maintains
community cohesion, abides by the consensus, and never leaves. Here is
community at work. But in other respects she is frustrated. She has needed
prescribed Valium, and she helps herself to too many Carlsberg Specials
– always a bad mix. A little drunk, she is outrageously sluttish in the Deacon Brodie pub after the court case, unforgivably infantilising Mark while
treating Begbie at his worst as an intimate and equal. She is apparently
deluded about the nature of Billy's relationship with Sharon (p.171 and
p.221), and she holds views of Mark's inner circle of friends that differ
sharply from Mark's own (and the reader's) view (p.198). Not a major
character in the *Trainspotting* story, nevertheless Cath Renton's presence
on the page should be considered a minor triumph for her creator. We all
know Cath Renton – in the 1980s there were thousands of her in the Junction Streets of Scotland every day, getting their messages. She is still there
today, but she knows fewer and fewer people in the shops and at the bus
stops going her way.

The women of Renton's age all have single, simple personal names; no
jokey or cruel nicknames for them. His cousin Nina is the youngest, her
angsty teenage feminine sensitivities, nicely told, nothing remarkable about
her, make her the kid next door. Alison is a needy junkie from beginning to
end. In the first episode she explicitly finds heroin more satisfying than sex,
which disconcerts Renton, and the last reference to her is Johnny Swan's
regret that he didn't pimp her out (p.312). Laura McEwan has a voracious
sexual appetite, and can be rough with it. The frigid Hazel is sympathetically drawn, and plays a part in moving the story on (p.187). June is almost
inarticulate in the face of Begbie's vicious onslaught, and her being alone in
her misery is left to speak for itself. Sharon is in a similar position; both are
isolated and vulnerable, their pregnancies neither respected nor valued.

The un-named woman in 'Her Man' is not condemned for being com-
plicit in her own abuse; her creator knows the complexities of domestic violence. Lesley departs the scene on the death of her baby, and the unforgiving
Johnny Swan ignores her pain and seeks to exploit her some more (p.204
and p.312). Dianne makes only one appearance. She has an attractive profile

as a young girl mature beyond her years. But if she is that smart, why on earth would she have unprotected sex with a stranger? (pp.141, 142). It looks like Welsh used that detail to keep alive the concerns about HIV/AIDS at that point in the book. Around 20 women are named, and several more are referred to or make an appearance.

Kelly, the one of the younger generation we get to know best, is first referred to in 'The Skag Boys, Jean-Claude Van Damme and Mother Superior' when Renton is uncertain about his relationship with her. Putting together things said in 'There is a Light That Never Goes Out' with 'Feeling Free', we gather that the father of her aborted baby was Des, Spud's cousin (p.266) who we never meet. She has the voice in 'Feeling Free' and she is abused as the bar girl in 'The Elusive Mr Hunt'. From the way it is left at the end of 'Straight Dilemmas no. 1', we take it that it is she who, having been twice abused, now does the abusing in 'Eating Out', in female form, and how! She has the ambition to get a university degree and she uses the incident as a practical for her philosophy course. In this detail she looks like a semi-autobiographical character.

Meanwhile, in 'Feeling Free', female companionship in this mixed age-group is consolidated as the new friends walk away from the hassle on the GPO building. With the statue of the Duke of Wellington on our right we go up the cut heading diagonally for St Andrew Square. I would be astonished if Welsh did not disguise one of his watering holes, the Café Royal, just there on the left, as 'Café Rio' (p.276) in the text. As they part from the wifies, one says she would do it differently if she was Kelly's age. Back at her place, wherever that is, with the two New Zealanders, we get a strong female perspective. Men 'cairry their reproductive organs on the ootside ay their bodies... all men are good for is the odd shag.' They imitate and reverse Begbie's misogynism. They get progressively stoned, and the double entendre of 'crack' (the meaning that may need an explanation is that it is common parlance in Scotland, meaning 'lively conversation', or 'gossip', or, simply, 'good company') seems hilarious (pp.276,277).

In the last sentence of 'Feeling Free' Welsh gives Kelly the line: 'Aye, when [men] are in the fucking minority thir OK, ah sais, wondering where the edge in ma voice had come fae, then no wantin tae wonder too much.' (p.277) This female self-empowerment and authority without having to analyse or justify it is less remarkable now than it was at the time of writing. We don't see much of Kelly, but she seems like an interesting character who would be worth developing. Welsh deserves some credit for sketching a disparate line-up of female characters with sensitivity and confidence.

SECTION IV
Heroin, Dealers, Sex and HIV/AIDS

CHAPTER 13

God's Own Medicine

THERE'S A LITTLE turreted room for a night watchman on the entrance to St Cuthbert's Kirkyard on King's Stables Road, just off Lothian Road in Edinburgh, put there two centuries ago to deter body snatchers. In the 1980s it did nothing to stop junkies using the plentiful hidden spaces to light candles which flickered in the dark as teaspoons of smack were heated. Bethany Christian Trust organised an excellent operation which offered an evening bowl of soup and a blanket for rough sleepers. Arrangements were made to collect the abandoned blankets in the morning, for reuse, but this was soon expressly forbidden because of the risk posed by concealed injecting equipment. The well-meaning donors were shocked.

We've come here to stand at the grave of Thomas De Quincey (1785–1859), author of Confessions of an English Opium Eater in which he wrote 'Nobody will laugh long who deals much with opium.' This kirkyard, with intimations of mortality all around us and strong connections with opium and its derivative heroin, is an excellent place in which to go over man's relationship with drugs, which has been a never ending evolutionary dance with various properties of plants and animals since the beginnings of the human race. Every society in the world except the Inuits has a plant-based drug of choice, along with elaborate rituals to minimise the dangers and maximise the enjoyment.

This leg of the *Trainspotting* tour is not so much on location as taking liberties with time and space, as though we had taken a shot, since we have huge expanses of both to cover. In a small sense it's a bad place: on the whole, religious authorities take a dim view of mind-altering drugs because they can take one into visions and experiences which are beyond doctrine and discipline. On the other hand, it's quite an appropriate place; as we see elsewhere, the modern Church of Scotland, and other churches, have been very concerned and active in harm reduction in the matter of substance abuse.

The term 'drug' describes a variety of substances that are introduced to the human body, by various means, which all fall into one or more of the following categories:

a) intended to enhance or prolong life, commonly also known as medicine, and often, in modern times, professionally dispensed and administered;
b) intended to produce a pleasant and temporary effect, legitimately acquired and recreationally used – a glass of wine or a cigarette, for example;
c) also producing a temporary effect, either body-enhancing or mind-altering, mild or powerful, generally illegally acquired and taken surreptitiously without the approval of society at large.

There can be some merging between any two and all three categories. There never was a clear dividing line between medicinal and recreational drugs, and the whole area is becoming not simpler but murkier as technology produces ever more refined substances. However, it is the mind-altering element of category c) that concerns us here. Among the general characteristics of drugs in this category is that they tend to be seductive, they have a negative impact on general health and well-being, they can be addictive, and they can be fatal.

And now there needs to be an understanding of the difference between dependence and addiction. A diabetic depends upon insulin for very survival; this is not addiction. Addiction is an acquired habit, a habit that can be so forceful that the addict continues to take the drug even though he knows very well that it is killing him. Death, when it occurs either as an overdose or in a slow decline with other health factors involved, is not normally recorded as suicide, since there was no wish or intention to die. Coroner's courts in the UK generally take the view that an overdose is accidental, and in other cases that the deceased was aware at some level that death was at least a known risk and sometimes known to be an inevitable consequence of the habit.

Since so many addicts are liars and cheats and some are involved in crime, it is often tempting to think of addiction as moral depravity, but this is not helpful. In many cases the addict was a criminal before becoming an addict. Besides, it is also true that many addicts lead normal, productive and responsible lives such that other people never know the true state of affairs. Neither is addiction an illness; that would require a metabolic disorder common to all addicts, which there isn't. As an acquired habit, each case has its own aetiology. The circumstances of the individual, his personality, and his own biological reaction to whatever drug is taken all have to be considered in order to come to an understanding of every addict. Some become addicts after first use of a drug, while others have a relatively prolonged period of opportunity to stop taking it before becoming addicted. But all too often, addiction leads to a downwards spiral of loss of autonomy, loss of moral direction, loss of health and personality, and even to loss of life.

* * * * * * *

Opium (derivatives are known as opiates) produces its effects in its natural state. It is a product of *Papaver Somniferum* (the poppy that makes sleep). It is harvested by scoring a gash in the ripening seed head and collecting the sticky liquid in the wound. People can be affected merely by handling the plant, or even by walking through a densely planted field. Over 4,000 years ago it was known as 'the joy plant' in Mesopotamia. The ancient Greeks used it to banish sorrows and to ease pain, despite warnings of its addictive properties. The Crusaders of a millennium ago brought it to Western Europe from the eastern Mediterranean. During the Middle Ages there was a comparatively large population of addicts within the wealthy and well-connected European classes. It was enthusiastically prescribed and taken for its narcotic, analgesic and palliative effects while at the same time it was vehemently decried as a substance that makes people feckless, unreliable and selfish. In Germany in the 16th century opium was given the name 'laudanum', which describes it as praiseworthy. Thomas Sydenham in England in the 1660s mixed it with alcohol, and this preparation became specifically known as laudanum.

Unless it has been overtaken recently by a modern drug lord, the British government of the 19th century was the biggest dealer and most forceful pusher in the history of opium. Two Opium Wars (1840–42 and 1856–60) with China were fronted by two Edinburgh-educated Scots, William Jardine and James Matheson. To be brief, they exploited the opportunity to sell good quality Indian opium to a near-virgin market in China in order to redress an imbalance of payments between Britain and China. The Chinese Emperor banned the import, forbade his subjects to buy it, and earnestly pleaded with Jardine and Matheson not to persist. Believing themselves to be above Chinese civil law, however, the two acted out the law of the free market, with all necessary associated strong arm tactics and the backing of the British armed forces. In London, the government's stated view was that the opium traders were meeting a demand and it was up to the Chinese to control consumption. The truth was that London had become dependent on the money that the trade yielded, and was prepared to back the East India Company – effectively an arm of government – with state military power. In the Opium Wars Britain polluted vast swathes of a population and acquired Hong Kong as a colony.

In 1806, there had been a breakthrough in Germany. A young pharmacist's assistant isolated the active elements of opium. He named it after

Morpheus, the Greek god of sleep and dreams. The new product, morphine, was, in effect, opium concentrate, highly significant because as opium the active content is a relatively small but variable percentage of volume. Despite the young discoverer's warning that it may have 'terrible effects', it was initially held to be a cure for opium addiction. When morphine became available in China in the wake of the second war, Christian missionaries issued it in the belief that it would help counter opium addiction. It didn't. It became known as 'the Jesus drug'. It was up to ten times more powerful by weight than opium and of course it was now possible to prescribe precise quantities with fairly predictable effects.

In 1853, Dr Alexander Wood of Edinburgh developed a combination of syringe and needle. The belief was that appetite and cravings were satisfied only by ingestion into the stomach – injecting through the skin would not lead to addiction. An enthusiastic injector, it may be that the death of Dr Wood's wife was the first recorded drug death by hypodermic needle. More expensive than opium, and injectable, morphine became a drug fashionable among the wealthy in Britain and elsewhere. Up to the early years of the 20th century, ingeniously concealed injecting equipment was often found in the make-up bags of ladies who discreetly absented themselves from their company in order to take a fix.

In the first two thirds of 19th-century Britain the notion that any substance could be made illegal, particularly one as useful as an opiate, was never entertained. Medicine had few cures for illness, and opium and morphine were highly effective painkillers and sedatives: God's own medicine indeed. It was the effective element in many a tincture that was readily available over the counter and issued not only to the sick and those in pain but also to fractious children, especially those with overworked and exhausted parents. There was no mention in promotional material of their addictive properties, just as there was no mention of tobacco's carcinogenic properties until late in the 20th century. Martin Booth makes another comparison with tobacco: 'For the average Victorian, opium taking was as much part of society as the drinking of alcohol and the smoking of tobacco. Indeed, opium was more widely available in 1870 than tobacco was in 1970: and, like tobacco in the present day, it was primarily purchased by the poor and lower classes...'[19] In 1868, legislation in Britain gave control over the dispensing of opium and morphine to an increasingly scientific and professional generation of doctors and pharmacists. It was effectively the beginning of the separation of medical use and recreational use of opium (and other drugs). By the end of the century opium had been more or less cleared from the nation's kitchen cupboards, but there was a wide spectrum of the population that knew just how pleasant and useful it could be.

Heroin was first manufactured at the Bayer Laboratories in Germany in 1898, and so named by the chemist who developed it because of its 'heroic' qualities. Being highly soluble in fats, heroin rapidly turns into morphine in the bloodstream, reaching the central nervous system more quickly than morphine. The recipe is fairly straightforward and does not require equipment or ingredients that are particularly difficult to obtain. It can be left as a powder for snorting or chasing the dragon. For medical use it is made into a water-soluble salt. In the absence of the necessary material and equipment for this slightly more difficult process, recreational users can make it soluble, for injection, by mixing it with citric acid, for example lemon juice or a citric acid powder and water. Mixing it only with water does not dissolve the grains of the powder. It is illegal to produce heroin probably in every jurisdiction in the world.

Heroin was mass-marketed at first as a non-addictive treatment for respiratory illnesses and coughs, even though as an analgesic (painkiller) it was up to eight times more powerful than morphine. It was thought to be non-addictive because the morphine molecular structure had been changed. Some even held it to be a cure for morphine addiction, but within ten years it was clear to the medical profession that it had no clinical use at all; indeed, it was by now known that it is more easily addictive than morphine. The timing of the arrival of heroin ensured that its use became both widespread and illegal. Cheaper than morphine, it was used as a leisure drug just as drug controls, especially in USA, came into force. Being concentrated and compact, carriers and dealers found it easy to evade detection. With an addicted market, profitability was guaranteed. It was the criminal world that created and has gone on to maintain the international heroin problem that has plagued the planet for over a century.

During the Crimean War (1853–56) and the American Civil War (1861–65) opium and morphine had been dispensed almost indiscriminately on the battlefields and in the field hospitals, creating a significant number of opiate addicts on both sides of the Atlantic. In Europe from 1914 again there were unstable circumstances. There were lots of soldiers in London, many Canadians and others from around the Empire mixing with working class men from the regions, many with recent experience of the horrors of war and others going wild in advance of departure for the front. Young women were unchaperoned for the first time, and there was a vivacious theatre land. In wartime London there were some alarming and unpredictable elements in play. The authorities could see an alcohol and drug epidemic spiralling out of control in the chaos of war.

The Defence of the Realm Act (DORA) (1914) provided for the Home Secretary to introduce whatever legislation he deemed necessary to achieve the purpose of the Act without having to take the normal procedure of going through Parliament. Clause 40B, passed in 1916, made possession of opium, heroin, and cocaine illegal, for the first time ever. The clause was mostly aimed at cocaine, but opium and heroin were included, and morphine would have been as well but for representations from doctors and chemists. Alcohol was also curtailed: pub opening hours were severely restricted to lunchtimes and early evenings. The immediate response was the formation of private drinking clubs which went underground, taking the drug scene with them. If the recreational use of opiates becoming illegal was conceived in the 1868 Act, its arrival was on 28 July, 1916, and was known at birth as DORA 40B.

In 1926 the situation that lasted for the next 35 years in UK was formalised. Addicts were treated as medical patients, and doctors could prescribe whatever was needed, including heroin, for their maintenance. Opiate addicts were reduced to a tiny and manageable number. Several famous figures were regular users, if not addicts, and they openly expressed the fact: Aldous Huxley, Pablo Picasso, Jean Cocteau, and Graham Greene were among them. But on the whole the drug scene disappeared out of British public awareness. In 1960 there was a total of 94 addicts known to the Home Office, and in 1970 there were 1174. This was a miniscule number within the population, but of course it was a highly significant percentage increase over a short period.

As the 1970s opened, a reassessment of drug-taking worldwide, and of national legislations, was badly needed. For ten years a young, prosperous, confident generation of westerners had gone forth on the hippy trail to discover the world. These people saw drugs, little known in the west, in common use in their native cultures, and brought them home, bursting through the existing international laws and protocols. It was a significant moment in human history: drugs which in their native environments were used and accommodated within well-established rules and etiquettes, were being moved in large quantities to parts of the world where no such familiarity, institutions and habits were in place. This had happened before, of course: the arrival of tobacco in Britain was deplored by James VI (and I) more than four centuries earlier; alcohol was introduced suddenly, by Christianised Europeans, to native North Americans, and Australians, for example; and we won't forget who introduced opium to China; all with ruinous consequences. The western establishments saw this large scale arrival of exotic drugs as a serious threat. In 1971 President Richard Nixon famously declared that drug abuse was public enemy number one, which was effectively the beginning of the 'War on Drugs'.

This declaration of war was effectively a prohibitionist stance, all the more astonishing coming from USA as though the abject failure of the prohibition of alcohol only a few short decades earlier had not been noticed. Any idea that people would stop using drugs, or that the authorities could stamp out the trade, was pure moonshine. If lamb meat and apples could be transported from New Zealand to Europe, highly lucrative drugs would find their way to their markets anywhere in the world. Drugs could not be stripped out of burgeoning globalisation. Nixon's declaration of war safely delivered the international drugs trade into the hands of criminals and racketeers. Over half a century they have become so powerful – the scale of the trade is now on a par with oil and arms – and violent that they have wrecked the economies and good governance of the drug-producing countries, the transit countries, and some of the consumer countries.

In the UK, without using American rhetoric, the position was much the same. The Misuse of Drugs Act (1971) did little more than tidy up existing legislation and set a tariff of punishment for breaches of its terms. It was not illegal to be under the influence of a proscribed drug, but to be in possession of anything in excess of a small amount that you could demonstrate was for your own immediate use could land you in court on a charge of being a dealer. An expert witness, normally a police officer, would give the court an estimate of its street value and, depending on that valuation and the particularities of your case, you could expect anything up to 14 years in prison and/or an unlimited fine. The top end would normally be reserved for the large scale or wholesale end of the market. It was still possible for doctors to prescribe heroin to addicts: 'pharmy gear', as it was known.

The official and popular attitudes, influenced by the rhetoric of war and the criminalisation of drugs as determined by the Act, combined to encourage polarisation, fear, and ignorance. *Trainspotting* is set towards the end of the second decade of this regime.

CHAPTER 14

From Eden to Leith

GENESIS CHAPTER 3: 'Now the serpent was more crafty than any other animal that the Lord God had made.' In one of the world's most ancient narratives, the serpent's sales pitch to Eve is perfect. He opens up with the insinuation of doubt: 'He said to the woman 'Did God say You shall not eat from any tree in the garden?'' Under a little pressure, what can Eve say? Did God really say that? Any tree? Her reply is cautious: only the tree in the middle of the garden is forbidden. God said that to eat from that tree would lead to death. The serpent expands the doubt: 'You will not die.' This is the first time Eve has heard God contradicted. The serpent goes on to question God's motives and press home his point: 'God knows that when you eat of it your eyes will be opened, and you will be like God, knowing good and evil.' With this angle on it, the tree looks different. Why should God keep things hidden? If she eats, she can judge for herself. Ignorance is foolish, an unnecessary and dangerous weakness. When Eve sees the possibilities, eating the fruit becomes irresistible. Apart from the simple prohibition, there is no warning of downsides and dangers; everyone except Eve – the author, the reader, the serpent, God – knows that with a little knowledge she will always want more, but she will never have enough. It's an addictive drug.

As in the Garden of Eden, so in modern life. It is recognisably the ancient process that is played out in Renton's flat in 'Cock Problems'. Tommy makes a genuine enquiry about the effects of heroin. Renton gives an upbeat manifesto; he is well aware of reservations, but fails to articulate them. Tommy is persistent: 'C'moan... Ah pure want tae try it' (p.90). Renton now becomes a reluctant salesman, but his counter-advice is half-hearted and too late. Just like Eve and the fruit, for Tommy smack is seductive and available. Having a shot is a necessary rite of passage, an initiation, a way of keeping up with his peers. He wants the experience, then he can judge for himself.

The aftermath is familiar, too. Exonerating Himself, God dreadfully curses the serpent: 'Because you have done this, cursed are you among all animals... Upon your belly you shall go, and dust you shall eat all the days of your life. I will put enmity between you and the woman, and between your offspring and hers; and he will strike your head, and you will strike his heel.' There is no lower form of life. Nothing is more sinister, devious and dangerous, striking from behind at humans' most exposed point. The serpent is friendless.

The attitude of the ancient author was embedded in 1980s drugs legislation. Heroin was highly illegal, and there were stiff penalties for possession of it. The legislation was supported by 1980s rhetoric: in President Nixon's long-lived 'War on Drugs' and in Nancy Reagan's 'Just Say No'. Even Sick Boy accuses Renton of turning Tommy onto the hard line dealers (p.174), and Mr Renton bitterly calls dealers 'scumbags' (p.193). In conversations at school gates and family meal tables in the late 1980s, imprecations on drug dealers were echos of God's curse on the serpent.

The reality is that very few drug users have their first experience as a result of an aggressive or predatory pusher who offers a free first shot with a view to acquiring a new addicted customer. Certainly in modern Scotland almost all first time uses are among familiar people in a casual setting. It is an experiment, conducted with peers and within prevailing norms; if others are using a drug, why should I not? Tommy's circumstances are a classic illustration: temporarily destabilised having been dumped by his girlfriend, a common enough youthful experience, his usual powers of critical judgement are weakened. It doesn't take much – as he says, not realising the full implications, 'One fuckin shot isnae gonnae hurt us' (p.90). People take drugs because they are curious, drugs are seductive and available, and we don't always take advice, however good and well-intentioned it may be.

You'll appreciate that it's not easy to meet a working dealer. An acquaintance offered to introduce me to a retired dealer from the 1980s who had done some time in prison, but word came back that she didn't want to see me. I did meet one dealer. He stood against a wall, with clear views over my shoulder in all directions. He knew he was receiving the very close attentions of the police, he knew he was cornered and a lengthy prison sentence was almost inevitable, but even that wouldn't solve his problems. He had been ostracised and rejected by his wife and children, his parents and siblings, and the pain was unbearable. And he understood all the reasons for his isolation: 'I know I'm a dealer in death and destruction' he said. 'And I associate with some very unpleasant and dangerous people, so the family is quite right to put me out of the house, for their own safety.'

Indeed, it was partly to protect them that he stayed away from them and refused to give out any information – which schools the children were going to, or where his wife worked. He was in debt to his suppliers, and to try and gain some money he had been cutting and overpricing his product; he had serious enemies on all sides. He didn't know what to do or, it seemed, how to live with himself. Suddenly he saw someone, and he melted away in a flash. In the marketplace he was no more than a stallholder whose business management had gone wrong. In his personal relationships and in public perception he was no more than a serpent.

The antiquity of the Genesis story, and its elevated, protected status in scripture, appears to make it a model narrative to justify a recurring refusal to engage with and manage some of life's complexities. It tells deep truths about the human condition. Among other things, it is an allegory of youth. It is irrelevant here that Eve is female – the point is she is young. We have all been Eve. Our higher, mature selves (God in the narrative) deplore our own vulnerability, our gullibility, our propensity for bad, destructive habits. Rather than accept that our weaknesses and foibles are inherent in our nature, we externalise it all, exporting what is so deplored onto the serpent.

This story is written by a theist who accords all righteousness and authority to God, with deistic tendencies: having created the world, God is now indifferent to it or regards it as a plaything. After all, He created a susceptible creature with a natural curiosity and put her in close proximity to seductive temptation, also created by Him. No good can come from eating the fruit; if she succumbs to it she will be damaged. She succumbs, as is her nature and as He knows she will, and in consequence He destines her to fulfil her female functions in childbirth with great pain. At this point the story is a creation myth, that is, a narrative explanation for the ways of the world.

It doesn't have to be like this. Other Gods are available. The situation in Eden could have been addressed by a God who understands and accepts that curiosity and temptation are in the natural order He has created, and that humans have the power to spoil and fail to get the best from the good world in which He has put them. This God will recognise that eating the fruit does not subvert His will. He accepts His responsibilities for some guidance and advice which does not remove Eve's autonomy, which He also gave her; a tricky balance. If Eve comes to harm, He will continue to love and support her. This God knows that simple prohibition of something that is seductive and available does not achieve its stated aim, but it does have the effect of putting His creatures at odds with each other. He loves all His creation, including the serpent. Banishment does not solve the problem or make it disappear. The serpent has a God-given place in nature, just as we cannot rid ourselves of this impulse to lose our innocence and gain experience.

Similarly, the drug dealer has a natural place in the market square that is part of human interaction. This is trade and capitalism: there is a supply chain in which everybody takes a cut and the end consumer gets what he pays for (Renton is not a dealer, but on this occasion he is the supplier, which amounts to the same thing for our purposes).

There will always be people who are struck on the heel by snakes, who will fall ill and perhaps die. There will always be a supply of and a demand for 'drugs'. Prohibition is useless. There will always be some people who fall foul of them, who will be damaged and who will not take a full part in conventional life. This is not a perfect world. To take the theology out of it and put it into policy terms, the task is not to attempt to banish, but to manage.

Johnny Swan

So we come to Trainspotting's dealer, Johnny Swan. He was first created in 'A Scottish Soldier', where he is a character more than a dealer; cynical, duplicitous, exploitative. When creating the second generation of episodes to form the book, however, Welsh realised that he needed to introduce a dealer to help carry the narrative. He also needed a character to top and tail what we are calling the 'junkie strand'. Thus Johnny Swan is recast to appear in 'The Skag Boys, Jean-Claude Van Damme and Mother Superior'; his significance to the book is conveyed in the presence of his nickname in the title of the first episode. There actually was an older dealer in Muirhouse in the 1970s, known variously as The Auld One and Mother Superior because of the length of his habit, quite a good joke, but the transfer to Johnny Swan doesn't work well. Johnny is a contemporary of Renton's, so hardly has the longevity to earn the soubriquet.

To launch the reader's introduction to him, Renton reflects that 'Some malicious demon had invaded [Swanney's] body and poisoned his mind' (p.9). Spud also reflects on this, apparently with sadness, as he sits on a bench at the Shore, looking at a swan (p.121).

In Swanney's cameo appearance in the Dockers' Club in 'House Arrest' he has no sympathy for Lesley and the death of her baby, rather resenting her for failing to turn him on to good quality Glasgow gear. In the second generation 'A Leg-Over Situation' his attitude to the sex life in Thailand, first on view way back in 'The Skag Boys...', remains intact. He describes how he could have pimped out Alison, which would be her just desserts for k.b.ing[20] his request for a sexual favour, especially after he had often let her have heroin (p.312). He embodies what Renton is leaving behind as Renton consciously walks away from the whole scene (p.314). As a portrayal of character, Johnny's appearances in the second generation of episodes are more or less in line with what Welsh first created in 'A Scottish Soldier'. He is thoroughly unpleasant.

The presentation of Johnny Swan's function as a dealer runs into trouble when Renton recalls in the opening two paragraphs of 'House Arrest' how Johnny (and Alison) took him outside, overdosed, put him in a taxi, and apparently gave the hospital his parents' address. Is he a nice guy or is he a dealer? He can't be both. Not even a friend, far less a dealer, would risk being identified like this. Look at the trouble they go to in 'keepin shoatie' (p.7). Johnny Swan 'was a junkie as well as dealer' (p.6). Although that is an unlikely combination, he would be looking at several years in prison as it seems the possession of more heroin than would be needed for his own use would not be a difficult case for the police to make.

And there is a further problem: you wouldn't expect a dealer to turn up in a traditional, community-orientated social club like the Dockers' as he does in 'House Arrest'. These well-informed people would have him out of the door before he got through it, unless they would keep him in until the police arrive. Remember what Mr Renton said what he would do to dealers (p.193). It's inconceivable that someone would have a conversation about a mutual friend and the present dealing scene with the dealer who dispensed the overdose from which he is just recovering, in full view of his parents and their friends. Johnny Swan is only present because Welsh is using this episode as a stepping stone in the structure of the book and he needs to keep Johnny Swan in play. In *Trainspotting* the combination of the dealer's character and his function in the narrative is poorly worked out.

CHAPTER 15

Needles and Sex

WE CAN EASILY picture Renton in Welsh's flat at no. 2 Wellington Place at the opening of 'The First Day of the Edinburgh Festival'. The only detail that doesn't fit is the payphone in the hall, but that can be readily borrowed from elsewhere and imagined here. We can whizz through the nearby Kirkgate with him as he does his shopping for the hard week ahead, then go for the bus. The no. 32 doesn't go through Leith now, but when it did the fare to Muirhouse was indeed 45p (p.16).

In 2004 I was asked by a journalist from *de Volkskrant* (Netherlands) to do an Irvine Welsh tour of Leith; a wonderful opportunity for an out-of-luck tour guide. He brought five colleagues. I left my glasses in a bar – unforgivable, really, for a wannabe literary guide. Waiting for the no. 32 bus with them to retrace Renton's route as he goes to score with Mikey Forrester, a man I knew happened past, and I asked him to read out the few paragraphs either side of Renton getting on the bus (pp.16,17). Bless him, he struggled through the profanities to the end. We got off at Pennywell Road opposite the Gunner pub and the bookie's shop, in Renton's footsteps, and passed through the shopping centre (which is now being demolished). I always think it was an angry man holding the pen when Welsh wrote: 'Ah pass the steel-shuttered units which have never been let and cross over the car park where cars have never parked' (p.18). And in the 30 years since that was written nothing has changed, except a library has been built where there was never going to be any cars. What hallucinatory drugs were those 1960s planners on?

From here Mikey Forrester's gaff can be envisaged. All the low level housing blocks have been demolished now and there is some new building. It was hardly a joke to say that in the 1980s you could go to almost any block and score some skag. A lot of opiates and injecting equipment was stolen from the nearby Western General Hospital, and Forrester selling the suppositories (p.22) is strongly related to reality.

I asked a Dutchman to read the relevant passage, but it wasn't easy. A woman passing by showed some curiosity in a group of seven men huddled together, and I was bold enough to ask her to read. 'Aye, nae bother, pal', and she made a start. The language was foul, and soon she accused me of setting her up. 'No, no' I protested, and there was something of a tussle for my precious book before she flung it down, proclaiming it to be filth. Storming off, she questioned our sexual orientation and the married status of our parents. I paraphrased the passage for my clients from memory.

The drug of choice in Leith has long been the traditional alcohol, together with the ubiquitous tobacco. In the 1960s and going into the 1970s the more exotic and illegal drug scene in Edinburgh was centred on the university and the art college, and had not much to do with working class Leith and the overspill council housing schemes. In various formats, amphetamines had been widely prescribed up till the late 1960s. During the war they were given to soldiers before battle to keep them awake and fearless. Prime Minister Anthony Eden made no secret that he was taking them as he handled the Suez crisis in 1956. Known as pep pills and purple hearts, they were prescribed to exhausted and isolated housewives in the new suburbs of the 1960s, and an ordinarily wholesome younger generation took a liking to them for their upbeat effects. For this reason they were outlawed in the 1971 Misuse of Drugs Act, but they remained easy to obtain. Half a dozen known dealers in Edinburgh offering purple hearts, uppers, downers, the ever-popular cannabis and the increasingly popular LSD, were watched and chased by a small handful of CID officers in a pretty well balanced and choreographed arrangement.

From Edinburgh you had to go to London or Amsterdam for supplies of various drugs, or the more adventurous came back from further afield: North Africa, Afghanistan, or the Caribbean. The best contacts were made in the pubs of Rose Street, Edinburgh, and The Antiquary (The Auntie Mary) in Stockbridge, although it was risky to do the deal there: most transactions took place in flats. Cannabis was an illegal substance, but there was no great surrounding criminality. Quite heavy smokers could get a month's supply for £10 or £15. LSD was also fashionable in certain quarters. The dealers covered their costs and not much more. Overall in the 1960s and the early 1970s the ambience of the drug-taking community was PEACE, MAN! As it presented no immediate threat to the establishment there was a consensual blind eye that permitted it to continue.

But, as Bob Dylan was singing, 'the times, they are a-changing'. Making an appearance, for the first time at street level, were cocaine and heroin.

Nico, the German-born heroin addict, sometime lover of Lou Reed and singer with Velvet Underground, and close associate of Andy Warhol, lived in Stockbridge, drawn to Edinburgh by the ready availability and good quality of heroin. The pharmaceutical factory known as Macfarlan's at Roseburn, just west of Edinburgh city centre, was the country's only licit manufacturer of heroin, from where there was a steadily increasing incidence of theft.

On a day in 1974 the attention of the policemen in a patrol car in Muirhouse was drawn to a pillar box red E-Type Jaguar, standing out dramatically from the drab surroundings. It was driven by a two-bit crook they knew well. As an ostentatious statement of new wealth it was unmistakable; as an invitation to make enquires it was irresistible. Within two weeks he was arrested and charged as a drug dealer, the first new style dealer in the area. On looking back, one of the policemen says, this incident marked the beginning of a ten-year period in which the drug scene changed from being fairly well contained to a picture of violence, with strong associations with other criminal activity.

For one young man in Muirhouse the introduction to heroin was gradual. He now divides the 1970s into three parts. The first began for him in HMP Saughton in 1973 where he saw older guys get co-codomol from the dentist, and syringes and needles from the hospital. They mixed the crushed tablets with milk and sieved it through bread before injecting. They got a hit of sorts, but paid for it with bad shits and cramps for a day or two. Back home, he and his pals got into stealing clinical drugs, from chemist shops and from the patients themselves: dihydrocodeine (a semi-synthetic opioid) and barbiturates were the favourites.

In the second period, 1975–77, he could go to parties where heroin was freely available, supplied by the girls who went onto the ships in Leith and who were paid or part paid in heroin. There was a particular family where there was always plenty – he doesn't remember ever paying for his shots. The first sellers that he was aware of were not locals (it seems he didn't notice the one in the red Jag). One was a hippy with an unfamiliar accent, and there was an architect and his very middle class wife, whose children ran about with bare arses and there was never any food in the house. It was clear they were feeding their own habit.

The third period began one day in 1978 when he saw his pal weighing out heroin. He knew the game had changed – this was business. People started putting drugs into packets. And it was being cut to the point where either you didn't get a hit or it was downright dangerous, or, quite possibly, both. He was stopped and searched several times by the police looking for drugs and drug paraphernalia. One man jumped through a high window because he lacked the courage to defend the stash of cannabis and heroin that was sought by intruders who had broken down his front door. The stuff belonged to two brothers in Leith for whom he was acting as a local sales-man. It wasn't difficult to work out that anybody could steal from a dealer's flat, and it would never be reported to the police.

Unemployment was taking hold in Muirhouse. Poverty is not the first reason for the temptation to use drugs – drug misuse is more a question of what to do with far too much time. A later academic work established a strong link between unemployment, escalating drug abuse generally and heroin addiction from 1979.[21] The surroundings were very bleak and drab. One policeman tells me he had every sympathy with the youngsters who yearned for a few hours during which it didn't matter where they were. He recalls the occasion when he apprehended one of two boys who were engaged in petty shoplifting in Pennywell shopping centre. With a colleague he took him to Drylaw police station, where it became clear the boy had taken a hit just before being picked up. When he calmed down a bit he was reasonably co-operative, and the police took him home to Silverknowes, the middle class owner-occupied housing scheme right beside Muirhouse. His father opened the door to them. 'We have caught your son with a wee bit of shoplifted stuff, nothing too serious. However, are you aware he is using dope?' Although his father was shocked and doubtful, needles were found in his room. Two years later the boy broke into an old woman's house in another area of the city to steal her ring; she resisted him, and he killed her. 'That boy was never a murderer,' said the policeman sadly. 'It was the drugs that caused that crime.'

There was a widespread surge in heroin use throughout Europe around 1979 and 1980. This followed the Soviet invasion of Afghanistan and it was brought to Leith in some of the many Russian ships. It was also a direct result of the overthrow of the Shah of Persia by the ayatollahs, who placed an absolute ban on heroin and opium. Vast quantities of good quality opi-ates entered the country in diplomatic bags and by other means. Young peo-ple, many with poor education, low expectations and too much time, were unfamiliar with this powerful drug. Using the highly efficient and dangerous means of delivery, injecting, there were many sudden deaths by overdose. It was distressing to find bodies with the needle still in their arms. In the very early 1980s when addicts turned up in hospital they were sometimes given a shot of heroin and discharged without delay. The hospitals were not set up to deal with them. But increasingly they presented with medical conditions which had to be treated.

Jinty Kerr, capable and aspiring police officer in the CID, came to know the local crooks in Leith and Edinburgh city centre very well: purse thieves, credit fraudsters, housebreakers. She went to police college for three years in 1980 and on her return was astonished to find that they had transferred to a much more lucrative line of business – drug dealing. Whereas in the previous decade drugs were barely mentioned in the daily CID briefing meetings, now drugs was the central recurring theme. By 1984 the CID reckoned that around 35 per cent to 40 per cent of acquisitive crime was drug related. This was not old-fashioned professional thieving. It was opportunistic house-breaking, shoplifting, purse-snatching, credit card fraud, all causing a great amount of pain and grief to the victims. Stolen items were usually small, easy to carry and to sell on, although the true value was rarely realised.

Kerr was appointed head of the newly formed Drug Squad (DS), which very quickly became very powerful. The judiciary didn't blink before signing search and arrest warrants on request. The DS busted a place in Annfield, Newhaven, finding a lot of drugs throughout the premises and in the back green (common garden). The CID was astonished – they had no intelligence on it at all, illustrating that drug dealing had become a specialist criminal activity, operating outside the usual suspects and justifying a dedicated team of police officers.

The DS was on a steep learning curve, and before long it was augmented by case hardened CID officers. They were very good at their job, with many arrests and successful convictions, filling the prisons almost to bursting point. But it didn't take them long to realise that they were having almost no impact on the supply and use of heroin. When a dealer was taken out of circulation, he would be replaced within 24 hours. The DS was trained to catch crooks. It was not geared up to manage a marketplace. In 1984 the Assistant Chief Constable said as much in public: increasing the number of police engaged in the war on drugs would not cure Edinburgh of its growing heroin problem, he said.

It is not clear that relations between the police and customs were good and effective in this period. Several interceptions of drugs were made at sea, particularly, it seems, off the Fife coast. It was well known that Burntisland was a good place to go; for some time cannabis had been brought in on the barges bringing bauxite off the ships from the West Indies to the local aluminium works, and there was a local network accustomed to the trans-mission of illegal drugs. As quota restrictions were squeezing the margins of the fishing industry, several vessels found it worth their while to rendez-vous with an incoming cargo ship in international waters and run the stuff ashore. There was a shore-side customs patrol man who went up and down the coast enquiring about who was spending money that couldn't obviously be accounted for.

Customs could board ships and inspect at will, a power that the police, who needed a search warrant in each case, would have loved to have. Deep searches, as they were known, were a dirty business, sometimes involving spending hours trawling through heavy oil. But Customs and Excise were set up to look for dutiable goods, mainly alcohol and tobacco. When they did find something on foreign flag ships, which was practically all of them, they didn't normally prosecute under British law, which the police might have preferred. Their system was to notify their colleagues worldwide, which amounted to pressure on the company to make sure that it didn't become a habit. No attempt was made to isolate the docks as a security zone, which was an open door for smuggling and prostitution. Good quality Russian and Polish greatcoats were to be had in any of the pawn and second hand shops in Leith Walk, and it was well known that for a little extra the customer would find something to his liking in one of the pockets.

The Drug Squad did not believe that Leith shipping was a significant route of drugs generally. There was a court conviction in May 1983 for the theft from Mcfarlan Smith at Roseburn of almost 1kg each of morphine and heroin. One source says that Edinburgh became the heroin hub for Scotland. Another says it was Glasgow. In 1985 the Edinburgh and East of Scotland Pakistan Association led a fact-finding trip to its home country with a view to stemming the supply of heroin. 'Our borders are not secure, and most of the drugs are smuggled through Pakistan to Afghanistan', said the chairman on their return.

Certainly as far as volume was concerned, seizures in Edinburgh were significantly smaller than, for example, in Manchester, Newcastle and Glasgow. This may be because the injecting habit, which was distinctive to Edinburgh, requires less heroin than snorting and smoking. Injecting with dirty gear is a poor man's hit. And how and why did Edinburgh pick up the injecting habit? The best guess is that it came through the Edinburgh Festival, with its international connections. San Francisco was known for its injecting habit – maybe it came from there. The authorities were catching up on a new criminal culture, and their own machinery for evaluating it was not yet fully operational. The casualty department at the Royal Infirmary,

Edinburgh reported in 1985 that it was seeing one addict a day, comparing it with one per month five years previously.

In 1982 the Church of Scotland opened a drug addiction unit in Queen Street, Edinburgh, and shortly afterwards a rehab centre at Haddington, entirely out of its own funds. The Kirk couldn't afford to run both for long – the day centre closed in November 1985. The following year a community initiative Support Help and Advice on Drug Addiction (SHADA) was begun, with a remit covering Leith, Muirhouse/Pilton, Wester Hailes, and Niddrie/Craigmillar – all poor quality post-war housing schemes in the city. The Drug Prevention Group sprang up in Prince Regent Street, Leith, also manned by volunteers and run on a shoestring, as were several groups. They formed relationships with the heroin scene that professional social workers could never have achieved.

The junkies' desperation was barely concealed. In December 1984 the *Edinburgh Evening News* published The Junkies' Psalm:

> King Heroin is my shepherd, I shall always want. He maketh me to lie down in the gutter. He leadeth me beside the troubled waters. He destroyeth my soul. He leadeth me in the path of wickedness, for the effort's sake. Yea shall I walk through the valley of poverty, and will fear all evil. For thou, heroin, art with me. Thy needle and capsule try to comfort me. Thou strippest away the groceries in the presence of my family. Thou robbest my head of reason. My cup of sorrow runneth over. Surely heroin addiction shall stalk me all the days of my life. And I shall dwell in the house of the damned for ever.[22]

Police activity during this period of steadily increasing drug taking, dominated by heroin injection, acquired a whole new dimension in April 1983. Sheila Anderson, a well-known local prostitute who worked what the lurid end of the press liked to call Leith's Blue Triangle of Coburg Street, Commercial Street, and North Junction Street, was run over several times by a vehicle and left for dead at Gypsy Brae, half a mile west of Granton. The killer was never found, but what the police did discover was that they were dangerously out of touch with the working girls. They wouldn't talk. The police realised that many of them were teenagers, many were pimped out, many were leading extremely chaotic lifestyles, and many had a heroin habit.

An outcome of the murder was that a Tolerance Zone was arranged. The understanding was that if the women stuck to the stretch of Coburg Street between Sandport Bridge and Couper Street, which had no residential accommodation, and provided they didn't behave outrageously, and they didn't deal in drugs either directly or indirectly for a pimp, then the police would have things to be getting on with other than coming along and harassing them. It worked well for over a decade. The Black Swan pub at 23-24 Sandport Place (two hundred yards west of Sandport Bridge, now renamed), and the Junction Bar (on the corner of Great Junction Street and Ferry Road, no longer a pub) became refuges on cold nights, but the women weren't supposed to do any business in there. The tolerance extended to a euphemistically named sauna opposite the library on Ferry Road, and the nearby chemist shop did brisk business in heavy duty condoms.

The Tolerance Zone was supported in 1986 by the Woman's Guild of the Church Scotland, celebrating its centenary, by providing two night time outreach workers who based themselves in the offices of nearby North Leith Parish Church on Madeira Street. It wasn't easy. One of the workers could see that the children of one of the women were exposed to dangers; although under an obligation of confidentiality she discussed it with professional colleagues, as a direct result of which the children were taken into care. The woman orchestrated a hate campaign against her, which was vicious at the time but short-lived as most people could see the problem. The project was later taken over by Scottish Prostitute Education Programme (SCOT-PEP), who acquired former office space for use as a drop-in centre which was open all night and from which advice, support, onward referrals, and condoms could be dispensed. It was very well placed, right on Coburg Street, and it later moved to Henderson Street.

The new Tolerance Zone wasn't a magic wand that solved all the problems, the least of which was that the women did have a tendency to stray down Dock Street and onto Commercial Street. Sometimes there were incidents that had to be dealt with and enquiries to be made. It certainly didn't put an end to pimping. But it put the whole situation onto a much better footing. The women told the police about ugly mugs (dangerous customers) and underage girls. At its best it was almost like going back to the good old days in Leith, as women plied their trade on Coburg Street of an evening and did their shopping on Great Junction Street by day – they were part of the general community. South Leith Parish Church held several Christmas parties for prostitutes and their families. Edinburgh was a leader in Britain of such a tolerant, pragmatic approach, and it significantly reduced criminality around the local sex industry.

Sheila Anderson's contribution, in death, was to make life much safer for her sisters. But it was partly the very success that led to the downfall of the arrangement. Women from elsewhere, attracted by the ease with which they could earn some money, lacked the commitment to the local understanding with the police. When this stretch of Coburg Street was later residentialised the arrangement was transferred to Salamander Place, but a vigilante group of local residents vociferously objected and the police ended their restraint saying they could only manage it with a broad consensus.

As a direct result of the 1983 murder, it was realised that the Leith drug scene was closely enmeshed with the world's oldest profession. The combination of drugs and sex was nothing new. From time immemorial prostitutes have used opiates both to help them through the physical and emotional pain of their business and, since it disturbs ovulation, as a rough-and-ready contraceptive. It was just about to be engulfed by something previously unknown to mankind.

Meanwhile, back on location in Muirhouse, I walked with my Dutch clients from the back of the Pennywell Shopping Centre onto the main road and past the Gunner pub. From the pavement we looked at the bookie's shop where, we can easily imagine, Welsh has Renton, on his way to the toilet, having to deal with an Elvis-like 'de-composing ex-Ted' (p.24) who prefers alcohol. There was the woman who had kindly offered to read from *Trainspotting* a little earlier. She was vigorously denouncing us to her friends as a bunch of poofters who couldnae read and didnae even speak English. I spotted the next bus we needed, a no 27, so we put on a burst of speed to catch it with a hail of ridicule and abuse behind us. In the write-up in *de Volkskrant* this moment was described as when 'Leith Walks' became 'Leith Runs'. This book was conceived.

CHAPTER 16

God's Own Wrath

THE NO. 27 bus comes every ten minutes, and we'll get on board with our Dutch friends. They'll be alighting at the High Street for the walking tour, but for us it's almost an hour's journey, on the top deck, of course, front seat, with the sunshine pouring in ahead of us as we head south across the city.

The very next stop is right opposite where Craigroyston school used to be before it was demolished and relocated. Both Spud and Begbie attended school here. Welsh himself lived close to here, although he walked to the more established Ainslie Park, which was about half a mile further along our journey. On Ferry Road we have a good view of Fettes College, one of the most expensive private schools in Scotland. As we cross the High Street near the castle we pass between what was the Sheriff court on the left and Deacon Brodies' pub on the right, scene of Renton's and Spud's encounter with the law and subsequent celebration in 'Courting Disaster'. On Lauriston Place we pass what used to be the Royal Infirmary of Edinburgh, now converted into residential accommodation. At the bottom of the hill is Tollcross, location for part of the first episode in *Trainspotting*, then we go up through Bruntsfield and on to Craiglockhart.

We get off when we see signposts for Milestone House, which is a short walk past Firrhill High School. Davie Mitchell could have been more generous than describing it as 'not unattractive' (p.245); it's very pleasant. But perceptions depend on circumstances, and in the previous paragraph he acknowledges that his circumstances have changed between the fictional action and the purported time of writing. Within the grounds of the old City Hospital, Milestone House was opened in 1991 by the newly-formed Waverley Care Trust, which was dedicated to caring for everyone who was HIV+ regardless of how the virus was acquired. Very soon after the opening Princess Diana visited. With recent developments in the treatment and management of HIV, the place has been re-furbished and now offers day and respite care for people with HIV and Hepatitis C, rather than end-of-life care which was its original function.

Around 1930, somewhere in West Africa, a man was bitten or scratched by a monkey, passing on to him a virus against which he had no defence. This date and location are inferences, based on modelling backwards from later events. No-one knows exactly how or when what was known in the early years as Human T-lymphotropic virus type 3 (HLTV-3) entered the human race. It was first identified and described in the USA in early 1981, where it was strongly associated with the gay community and also known as Gay-Related Immune Deficiency Syndrome (GRIDS). This alien virus compromises the immune system so that the first symptoms to show are often almost indistinguishable from common, minor, passing infections. They become recognisable as what is now known as Human Immunodeficiency Virus (HIV) only when they persist and form a syndrome. Left untreated, it will almost inevitably progress into Acquired Immune Deficiency Syndrome (AIDS), a dangerous development bringing with it serious bowel infections and debilitating diarrhoea, sometimes leading to unusual tumours. When it invades the central nervous system there can be delirium and dementia. This can be the specific, immediate cause of death, or eventually the whole organism that is a human body is overwhelmed by a wave of opportunistic infections.

The virus is spread by body fluid: semen, vaginal and rectal fluids, blood and breast milk, although this was not properly understood in the early 1980s. Because there can be several months, or perhaps years, between contracting the virus and the first show of symptoms, normal behaviour is continued; you may not know you have acquired it until you have had plenty of opportunity to pass it on unknowingly.

In early 1982 Dr Sandy McMillan, Consultant Venereologist at the Department of Genito-Urinary Medicine (GUM) at the Royal Infirmary, Edinburgh, attended a conference in New York on Sexually Transmitted Diseases (STDs) and GRIDS. He reported back to his professional Society, but as there were no cases in Scotland, apart from the death of one man, who had connections with Africa, there seemed to be no need for a screening programme. Edinburgh's gay community implicitly agreed – they had a motto not to have sex with Americans. But this was, in truth, an attitude of complacent isolationism, which couldn't last long. In early 1983 BBC TV screened a *Horizon* programme titled 'The Killer in the Village', describing the way in which the disease was rampant in the American gay community and drawing the inevitable conclusion that it would soon arrive in UK. In May GUM and Dermatology consultants were asked to report cases of HLTV-3.

Two cases turned up in Scotland in the summer of 1983. McMillan, who was widely respected in the gay community, wrote in the July/August issue of *Gay Scotland* advising gay men to go to a GUM clinic for regular check-ups. In the absence of diagnostic tests, doctors relied on spotting observable symptoms. The gay community was hyper-sensitive to anything which singled it out for special attention, but the fact was inescapable that it was the focus of concern. The discovery in 1983 that HLTV-3 could be transmitted through blood was very worrying. Haemophiliacs in USA and Spain had acquired it, and first suspicions were directed at American blood products. The British Blood Transfusion Service (BTS) chose not to ask gay men to refrain from donating blood, but did issue general information on who was at risk.

The Scottish gay community reacted angrily – even though they acknowledged their own vulnerability, they pointed out that women and heterosexuals also carried and were affected by HLTV-3. They complained bitterly that this sort of advice fed the media presentation of the whole thing as 'The Gay Plague'. After urgent consultation with the gay community, BTS Scotland revised its leaflet to make it less discriminatory, and issued it more widely than usual, into the pubs and clubs of Scotland. Dr Ray Brettle, Consultant in Infectious Diseases at the City Hospital, who had studied HLTV-3 in USA in 1982/3, set about disseminating his knowledge publicly and to hospital staff, where some rejected him as 'mad'. 1983 was a bad year.

In unprecedented co-operation between the medical professionals and the gay community in Edinburgh, the Scottish AIDS Monitor (SAM) was set up. Its main function was to disseminate good quality information about HLTV-3 based on the latest research, and it was supported by the medics. The medics took the view that it would be dangerous to be at odds with the gay community. The Monitor itself, however, was ultra-cautious about giving advice. Although the evidence was overwhelming that gay men were disproportionately vulnerable (70 per cent of American HIV+ people were gay), it hid behind that fact that it was not known what *caused* it not to give advice on sexual practice and partners. The warning to '...take sensible hygiene precautions, keep to a decent diet, and don't be slow to visit the clinic if you are worried about symptoms'[23] was as far as it was prepared to go.

Things worsened in 1984. A haemophiliac with AIDS turned up in Scotland. The professionals knew that Scottish blood was not to blame. He had recently arrived from England, where he had been treated with imported Factor VIII. But BTS Scotland was very concerned not to let the story get out into the press, certain sections of which were certainly not careful with

their 'facts' and opinions. Nevertheless, BTS Scotland did have to take steps
to ensure the safety of its supply, in the process inevitably singling out gay
men as being in an AIDS high-risk group. The gay community worried on
two fronts: firstly that in the popular mind they were being judged for being
gay, a conflation of alleged promiscuity and being morally reprehensible,
and secondly that they were being medicalised. When would they ever be
free from special attention, of whatever sort? However, in the November/
December issue of the Monitor, they were a bit more specific about how to
reduce the risk of acquiring and passing on AIDS.

In various editions towards the end of 1984 the Edinburgh Evening
News tried to be reassuring. By then there were 20 or so known haemophiliacs in Scotland with AIDS, and the News told its readers that not one of them
had acquired the disease through Scottish blood products. As a by-product
of this development, the press had to concede that AIDS was now striking at
both male and female, gay and straight – but it was still easy to blame gay
men for the way it all started and was continuing. Things were not going
well.

1985 was even worse. This was the year in which it was discovered that
HIV was rampant among intravenous drug abusers (IVDAS). In the early part
of the year Dr John Peutherer, Consultant Virologist at the Department of
Bacteriology, University of Edinburgh Medical School, set about working
with some new screening kit. His task was to compare a random sample
of blood donations from known high-risk groups against a control group.
This, he decided, would be stored serum from Edinburgh IVDAS who were
being followed up for Hepatitis B. The astonishing result was that the control group contained more HIV+ samples than the known high-risk group.
He had his findings checked and verified. There could be no doubt – HLTV-3,
as it was still known, had significantly entered the heterosexual population, and IVDAS were the new main vectors of the virus. Furthermore, these
findings were not paralleled anywhere else in the UK. Edinburgh, or, in the
required way of compiling these statistics, Lothian, stood alone.

There was a great deal of rapid, urgent discussion and activity that summer. SAM, now a respected lay body which had achieved charitable Trust
status, immediately added haemophiliacs and drugs mis-users to their at-risk
groups. With the help of the largest-ever grant to a gay group in Scotland,
SAM launched an office, a part-time secretary, and several education and
advice leaflets. Lothian Health Board (LHB) was quick to draw up new
practice guidelines for nursing and medical staff, and spelled out the need

for confidentiality and patient protection from stigma. In doing this, it was drawing on experience of an outbreak of Hepatitis B a decade earlier.

There was disagreement about opening an open-access clinic. The GUM service regarded itself as the best equipped to deal with the sensitivities involved with the virus acquired as an STD, and advocated that haemophiliacs should be dealt with in their own department, and IVDAS by General Practitioners (GPs). However, from the medical point of view the means of acquisition hardly matters, even if it could be reliably established, although it was recognised that personal sensibilities could run strong. On pragmatic grounds, an open-access clinic was opened in the City Hospital – the former Isolation Hospital – and all surgery for HIV+ patients, whatever the speciality, was carried out at the City.

This was the heyday of Thatcherism, and the issue was politically messy. Apart from making the grant to SAM, the Scottish Home and Health Department (SHHD) was reluctant to get involved further. For example, under pressure from professional and lay groups to authorise the free issue of needles and syringes, it pointed out that this equipment was not subject to any legal restriction and left it at that. But it was not so simple. Only very recently there had been successful prosecutions of shopkeepers for selling glue knowing that it could be 'injurious to health'. What would be the legal distinction between glue and hypodermic equipment except, probably, that the latter would seem to have rather more obvious potential for being injurious to health? Chemists demanded immunity, but there was no help from SHHD.

There was another difficulty: chemists had to operate as commercial outlets in the market place, and they had no wish to attract addicts who could be noisy and demanding and who were also very likely to be shoplifters. Feelings ran high. Over the next few months several GPs began issuing clean needles and syringes from their surgeries, when possible on an exchange basis. They did this well aware of the reservations and outright criticism from the police and judiciary, who took the view that this amounted to an encouragement to inject. The doctors defended their action saying that the issue was always accompanied by an expression of concern and a warning of the dangers, and that the intention was to keep the addict alive until s/he was able to address the addiction with a view to bringing it to an end.

Even if certain sections of the Scottish press remained pretty homophobic, in general they sought to reassure the public concerning the virus itself. In November *The Scotsman* ran a piece from Dr Brettle explaining the current state of scientific and medical knowledge: 'AIDS does not seem to be an airborne disease: it does not hop across the room like Lassa fever, for example, or measles, or chicken-pox. If it did, all the blood tests and surveys being done around the world would have turned up literally millions of AIDS cases by now, and they haven't.'[24] But the dangers spoke for themselves. The general advice was to choose sexual partners carefully, use a condom, and don't share needles.

But the worst news of all came right at the end of 1985. Dr Roy Robertson, the well-respected, hard-working Muirhouse GP, meticulous in his record-keeping, reported that he had found 51 per cent of a sample of 164 IVDAS to be HIV+. In Muirhouse there was a very high concentration of Dr Peutherer's findings of a few months earlier.

Dr Robertson knew that this would require a radically new response from those concerned with public health. He also knew that sharing needles was part of the culture of intravenous drug-taking; it was what the shooting galleries were all about. He concurred with the opinion of practically everyone with any knowledge of the subject that the closure, under police pressure, of a medical supplies shop in Bread Street, Edinburgh, some years previously led directly to the shooting galleries and shared needles. The situation was made worse by the habit of the police to confiscate the injecting gear when they found it – and they had a habit of looking for it. He said that sometimes the street value of injecting equipment was greater than that of the drug itself. Dr Robertson was reluctant to criticise the police and the judiciary, but asked for the drug scene not to be treated simply as a law-enforcement matter. He was appalled to see so many youngsters being sent to prison on long, harsh sentences having been caught selling amounts as small as 1mg of heroin to their friends – it was clear to him that they weren't dealers. There were, he insisted, personal, social and medical elements of the situation which had to be taken into account. Regardless of all the surrounding issues and considerations, two brute facts stood towering over everything:

> 1. Two enduring human habits, sex and drugs, were spreading the virus around particular communities like wildfire, and the prospect of it leaking out into the wider community was no longer a worry – it was already happening.
>
> 2. Lothian, or to be more exact, Edinburgh, and in the case of IVDAS, Muirhouse, was host to the problem in proportions that were quite exceptional in the whole of Europe. The nature, the scale, and the dangers of the impending epidemic were unprecedented in modern times.

It was not until the first week of December 1986 that the issue was brought into the open and aired publicly. The *Edinburgh Evening News* ran a series of hard-hitting main features on HIV/AIDS. The series was branded throughout the week by a box reading: EDINBURGH'S PROBLEM – AIDS AND YOU – PUBLIC WARNING, and was accompanied each day by a list of places and telephone numbers under the heading 'Where to turn for help...' The strap line on Day 1 read: 'AIDS has already crippled New York... Edinburgh is notorious for having one of the highest rates of infected people among its drug addicts... there is no cure... [we] must change our personal habits... this series is explicit – it has to be, so no-one misunderstands... it may offend some people – but only knowledge will save lives.' During the week it described near-panic in New York. It profiled a young prostitute working in Leith, who was also a mother, who knew she was infected and felt sorry if she infected her customers but said she needed the money. It reported on the ongoing concerns of the Blood Transfusion Service, and it carried a three-point plan unanimously passed by the Edinburgh & District Trades Council: free needles to be issued at doctors' surgeries; free condoms to be issued at surgeries, clinics, and chemists; and the allocation of major resources and counselling for AIDS victims. On the last day the reporter, Ian Burrell, was given space to write for himself, which he summarised in seven points:

> ➢ No-one can afford to sleep around casually any more. It's too risky.
> ➢ We must educate now – the USA did, but 5 years too late.
> ➢ The government campaign must be blunt – forget vote-catching.
> ➢ Condoms must be made freely available to all.
> ➢ Doctors must be able to hand out needles to drug addicts.
> ➢ £20 million is not enough – we must have more research cash.
> ➢ Sufferers must be treated with compassion – they are not outcasts.

Burrell did well to make the first point the most weighty and the most difficult to implement. A whole generation had grown up unused to having to negotiate safe sex. For 20 years and more, since the arrival of the readily available contraceptive pill, women were able to safely and temporarily suspend their own fertility. The free love of the 1960s had truly taken hold. There remained the risk of various STDs, of course, which could be embarrassing but which were generally treatable. The possibility of pregnancy from sexual intercourse had been replaced by a fatal, incurable disease that could strike male and female alike. Everything else in the Burrell's list was a matter of policy and education. This was a matter of personal habits and attitudes.

The *Evening News* could look back on a good week's work. It had put the key facts and issues to Edinburgh in an urgent, coherent and accessible manner that ensured they were discussed round kitchen tables and in the pubs of the city. Edinburgh (and the world) had to learn fast. The facing-down of the moralists and the prohibitionists was urgent. It had to be understood that the free issue of condoms and needles was intended neither to encourage nor to condone promiscuous sex or drug-taking, but to keep people alive and prevent an epidemic. The risk of people living with HIV being demonised and isolated was very real; if they were to be treated as outcasts, the problem would not go with them into the wilderness but would be exacerbated and rapidly get out of control. The mind-changes, the policy shifts, and the allocation of real resources were all a challenge.

In January 1987 the UK-wide Department of Health and Social Security issued a leaflet to every household in the country: 'Don't Die of Ignorance'. Secretary of State for Health Norman Fowler, who had studied the situation in USA, deserves great credit for the initiative. Prime Minister Margaret Thatcher was against it on the grounds that it could have a bad influence on impressionable young people. Addressed to the general population, the leaflet was more concerned with the transmission of HIV/AIDS by sex than by sharing injecting equipment: '...three hundred people in UK have died; ...there is no cure; ...it kills; ...HIV/AIDS is initially symptomless, so never take chances; use condoms; ...fewer sexual partners makes for less risk; ...it can't be transmitted by shaking hands; ...blood transfusions are safe; ...we all have to take this seriously to avoid an epidemic getting out of control.' It formed the basis for a wide-ranging public awareness campaign.

Later that year a needle exchange was arranged at Leith Hospital on a cautious one afternoon per week, but the police, who still had to enforce the law, saw it as a golden opportunity for surveillance that would lead them to the dealers which, naturally enough, discouraged the users. A phlebotomy room was set up alongside, specifically to take blood for testing for HIV. A senior advisor in the Social Work Department who needed to see the situation for himself and meet the real people, trained as a phlebotomist to give himself an obvious role. He saw some very worried men and women, including professionals, some of whom had travelled from Glasgow, Newcastle and Aberdeen to get out of their home areas.

Early in 1988 the UK government's Advisory Council on the Misuse of Drugs reported that time had been lost in Scotland. In September the Scottish Home and Health Department resolved the legal situation by authorising guidelines to GPs to supply injecting equipment. By this time there were

47 known cases of AIDS and 23 deaths by AIDS in Scotland – this is not including death by drug abuse and injecting – and rising every month in an atmosphere of ignorance and fear. One retail chemist recalls for me how she was discussing the situation with friends and colleagues in a posh restaurant in Edinburgh when the waitress risked a reprimand by stepping out of line: 'Give them what they want. Just keep it out of the general population' she said.

Edinburgh was horrified in April 1987 as *The Sunday Telegraph* ran a piece entitled 'Babies of the AIDS capital: ...Stately Edinburgh is now the AIDS capital of Europe... at least 50 per cent – and possibly 80 per cent – of Edinburgh's 2,000 drug addicts are carriers... Just six per cent of London's addicts carry the virus' it reported. One newly diagnosed man, it went on, returned home 'after an evening out to find his house wrecked and AIDS graffiti scrawled on the walls'. There was an air of apocalypse in the final paragraph, quoting a speech in the House of Commons in 1855 by John Bright: 'The Angel of Death has been abroad throughout the land: you may almost hear the beating of his wings'.[25] The soubriquet 'AIDS Capital of Europe' stuck.

All this was dramatically brought out in the same year when it was proposed to open an HIV-dedicated hospice in the small village of Wallhouse, near Torphichen, West Lothian, 15 miles west of Edinburgh. The building in question was a large old family house that had recently been closed as a children's home. They were going to call it Milestone House, after a stone of that name in the village kirkyard. The stone is one of several refuge stones which in the medieval period offered refuge and respite to debtors and criminals who stayed within a circle of them. A kirk elder and local teacher expressed a strand of opinion succinctly: 'The people who would be in the hospice will no doubt predominantly come from the homosexual and drug-taking community. No doubt those who come to visit them will be from the same sections of society. They will be less than welcome in Torphichen.'[26] In the event, the proposal was withdrawn when it was found that the building had serious problems and was unsuitable. Fear and feelings were still running high a couple of years later. The newly founded Waverley Care, having established this dedicated hospice in Firrhill – named Milestone House in recognition of the gay community's major contribution to developing HIV/AIDS awareness and making provision for caring for those with the virus in the 1980s – was proposing a second hospice within a stone's throw of the fictional Mikey Forrester's flat in Muirhouse and right beside the Varicose Veins flats where, in the fiction, Tommy, with HIV, approaches death in dreadful circumstances in 'Winter in West Granton'. A local man said: 'Hospices should be put somewhere in the country.'[27]

For Welsh, all this is not some recorded history to be coolly considered. He was writing in the thick of it. To enter his world at the time of writing, let's take a no. 27 bus back to Tollcross, scene of the first shooting gallery in *Trainspotting*. Here we get into a Tardis bubble that carries us back to the first year or so of the 1990s, as Welsh is finishing his book. We'll walk north up Earl Grey Street and Lothian Road.

Heroin injection is fading away fast; as a substitute people are now using Temgesic, a narcotic pain reliever, and Temazepam, a tranquiliser, both available on prescription and both soluble and suitable for injection. If anything, that is more dangerous than injecting heroin. The recreational drugs of choice are now Speed and Ecstasy, taken orally. These things go in fashions, influenced, of course, by availability. Leith and Edinburgh are left to deal with the aftermath of the collision between sex, drugs and HIV/AIDS during the 1980s. In 1987, only three years ago, Princess Diana ostentatiously shook hands with an HIV+ person without wearing gloves – such was the level of ignorance and fear that this was widely reported, but by now it is known and understood that the virus is not transmitted in normal social intercourse of this sort. Since then she has been openly involved in supporting HIV/AIDS causes around the world.

Nevertheless, there has been some vociferous vocalising from moralisers and prohibitionists, some of whom are saying that HIV/AIDS is the wrath of God, and they feed apocalyptic visions of the end of the second millennium. But the authorities have learned from the USA, New York and San Francisco in particular, that it is essential to not demonise and isolate people with HIV/AIDS. They are doing their best to both respect and care for the victims as well as educate the general public. There are some cases of HIV+ individuals who have delayed the onset of AIDS, so the possibility of longer-term survival with the virus is beginning to emerge. But once AIDS has developed, people invariably die, generally within a very few months.

The newly founded Waverley Care Trust has just opened the country's first hospice dedicated to this completely new condition, at Firrhill, using a parcel of land within the grounds of the City Hospital, the former isolation hospital. The charity SOLAS (from a Gaelic word meaning comfort and light) has acquired pleasant premises at Abbeymount, just east of the city centre, offering a cheap healthy café and food shop, nice activity rooms and, of course, mutual support.

It is officially estimated that, compared to England's 25 per 100,000 of the population who are HIV+, and Scotland's 35 per 100,000, in Lothian Region there are a staggering 144 per 100,000.[28] The Waverley Care Trust estimates that the 40 people living with AIDS in Lothian in 1989 will balloon to 500 in five years, by 1994.[29] The Edinburgh District Council Women's Committee has just published a children's story book, written by an HIV+ mother, that says in the introduction that almost half the children born with HIV in Britain live in and around Edinburgh. Two researchers are studying the 'invisible' carers of Muirhouse and Pilton, municipal housing schemes occupied by many of the post-war Leith diaspora and epicentre of these statistics which are diluted by including the whole city and the surrounding area: Lothian Region. Mothers and partners of drug users become proxy nurses, dieticians, house-keepers, drugs counsellors, and sometimes, on behalf of the prescribing doctor, monitors of the methadone intake. It is an exhausting, unrecognised multiplicity of roles.

The researchers are noticing that younger women partners of male addicts often feel under some pressure to show their love and commitment to them by eschewing safe sex: 'He wouldn't like it if I rejected him' and 'He wouldn't like a condom' are both quoted. Many feel themselves under an additional obligation to give their men the satisfaction of becoming fathers, thus knowingly exposing themselves and the baby to the high risk of infection.[30] There is no certainty that HIV/AIDS will not sweep through society like a medieval plague.

At the second traffic lights we turn right into Bread Street. Here was the medical supplies shop, where you could buy injecting equipment; the consensus among the professionals is that its closure led directly to the shooting galleries and thus in making intra-venous drug abusers (IVDAs) bigger carriers of HIV than gay men. So it seems fitting that there some agencies here dealing with the consequences. The Salvation Army now runs a help centre here, offering a safe place for people with HIV for conversation, some counselling, and practical help such as transport to hospital.

Left down Spittal Street is the Spittal Street Centre, on the corner with Lady Lawson Street, owned, staffed and managed by Lothian Health Board. It offers not only a walk-in clinic and advice centre, including a harm reduction team and a needle exchange programme but, with senior staff on the premises and eminent people available as consultants, it is also set up to co-ordinate HIV/AIDS policy across the Region. It takes referrals from and offers support to a variety of professions: medical, social work, education, housing. Its own education programme disseminates HIV/AIDS material aimed at 11 – 25 year olds.

The Housing Department, anxious to play its important part in supporting people with HIV/AIDS, has issued a flyer to all tenants on the subject. A young fellow you haven't heard of, Irvine Welsh, working as an official within the Housing Department, may well have had a hand in drafting it. Included is the following sentence, prominently placed and in capitals: All Housing Staff Who Meet The Public Have Received Training On Working In A Sensitive Way With People Who Have HIV Or AIDS, And Are Aware That They Must Maintain Strict Confidentiality. If, as a Council tenant, it goes on, you are being harassed, the Department will investigate and possibly re-locate you or take action against the perpetrators of the harassment. It will also arrange for obscene graffiti to be removed.

We can't miss how Welsh incorporates both the general fear as well as many specific details into the fiction that we are reading in *Trainspotting*.

SECTION V

What sort of book?

CHAPTER 17

Is Welsh Scottish?

IN AN EXPANSIVE Edinburgh-style literary mood, let's go to Rutherford's Bar, a pleasant enough pub on Drummond Street, where we will read a little Robert Louis Stevenson on location. The Speculative Society of the university, of which RLS was a member in the early 1870s, used to meet here. On the end of the street, a few steps away, is a plaque with an extended inscription, penned by Stevenson under a blanket on his yacht in the South Seas:

> And when I remember all I hoped and feared as I pickled about Rutherford's in the rain and the east wind; how I feared I should make a mere shipwreck, yet I timidly hoped not; how I feared I should never have a friend, far less a wife, and yet passionately hoped I might; how I hoped (if I did not take to drink) I should possibly write one little book, etc. And then now – what a change! I feel as if I should like the incident set upon a brass plate at the corner of that dreary thoroughfare, for all students to read, poor devils, when their hearts are down.

This is university territory, with Old College just off the end of the street to the west, and the sports and recreational centre, The Pleasance, a few hundred yards to the east. Stevenson wrote recollections of his childhood and of Edinburgh, but the comparison with Welsh is not strong: Stevenson's work is poetic and 'picturesque' (his word), not the harsh, excoriating, scandalous work of Welsh. J M Barrie wrote a fictional account of an encounter with RLS in this bar, and the creator of Sherlock Holmes, Arthur Conan Doyle, used to come here. It seems to have been because of the pub's literary connections that a young Sorley Maclean was introduced to Hugh McDiarmid here, both giants of Scottish letters, in 1934.

We become aware of several young men being boisterous, and the bar girl looking increasingly harassed. We try to ignore them, but we are startled when she seems to call out in a loud voice: 'Has anyone seen my cunt?' There are howls of laughter, not nice laughter, more like the baying of a lynch mob. 'Naw, but ah'd like tae' (p.178) is guffawed across the room.

It's not clear why Welsh chose Rutherford's Bar for his short story 'The Elusive Mr Hunt'. It may be that he wanted to make a pitch for literary greatness by association, or maybe he wanted to bring literary greatness down to his own level. It may be that he was placing it here because Kelly is a student. Sick Boy is the main other character in the episode, and we should note that this is Sick Boy's second territory: he is at home cruising on The Bridges, just to the north, and he entertains women at the Minto Hotel, half a mile to the south. We learn in *Porno* and again in *Skagboys* that his mother, father and sisters have left Leith Banana flats, and moved to the South Side, where Rutherford's Bar was a local pub. Or it may be none of the above: maybe one of Welsh's writing groups met here, or he just liked the idea of playing an away game. Anyway, this fictional episode couldn't be set here now; the pub has been merged into an RLS-themed Italian restaurant with the premises next door.

It's August 1990, Edinburgh's festival month. Let's go onto South Bridge, where Sick Boy enjoys cruising the mantovani in 'In Overdrive'. Turning left up the High Street, we find the Fringe at its open air best, with street performers in full flow. The Fringe was probably at its strongest in the 1980s: mature, confident, flexible, subversive, aspirational, funny, open, and cheap, before it became a shop window for professionals and a sequence of television studios having a month on the road. Sick Boy is not here to enjoy the fun in any generous or open way, but to personally take advantage of the 'fanny of every race, colour, creed and nationality present'. Playing up his own origins in working class culture, he derides 'zit-encrusted, squeaky-voiced wankers': students who are enjoying their liberal education at public expense before going on to lucrative careers shutting down workplaces and throwing people into poverty (p.29).

We go down Cockburn Street and cut down Anchor Close. We drop down to Market Street at the bottom and into Waverley Station opposite, which, presumably arising out of Welsh's frequent journeys to and from London, comes into *Trainspotting* several times. It is perhaps the only station in the world named after works of fiction, the Waverley novels by Walter Scott. Scattered throughout it are three dozen quotes from Scott's writings, for example: '... when we had a king, and a chancellor, and parliament – men o' our ain, we could aye peeble them wi' stanes when they werena gude bairns – But naebody's nails can reach the length o' Lunnon...' (from *The Heart of Midlothian*). A nationalist sentiment, expressed in the vernacular but, as we shall shortly see, not in Welsh's trademark subversive and scurrilous language.

Crossing the bridge into the gardens, we approach the largest monument to a writer anywhere in the world, the Scott Monument, on top of
which Sick Boy takes a photo of his French girlfriend (p.199). Walter Scott
(1771–1832) was hugely influential in the development of historical fiction
in modern times in English, making Welsh a latter-day exponent of the genre.
It's doubtful in the extreme that Welsh was consciously paying any sort of
tribute to Sir Walter Scott. The locations referred to are, quite simply, part of
Edinburgh's familiar townscape.

We walk in the gardens parallel to Princes Street. If in the 1980s Princes
Street was exotic, pleasant and dramatic for visitors, for Renton with Spud
it is 'hideous'. They register the castle as 'just another building... just like
British Home Stores or Virgin Records'. In the same paragraph, however,
Renton, on coming out of the station and catching his first view of the dra-
matic castle, thinks 'this isnae bad' (p.228). It all depends, according to
Renton, how familiar you are with it and how long you have been away.

We'll step onto The Mound, with the railway lines heading to all parts
of Scotland tunnelled below and its art galleries above. Let's stand on the
low plinth which marks Edinburgh's status as a UNESCO World Heritage
Site, since 1996. Whereas most cultural Sites are single buildings or small
complexes, Edinburgh is most unusual in being an extended city centre, with
thousands of property owners and fully functioning in the modern world.
Recognition of a centre of living culture would be incomplete without a
360-degree inclusion of dissent and counter culture; which is where Welsh
has a rightful place.

Crossing Princes Street to Hanover Street, we'll cast a glance to the west,
to number 124 Princes Street. It formerly belonged to John Menzies, the stationers; this is the location for the film shoot in which Sick Boy leads the way
for the shoplifting spree that culminates in Spud and Renton being caught
and brought before the sheriff. It has changed hands now. The distinctive
lintel at 45 degrees is still there, but without the mirror that produces such
a good effect on the screen. We go up Hanover Street and turn right into
Rose Street.

First on the left used to be a pub known as The Cottar's Howff, and
Macnair says that Welsh witnessed a scene here that inspired 'The Glass'.
Certainly, he puts the fiction in Rose Street, where, Renton reflects, 'only
arseholes, wankers and tourists set fit' (p.76). But, more to the point, we
should look at Renton's reflections on his own countrymen. Scots are 'Fuckin
failures in a country of failures'; Scots, having been colonised by 'wankers'
(the English), are '[t]he lowest of the fuckin low... Ah hate the Scots' (p.78).

Renton's manifesto of what it is to be Scottish is certainly not couched in ringing, declamatory terms. It's the reverse of inspirational or aspirational. It can be put alongside his reflection in London: 'Scotland the brave, ma arse; Scotland the shitein cunt' (p.228). It's a view of history that sustains Scottish identity politics: Scotland's pride is in having survived all this abuse and still having some fight left! But Spud is under no illusions. As this young man of Catholic Irish descent and his mixed-race uncle are heading for the Persevere pub where the Orange Order is mixing with the British National Party he casts doubt on the idea that Scots are not racist: 'Ah jist sortay laugh whin some cats say racism's an English thing...' (p.126)

The location is important. Right next door to the Cottar's Howff is Milne's Bar, where, famously, Hugh MacDiarmid used to meet fellow writers – and in one or two other pubs in the area – consciously trying to revive Scottish literature, particularly in the form of poetry and in the languages of Lallans (Lowland Scots) and Gaelic. In the 1960s and 1970s this had a subversive edge to it, earning the bar, deservedly or not, the soubriquet The Little Kremlin. Alexander Moffat's compilation portrait of MacDiarmid holding court with Sorley Maclean, Norman MacCaig, Iain Crichton Smith, George Mackay Brown, Sydney Goodsir Smith, Edwin Morgan and Robert Garioch, who are all taught in schools now, hangs in the Portrait Gallery on York Place. Maybe, once again, Welsh is trying to take on received views in the very places where these received views are most strongly associated. Or, maybe, Welsh is deliberately adding to and updating McDiarmid's work. *Trainspotting* was taught in schools within five years of publication, and Welsh's portrait (it was actually little more than a studio mug shot), along with other local luminaries, was displayed on Leith Walk a few yards from Leith Central Station for three or four years up to early 2014. Clearly, the authorities have given Welsh more public recognition, and earlier in his career, than some very illustrious forbears enjoyed.

* * * * * *

But the positive recognition didn't come immediately. Following the publication of *Trainspotting*, Welsh spent about a decade as an outcast of the establishment. He seemed to be doing everything he could to remain there; he published *Filth* (1998), and *Porno* (2002), both titles, and their contents, seemingly calculated to cause offence and reject recognition, which, of course, generated recognition. He thrived on it. *Trainspotting* the play and *Trainspotting* the film were feeding off each other to produce a cultural and commercial fireball, and not even the middle classes or literary establishments can counter that. Welsh was a beneficiary of writing about and for the first generation that was using cyberspace to discuss and rave about his work. Some online comments were sensitive and sensible and a lot were rubbish, but the quality hardly mattered; it generated an interest in Irvine Welsh and *Trainspotting* that was beyond the wildest dreams of a publisher's marketing team. He also benefitted from the collapse of the Net Book Agreement, which magnified the importance of prizes and awards and encouraged the promotion of blockbusters: pile 'em high and sell 'em cheap. He was awarded a clutch of end-of-century accolades. All this is well documented elsewhere.

Things were perceptibly changing a decade after his meteoric rise to prominence. An unlikely source brought it to a head. In January 2004 Alexander McCall Smith launched an outright attack on Welsh in the South African *Sunday Times*, which *The Herald* quoted and paraphrased:

> ... Welsh's books, such as *Trainspotting*, portray a notion of 'Scottish miserabilism' that is at odds with reality... 'I think Irvine Welsh has been a travesty for Scotland [said McCall Smith]... but most people in Scotland aren't like that... I've got complete contempt for that. I feel that writing is a moral act. I feel that those who portray an aggressive, vulgar, debased attitude towards life are conniving in that life, and I think publishers should reject them.' He said he would never allow any of the characters in his books to swear. 'No, no, no! Because it's an act of verbal permissiveness and sexual aggression. I will not do it and I've got no time for it. It sounds terribly pompous, but it's true.[31]

Realising he had been quoted in Scotland, McCall Smith immediately claimed his remarks had been 'misinterpreted'. The following day *The Herald* quoted him:

> All I said is that I do not agree with the vision of Scotland that [the novels of Irvine Welsh] represent. Some people like that view, and that's up to them... this is a storm in a teacup. I have nothing against Mr Welsh. I do not know him, and I believe he is a perfectly agreeable and charming man. I certainly have no dispute with him – none at all.[32]

However, his original comments had some support. A couple of days later the correspondence page carried two letters, both from Edinburgh residents:

> It is not at all pompous of Alexander McCall Smith to castigate such writers as Irvine Welsh... [who] may claim that he draws

attention to the health problems of the poor and marginalised in Scottish society. Far from offering a solution, his language encourages a certain middle-class view that drug-taking, copious use of F and related words, rough trade, inter alia, are somehow chic, or in the new parlance, sexy... Have Welsh and his ilk ever considered that their repeated use of such words effectively condones sexual aggression and advocates gratuitous violence? Rather than mirroring a cultural and social malaise, they adorn it with rosy footlights, which stultify the imagination and kill vision. Others suggest that Welsh's work has at least encouraged deprived people to actually read books. Where is the evidence? I fail to see how *Filth* and *Porno* can nourish young minds or offer them anything other than a circular route to their Dantean inferno. In this respect Irvine Welsh and his cohorts have had a deeply damaging influence on Scottish life and perceptions of literature.[33]

The other letter was from me: 'I'm glad to see Alexander McCall Smith has climbed down from his too high-minded denunciation of Irvine Welsh and his novels. *Trainspotting* (his example) isn't miserable, writing it and publishing it isn't immoral, and it isn't an aim of an author to describe what "most people" are like. Far from it being "at odds with reality" it vividly portrays [a] familiar lifestyle... [and] conveys a sense of humour and courage which isn't always there in real life. Dealing in the world of skag, [*Trainspotting*] could be really miserable.'[34]

In the next *Sunday Herald* Ian Bell (no relation) waded in to get this sorted. Since when, he demanded, did a novelist, 'a person who makes things up, acquire a patriotic duty to act as a kind of tribal scribe?' Did Walter Scott, or Lewis Grassic Gibbon, describe some form of Scotland that everyone could agree is accurate and nobody quarrel with? If authors who describe 'an aggressive, vulgar, debased attitude towards life are conniving in that life' and publishers should reject them, then McCall Smith seems to be conniving in crime (a reference to his Mma Ramotswe series), and he himself shouldn't be published. 'Welsh is a limited writer. He vamps with a few chords; a symphony is beyond him. But false?... Welsh may not tell the whole truth about [Scotland], but who does? Who can? What matters, surely, is to make the attempt.'[35]

At the time McCall Smith was preparing his series *44 Scotland Street*. It involves a young woman in her second gap year, a young man whose wealthy father has set him up in an art gallery, a stolen painting that is given as a raffle prize to South Edinburgh Conservative Association, and a bilingual five-year-old who goes for psychotherapy. Amusing it may be. A description of what 'most people are like' it certainly isn't. McCall Smith got the point. He regretted his remarks and apologised.

But probably most instrumental in transforming Welsh's standing was the formation of Edinburgh's status as the first UNESCO City of Literature in 2004. It was slow to get off the mark, but when it got going it could really do no other than fully embrace Welsh as a major literary figure, whether judged by sheer sales figures or by his personal/professional profile. So now he takes his place in the pantheon of Scottish Greats, entitled to be mentioned in the same breath as Robert Burns, RLS, Walter Scott, Conan Doyle, Muriel Spark, Ian Rankin, JK Rowling, just to mention a few from the Edinburgh Collection.

The process was complete in 2006 when ITV's *South Bank Show*, presented by the polymath Melvyn Bragg, screened a 50-minute show, mostly featuring Welsh's most recent output, the film *Wedding Belles* and the book *Bedroom Secrets of a Master Chef*, with a little about the man himself. It was the line-up of some of Bragg's other guests that season that announced Welsh's acceptance into the ranks of the great and the good: Robbie Coltrane, JG Ballard, Sue Townsend and Steve Reich. Of course, this was in large part a reflection of the runaway success of the play and the film, but it's useless putting up barriers between different art forms, particularly when they combine in one man. The decade in which Welsh both endured and enjoyed people taking free pot shots at him was coming to an end.

Welsh contributed a short story to an anthology published in support of the One City Trust.[36] The other contributors were Ian Rankin and Alexander McCall Smith. There is a heart-felt introduction by JK Rowling about the importance of good, strong community, to which, presumably, all the contributors subscribe. A subsequent One City Trust anthology appeared, for which Welsh wrote the introduction. In the foreword, Rev Councillor Rt Hon George Grubb, Lord Provost, hails Welsh as 'an iconic chronicler of our city'.[37]

In 2013 The Scottish Book Trust conducted a worldwide poll which asked for the public's favourite Scottish novel of the past half-century. *Trainspotting* was the winner. They put a copy (not a first edition) in a display case in the august National Library of Scotland. If the question had been: 'Which Scottish work of fiction in the last fifty years has had most impact in public life?' it would be difficult even for its detractors not to vote for *Trainspotting*. Welsh's transformation into a recognised literary figure, who is now feted by the BBC, production companies, and book festivals around the world, and is a sought-after ambassador and patron for a variety causes, seems to be complete. On a personal note, in 2012, visiting family in Goa (India), an international holiday destination, I went into a small multi-language bookshop where a full range of Welsh titles, untranslated, was stacked flat on the shelf to pack in the most volumes possible. 'Welsh is my best-selling author,' I was assured.

Welsh has views on whether he is Scottish or not. Speaking at the World Writers' Conference as part of the Edinburgh International Book Festival in 2012 he said:

> As I know through my own experience, the market will always convert art and culture into mass entertainment. When my first novel sold 10,000 copies, I was a local hero. When it sold 100,000, people grew more dubious. At a million copies I was a sell-out, whoring out my culture for the entertainment of outsiders. Now … I can't even think about it. The point is, that many people locally felt an ownership of the book, and a pride in it. What was an affirmation, an attestation to a place, a way of life, a language, a class, a culture and an attitude, became seen as something else. Obviously, the book was the same; I hadn't changed a word of it. Let me make it clear that I'm not complaining about making money – any writer that does is either a liar or crazy – just stressing that the marketplace can force the writer into a set of relationships and perspectives they might not have recalled signing up for.[38]

The author has his own life; the book also has its own life. Let's go into The Cottar's Howff and have a drink to all this. Except we can't – like Rutherford's Bar, it has merged with next door, Milne's Bar in this case. There are some changes of floor level, which may have given rise, as Macnair suggests, to the glass throwing incident from which the episode has its title. As with the discussion at Rutherford's Bar, there is no knowing for sure what inspired Welsh to locate some of his fiction where he does, and it may be that these associations are nothing more than abstract speculations that we literary types enjoy so much.

CHAPTER 18

Influences, Context and Genre

Influences

WELSH IS ENTITLED – he went out of his way – to say that he avoided using models, and indeed there is much evidence that his writing was speculative and innovative. However, it is inconceivable that there are no similarities with other writings in the vast world of published literature. For example, there are some striking resemblances between *Trainspotting* and Hunter S Thompson's *Fear and Loathing in Las Vegas: A Savage Journey to the Heart of the American Dream*. Both flip, without notice, from fiction to real life references; both have a drug-fuelled background; both are clearly, at least in part, auto-biographical; both are, to some extent, a chronicle of and comment on their times from the point of view of rebellious youth, with conventional society being ridiculed and rejected; and the structure of both is a jagged, episodic, fictional framework. Both, as it happens, are the first efforts of authors who never gained the same critical acclaim for their other works. The title of *Trainspotting*'s episode *Grieving and Mourning in Port Sunshine* strongly suggests that Welsh took some inspiration from the Thompson's text, although the content of the episode is hardly in line with the model. Welsh has said that Iceberg Slim's *Pimp* (1967) had more immediate impact, giving him the confidence to get inside Begbie's head and fill out the character without any attempt at providing a context or mitigation for his depravity.

Twenty-odd years after the publication of *Trainspotting* Welsh complained that it would not then be published by a London publisher, and maybe he was right. Neither, if his writings weren't already 600 years old, would Geoffrey Chaucer (c.1343–1400) who didn't hold back on graphic bawdiness. Chaucer took on the church, which was greatly more to be feared in the late Middle Ages than the literary establishment is now:

> '...You there, Satan! Lift up your tail' said he,/'Show us your
> arse and let the friar see/The place where all the friars have their

nest!'/And in a minute or two, more or less,/Just as bees come swarming from a hive,/A troop of twenty thousand friars drove/ Out of the devil's arse, and swarmed through hell,/And then swarmed back, as fast possible/And crept into his arsehole, one and all.[39]

Chaucer takes no lessons from Welsh in causing offence. But they have in common a sharp eye and a sympathetic voice for ordinary folk, and their triumph is to put their characters on the page on their own terms, without apology or explanation. Chaucer combined his scholarship (he would be expected to write in French or Latin) with his sharp ear and common touch to write in the vernacular, and his writings make him the father of literature in English.

Welsh cannot claim to be as ground breaking as this, but he deserves credit for a new phonetic rendering of demotic speech that may even catch on. It has to be recognised that here Welsh joins the company of James Kelman, who had recently done some heavy lifting in Glasgow-speak, and there was a general revival of Lallans in literature. But in Welsh's case, it's more than just spelling; it's the language, and not just the odd expletive for effect. It is strings of the most foul words in the vocabulary, most of them sexual obscenities, often several in a sentence, indiscriminately used. Do people really speak like that? The answer is: yes, some do. They don't advance far into mainstream society, which is why the question is asked and the offence is caused. One effect of this uncompromising language is that it limits the forums in which *Trainspotting* can be openly quoted. Public broadcasting, for example, is ruled out. You can pay to knowingly expose yourself to language like this – buy a ticket for a play or a film, or buy a book – but you are protected by law (in the UK) from having this sort of stuff thrust in front of you in the public realm.

And then there is the dialect. Much of the dialogue and some of the narrative is more or less phonetically spelled street level Leith patois. This breaks the rules of conventional rendering of the Scottish dialect and pays little or no respect to the emerging written Lallans. For example, the word 'of' is conventionally rendered as o', the apostrophe representing the missing 'f'. But for Welsh, nothing is missing. Besides, it is not pronounced as an 'o', but as somewhere between a hard 'e' and a hard 'i', which he makes into 'ay'. Similarly, there is no final 'g' missing at the end of present participles such as 'tryin'. To make matters worse, he is quite prepared to make up words that have never been on the page before, and they are in no dictionaries, although if you can hear them off the page it helps to work them out. It depends how familiar you are with the spoken language. For instance, 'always' becomes 'eywis' and 'off of' (itself an expression unfamiliar to non-Scots) becomes 'oafay'. All these examples are on the opening page. It's no way to encourage a wide readership. Or maybe it is. The same applies to Welsh's dogged insistence in locating the action in places known only to locals that lack the multiple referencing of, say, Edinburgh city centre.

Behind the punkish defiance there is a deeper intention and effect: in putting an obstacle to understanding between his texts and the literati and academics, Welsh puts ownership and control over them into the hands of the people of and for whom he is writing. Professionals have to defer to the native speakers and the locals. If *Trainspotting* is to have a long life, it needs to become an object of study, not only as a literary effort but also as a product or a version of its environment; thus the environment will need to be studied. Students have to enter Welsh's world, much as we need to understand Chaucer's world to fully appreciate the literature. As has been pointed out, Welsh writes of his community in its own language much as Jane Austen writes of hers.

Chaucer and Welsh both write of drug abuse; alcohol, in Chaucer's case. They both make creative use of material that is already in the common domain and is readily recognisable. And this, too, Chaucer and Welsh have in common: both are writers of bits and pieces, whose idea for the final composition (*The Canterbury Tales* and *Trainspotting* respectively) grew in the course of the piecemeal composing. In both cases the result is a collection of short stories making a whole, with erratic references between them, insertion of scraps that hardly fit into the composition, a multiplicity of voices, confusion and similarity of identity, lots of laughs, some sober and serious moments, and no conclusions. Both books can both be read as social commentary, and, in places, satire.

Is it Junk Literature?

Thomas De Quincey (1785–1859) was a brilliant intellect but with a patchy education. He should have been, by his own estimation at least, a philosopher the equal of his older German contemporary Immanuel Kant, but his opium habit clearly interfered with his personal discipline and therefore his output. Thomas Carlyle wrote a note saying De Quincey had said he would call on him, but 'he will do no such thing, poor little fellow... [he has] been once seen out this winter.' He almost certainly understated the true level of his consumption of opium, but he managed to keep some measure of control over it and he lived to a good age. He is chiefly remembered now for the literary quality and the vividness of his accounts of the effects of opium. For example:

> The sense of space, and in the end, the sense of time, were both powerfully affected. Buildings, landscapes, &c. were exhibited in proportions so vast as the bodily eye is not fitted to conceive. Space swelled, and was amplified to an extent of unutterable infinity. This, however, did not disturb me so much as the vast expansion of time; I sometimes seemed to have lived for 70 or 100 years in one night; nay, sometimes had feelings representative of a millennium passed in that time, or, however, of a duration far beyond the limits of any human experience.

De Quincey's grandiloquent descriptions of the effects of opium are matched by others: 'It was a grand night, and strange to feel so utterly self-sufficient – more like... God before he made the world or his son...' (Lady Diana Manners, 1892–1986). Or this: 'Without opium, plans, marriages and journeys appear to me just as foolish as if someone falling out of a window were to hope to make friends with the occupants of the room before which he passes.' (Jean Cocteau 1889–1963). Why can't Welsh write like this?

There are two reasons. Firstly, De Quincey, Manners, and Cocteau were describing the effects of opium, which permits these expansive visions and experiences as well as permitting relatively lucid intervals in which they can be recalled and put to paper. Heroin is much harsher. It offers release from responsibility and anxiety and, as Renton says, a feeling of immortality (p.89), but there is little respite before the compulsion to take more becomes all-consuming. The second difference is that De Quincey, Manners, and Cocteau were all well-to-do and beautifully educated; they could, as it were, afford their habit, enjoy it and reflect on it. Welsh, on the other hand, was writing for people who, as he has put it, didn't have a 'fucking scoobie' as to what was going on: poor, poorly educated, and desperate. These are the people who don't normally have the tools to tell their story. Welsh is their scribe.

And yet some of Welsh's descriptions of the junkie experience may go down among the all-time quotables. The recurring theme of the harrowing 'Junk Dilemmas' is that there is really no dilemma at all; in 'Junk Dilemmas no. 67' he (it seems to be Renton, but we can't be certain) is fully aware that there are two 'me's' and he is dicing with death. He is under no illusion about the nature of death, but it's not enough to prevent him taking another fix. In 'Junk Dilemmas no. 64' Renton wishes he could find a replacement son for his mother. Or maybe it's the honesty of the experience without junk that will be best remembered. Nothing is spared in his description of cold turkey, likening it to lying on top of sharp rods below a skip being loaded: 'Every cell in ma body wants tae leave it, every cell is sick hurting marinated in pure fuckin poison...' (p.194). And in temporary remission, which hasn't been easy, at the end of the carefully titled 'Straight Dilemmas No.1' he finds that being without drugs is even more boring than using (p.301). It's a dangerous stage in rehab, when it's all too easy to slip back.

Can we say that *Trainspotting* is junk literature? Heroin defeats the sustained exertion or concentration needed to produce something like a work of art. Welsh's earliest writings are pretty short; the more distance he put between himself and the use of heroin, the longer, more considered, and more inter-connected his writings become. It is beyond the authority of this book to state that there is a causal link between the two facts. But there is room to speculate. Maybe the output of the earlier creative period (we are calling it the First Generation of episodes) can be called junk literature. But in the second generation of *Trainspotting*'s episodes Welsh clearly has a larger vision: this is the early stages of Welsh the novelist, and it is certainly not junk literature.

Is it Journalism or History or Fiction?

When I first read *Trainspotting*, here in Leith, I was bowled along by the pace, the cheek, the colour, the freshness of the voices, the authenticity, and, of course, it was fun to recognise so many familiar locations set in fiction. 'Nice try, Mr Welsh' I thought. 'But it's too topical and it's too local. It won't last and it won't travel.'

Welsh has said that *Trainspotting* is 'all about generation and geography'. This isn't new. In 1621 Peter Heylyn wrote '...History without Geography, like a dead carkasse, hath neither life nor motion at all...' One of the steps in the formation of modern Scotland was the making of maps, which realigned peoples' self-identification from loyalty to clan, or king, or church, to their place in the topography: on the coast, or by a river, or up a glen. The daily preoccupations of a sheep farmer's lad are necessarily different from those of his contemporary in a declining port town. Identity and culture are acted out – history is made – on location. Some literary pundits will have it that in *Trainspotting* location has a presence like a character. I prefer to think of it as a literary form of cartography.

From the beginning, *Trainspotting* was described as a novel without any attempt to mark out what makes it different from an anthology of short stories. To be sure, the stories have themes and characters in common, and they make some sort of progress towards an ending, which means they become also episodes; but a novel needs to be more than one thing after another. There needs to be artful clues, themes, plots, surprises, structures, which the reader discovers and unravels along the way.

Richard Pevear wrote this in the introduction to his translation of *War and Peace*, which has always been called a novel:

> The first readers of *War and Peace* were certainly surprised, but often also bewildered and dismayed by the book. They found it hard to identify the main characters, to discover anything like a plot, to see any connection between episodes, to understand the sudden leaps from fiction to history, from narration to philosophising. There seemed to be no focus, no artistic unity to the work, no real beginning and no real resolution...[40]

A quarter-century after Irvine Welsh burst onto the literary scene I could write exactly this about *Trainspotting*. Pevear goes on:

> The formal structure of *War and Peace* and the texture of its prose are indeed strange. Those who did not simply declare the book a failure, dismissing the newness [...] of what Tolstoy was doing as artistic helplessness and naïveté, often said that it succeeded in spite of its artistic flaws. But that is a false distinction. *War and Peace* is a work of art, and if it succeeds, it cannot be in spite of its formal deficiencies, but only because Tolstoy created a new form that was adequate to his vision.[41]

I couldn't have put it better myself if I was referring to *Trainspotting* and Welsh. *Trainspotting* is Welsh's best effort to convey his vision, to tell a truth. Don't wait for 'the truth' to be made apparent and laid before you. No sooner do you establish a truth than you and it move on. Truth is held in tension. Slippery stuff, truth. We could say that *Trainspotting*, written during and in the immediate aftermath of the period in which it is set (in contrast to *War and Peace* which was written within living memory of the period in which it is set but well after formal histories had been assembled), is a form of journalism, the first draft of history. They tell journalists not to file a story until they have been close enough to smell it. Welsh smelled the action of which he wrote. Dr Roy Robertson, GP in Muirhouse and in the forefront of dealing with the collision of heroin and HIV, is quoted as saying 'I think we owe Irvine Welsh a great debt because he brought it out in the open. He definitely humanised drug users.'[42] Look on it as a first draft of history, in fictionalised form.

In 2017 Jon Snow led a collective mea culpa on behalf of journalism for failing to tell the real story of what was happening in the wealthy London

Borough of Kensington and Chelsea before the ghastly fire in Grenfell Tower
in June of that year which killed so many unwealthy people. It can be said
that Welsh told the true story of what was happening in Muirhouse (not
so much in *Trainspotting* as in other fiction, as outlined in Chapter 11:
Meanwhile in the schemes). I was very struck, talking to someone who lived
and worked with children in Muirhouse, that, having read *Marabou Stork
Nightmares* he identified strongly with the line: 'In Muirhoose nae cunt can
hear you scream... well, they can hear ye, they just dinnae gie a fuck'(*MSN*,
p.141). This was after I had selected it for inclusion in my chapter 'Meanwhile in the schemes'. When Welsh wrote: 'All those dull broadsheet newspaper articles on the scheme where we lived tended to focus on how deprived
it was. Maybe it was, but I'd always defined the place as less characterised
by poverty than by boredom, although the relationship between the two is
pretty evident' (*MSN*, p19) he was ahead of the academics who much later
established a strong link between too much time and little purpose in life
with heroin abuse.[43] This is journalism, buried in fiction; but nobody read it
in the next day's newspapers, and since it didn't appear for as long as it takes
for fiction to appear, maybe it is history.

When Welsh announced in 2018 that his next novel is to be set in American gun culture, *The Scotsman* ran a surprising editorial. Citing Harriet
Beecher Stowe's *Uncle Tom's Cabin* laying bare the horrors of slavery and
thus in part paving the way to American Civil War; John Steinbeck's *The
Grapes of Wrath* exposing the extreme poverty of the Depression; and
George Orwell's *1984* as 'a powerful warning about the dangers of totalitar-
ianism', it said *Trainspotting* had, similarly, 'got people talking about drug
addicts in a different way'. It went on to wonder if his next novel might also
join the ranks of 'the relatively small list of genuinely life-changing books'.[44]
Putting Welsh on such an elevated pedestal once is quite a tribute; hoping for
a second time is asking a lot. Maybe the connecting theme between out-of-
control heroin abuse and out-of-control gun abuse is social malfunction. If
Welsh tunes into that, we await his next output with great interest.

Crossing art forms, it appears that a soulmate of Welsh has emerged.
Graham MacIndoe, five years Welsh's junior and with strong associations
with Edinburgh (and a much more marked local accent than Welsh), tracked
his descent into heroin addiction through photography. Married and with
a son in New York, at the top of his game as a photographer of celebrities
and flying around the world, he refuses to blame the pressured lifestyle alone
for his downfall; his compulsive personality led him towards heroin, among
other drugs, which were readily available. In the depths of his squalor he

didn't stop thinking like a photographer. He set up cheap digital cameras on a delay function to record some of his bad moments. The best of his raw, vulnerable, intimate, uncompromising shots have gone on exhibition around the world, including the Scottish National Potrait Gallery, Edinburgh, and he has co-written a documentary account of it with his partner who went through some of it with him and with whom he emerged strong enough to tell the tale in *Chancers: Addiction, Prison, Recovery, Love – One Couple's Memoir.*[45]

Edward St Aubyn is another survivor of the heroin epidemic of Welsh's generation who has told his story. His circumstances are rather different: aristocratic family, posh private school, Oxford University. Raped by his father as a child, he has written semi-autobiographical novels of his encounter with heroin mostly in five books whose central figure is Patrick Melrose, adapted for television in a 2018 series. John Crace, also abused as a child and later a junkie, previewing the series in a piece titled 'Patrick Melrose and I are the lucky ones – we finally got help' found a lot of common ground:

> I never set out to be an addict... I thought I would be the exception that proved the rule, the person who beat the system. It would be me who controlled the drugs, not the other way round... In many films and literary depictions of using, the drugs are often relegated to an incidental role because the nature of addiction is so profoundly boring. Here, they get pride of place, centre stage. For a heroin addict it's the living that's incidental...[46]

Insightful and forceful though the piece is, it is let down by its strapline: the series '...captures the untold truth of heroin addiction – the blood, dirty hits, and banality...' as though Welsh and *Trainspotting* didn't exist.

David France has written an account of his own closeness to the arrival of HIV in the early 1980s to the mid-1990s in *How to Survive a Plague*[47], winner of the Baillie Gifford Prize, 2017. Having been told in 2012 that the literary canon for HIV was full, the story first appeared in an Oscar-nominated film of the same name.

Trainspotting is an artistic form of Welsh's truth. It was written urgently, while the Muse was upon him. It's very doubtful that Welsh's truth would ever have appeared between book covers if he had been reconstructing it while attending a creative writing course ten years after the period in which it is set.

Whatever else it may be, remember always that *Trainspotting* is fiction, it's not an academic history in which all relevant factors are coolly considered. Welsh, like all creative writers, is a liar and a thief. Some stuff is not there. The police have lodged a complaint with me that their role has gone missing from *Trainspotting*. Missing also is the role of the doctors, the churches, the community of prostitutes, and ordinary people, some of whom saw and knew and others of whom were blithely ignorant of the scale of the drama going on in their own community.

If *Trainspotting* is a fable, it's a Leith fable, and the moral is directed at politicians and planners who influence so profoundly the fate of people and communities. Widespread, out-of-control heroin abuse is a symptom of community malfunction. When an exotic drug is introduced new rituals, restraints and moralities need to be worked out very quickly. In this area, *Trainspotting* is a snapshot of work in progress.

Welsh's attempt to express it in this art form requires a variety of voices and no settled style of approach. From the hell hole of the 'Junk Dilemmas' and 'It Goes Without Saying', to the anger of 'Trainspotting at Leith Central Station', to the upbeat endings of 'Bad Blood' and 'Station to Station', to the pathos and ironies of 'Winter in West Granton', to the cynicism of 'In Overdrive', to the youthfulness of 'The First Shag In Ages', to the philosophising of 'Searching for the Inner Man', to the brio and insolence of 'Speedy Recruitment', *Trainspotting* contains and conveys some sort of truth. There is a universal truth about the heroin experience, and any who lived in Leith at the time recognises local truths. Others should respect their truth and not find fault with the presentation of it. It is, as Pevear says, 'a new form that was adequate to [Welsh's] vision'. The word 'adequate' is the right one. *Trainspotting* is scrappy, and if you insist, incomplete. But it's adequate. And the cleverly inserted threads and structure that hold it together qualify it as a novel.

Indeed, we can say that *Trainspotting* is a good format for its subject matter of mind-altering heroin in a changing community as told by a young man in transit. The many voices and jerky timeline fit with the junkie experience. Call it Cubist literature if you like. If a Picasso portrait can have square breasts and eyes where they 'shouldn't be', Welsh can have episodes outside any secure narrative order and characters acting 'out of character'. This is the product of a generation that grew up during Mrs Thatcher's government, which introduced lurching from one confrontation, crisis and scandal to the next as a form of government. Public life during John Major's governments of the 1990s, when *Trainspotting* appeared and was being read, was even more chaotic. Elected politicians, in office because of trust placed in them by the electorate, were acting in their own interests. This generation was brought up on video games, television interrupted by advertising, graphic novels, personal stereos, Tracy Emin's pop art, and get-rich-quick consumerism. *Trainspotting*'s format is a mirror image of life for many people.

Sailing close to an oxymoron, Lucy Hughes-Hallet wrote in the *The Sunday Times*, and quoted on the cover of early editions of the book: '*Trainspotting* is the voice of punk, grown up, grown wiser, and grown eloquent.' David Borthwick says it is a 'subversive alternative to the centripetally inclined novel [which caters]... to popular needs and tastes outside the elitist strongholds of literary culture'.[48] Punk depends on a DIY approach. It is quick, rough, and insolent. Stuff the professionals. A key aim is to defy conventional analysis and consideration.

Every work of art is singular and distinctive, just as each tree is itself. But each one relates to others of its kind as well as to the ground it stands in, the air that blows through it, and the birds that nest in it. No work of art is *sui generis*, even if some of its relationships are in other art forms.

It may well be the eventual judgement of Welsh that he is a one-book wonder. But what a book! As an exposé of a sub-culture in a prosperous city in modern Britain, it compares with Charles Dickens. As a description and discussion of the highs and lows of taking heroin, along with the hitherto unknown attendant risks of HIV, it is groundbreaking. As a description of what can happen to the emerging generation of a community that has been dispersed as carelessly as Leith was in the 1950s and 1960s, politicians and planners should read it. As an example of demotic speech phonetically spelt, the linguists pore over it. And as a celebration of life despite everything, and as a platform for voices that are not often heard, it deserves respect far more than the vilification it has generally received.

Trainspotting may be charmless for the literary elite and the bulk of the book-buying public. But claims that it found and indeed created a whole new group of readers are not exaggerated. The disorderly text and the localism of language and location appealed to the young, to the junk scene, to Scots, and to many others around the world looking for a fresh new voice. And you.

A correspondent of mine wrote in an email in 2017: 'Just finished Trainspotting a few minutes ago... as brilliant, as funny – gut achingly so at times, as insightful, as effervescent, as sad, as despairing... as I found it in 1993. With this book, Welsh indeed proves his brilliance as a writer. A book that brilliantly captures a zeitgeist – a bitter and painful one yes, but a zeitgeist nevertheless, [of] a particular time and place... a gifted writer... writing with courage... no cow is sacred, no territory off limits, no behaviour swept aside... [Welsh had] bottle... linguistic supernovae exploding and radiating out on every page! A book that will endure: yes, I liked it!'

SECTION VI

Trainspotting the Play

CHAPTER 19

In-Yer-Face Theatre

IN THE EARLY 1990s British and Scottish theatre was generally in a pretty poor state. Overall, public funding for the creative arts had dried up during the previous decade of Mrs Thatcher's antipathy to such things, and theatres were finding it hard to put bums on seats. Critics were grumbling that since John Osborne's *Look Back in Anger* (1956) caught the end of Empire and post-war mood of the moment with arresting potency, new writing for the British theatre lacked real urgency and punch.

This was so even though a new generation of theatre companies had grown up since the war. Doing away with proscenium and curtains, 'Theatre in the round' was developed, in which the stage was among the audience rather than in front of it. The intention was to recover some of the immediacy of the pre-modern age of theatre, to engage more directly with the audience. Theatre was something to be experienced rather than something for cool consideration and analysis. It was suited to smaller auditoria, and so also to smaller and amateur productions. Many new creative companies were innovative in the close collaboration they had with the playwrights or, quite often, they generated their own scripts. Scripts were not to be written with an ivory tower detachment, nor to be slavishly adhered to on stage.

British censorship laws were removed in 1968, and the taboo of onstage nudity had been breached in the musical *Hair* (1968). Kenneth Tynan's *Oh! Calcutta* (1969) took it a stage further to include simulated sex. The word 'fuck' had become commonplace; the word 'cunt' was next to be exaggerated. And, praise the Lord! – in Britain there is no law of blasphemy, so provided a production doesn't offend other legislation, such as the Race Relations Act, and provided there is no actual onstage violence or exploitation and it doesn't become a sex show, British theatre is free to shock.

And, in the 1990s, shock is what it set out to do. New playwriting of 'The Nasty Nineties' caught the soubriquet 'In-Yer-Face Theatre' (IYFT). Others were tried, but they didn't catch on: 'new brutalism' and 'theatre of urban ennui' did not convey the insolence, the aggression, the darkness and the vulnerability that were all, variously, intended in the new works. IYFT is unsubtle; it is deliberately provocative, impossible to ignore or avoid. It involves blatant extremism. It does not aim to charm, it aims to provoke. The audience is expected to experience the onstage raw emotions. While the serious purpose of IYFT was to question and push the boundaries of what is acceptable, it was always close to being puerile. It thrived on irate letters to the press demanding that the company should have its Arts Council grant withdrawn.

New political theatre of the 1980s reflected political realities – a cause and a victim were the main ingredients. But when, within a few months of each other in 1989/90, the Berlin Wall fell and Nelson Mandela walked free, the familiar causes and victims melted away. People in Britain in their early 20s had known nothing throughout their formative years but Margaret Thatcher as Prime Minister, with her shrill triumphalism. In 1992 John Major continued Thatcherism by winning a further five years of Tory rule, against the odds, and breaking the political cycle. Major laughably launched his Back to Basics campaign in support of traditional moral rearmament, only to have it revealed within weeks that MPs of his own party, right up to senior level, were mired in sleazy corruption of privilege, and that several of them – himself included, a little later – couldn't keep their trousers on. Thatcher's focussed zeal became Major's chaos, and throughout the 1990s the elected government progressively lost its moral authority.

But IYFT was not just a response to present circumstances; it was also a reflection. Shocking images and stories from Iraq, Bosnia, Rwanda, and Tiananmen Square were in the news bulletins. Violence in Northern Ireland continued into its third decade frequently spilling over into mainland Britain. Long before the courts quashed the convictions of the Birmingham Six and the Guildford Four, ten people found guilty in court of perpetrating Irish-related bombings and doing very long prison sentences, the public strongly sensed that major miscarriages of justice had been perpetrated in their name by corrupt authorities and an arrogant, incompetent political class. Meanwhile, portable personal sound systems and a nascent mobile phone industry were enabling people to put themselves in a bubble. Public life had a bad stench, and community life was breaking up into atomised units. This was the world the young play writers were writing about.

IYFT does not lend itself to traditional methods of criticism. If you are looking for a good plot you will find experiential confrontation. If you are looking for complex, developed characters, you will find types. If you are looking for theatrical speeches, you will find curt televisual dialogues.

If you're looking for moral ambiguities, you will find unresolved contradictions.[49] IYFT was not overtly political, there may be no clear narrative or conclusion, and much of IYFT can seem chaotic. The dark, brooding, violent cruelty and depravity was both a response to and a reflection of the world seen by the young play writers of the 1990s. And it had box office success. With the Royal Court and the Bush in London and the Traverse in Edinburgh in the forefront – but by no means were they the only venues – theatre suddenly became relevant to the student generation. Theatre was cool.

Aleks Sierz calls the effect of IYFT a shock fest. He points out that what shocks in this decade is the syllabus fodder of the next; the causes of anger, the tensions in play, the public issues at stake, and the humour, all move on and become historical. There are always new matters to tackle, new taboos to be challenged. The ancient Greeks understood that people and society are healthier for facing their personal and shared concerns; Greek theatre aimed not to attack but to help and heal its audiences even, and perhaps especially, when the healing might seem like shock therapy. Or, to come from a different angle, as George Bernard Shaw said of *The Doll's House* (Ibsen, 1879), a play's real strength will be judged by what it does in the world.

In-Yer-Face-Theatre is a good name, but the genre was small and shortlived. It was explicit, violent, and, generally, amoral. At the end of 1995 the *Evening Standard*'s Nicholas de Jongh wrote that that this 'was the year in which theatre caught up with the increasingly violent, alienated Britain of the closing years of the century'.[50] In 1996 the longstanding and widely respected critic Michael Billington wrote: 'I cannot recall a time when there were so many exciting dramatists in the 20-something age group: what is more, they are speaking to audiences of their own generation'. In *The Times* Benedict Nightingale said that there was a buzz in the air similar to 1956.[51] The *Look Back in Anger* moment that had been anticipated five years earlier had arrived.

It is into this pool that *Trainspotting* the play dropped in 1994, making a noisy, spectacular splash as it arrived. Almost certainly the best known play of the period, the biggest box office success, the most widely travelled, and the longest living, it is far from a classic of the genre. Except for some elements of the play and the accident of timing, it would hardly qualify for inclusion. Before considering it in its own right, we will make comparisons with the contemporary output.

It is a derivation. *Trainspotting* the book had already achieved some fame and infamy, making it impossible for the play to find its way onto the stage entirely on its own merits; it already had a brand name and an enormous potential public and market. Partly as a result of its particular branding, character is important and *Trainspotting*'s characters lend themselves to more conventional analysis than is generally the case in IYFT. There are many moments in *Trainspotting* that can be played for laughs; the play depicts young characters trying to have a good time that goes wrong, and despite some darkness and chaos, it is less dark and chaotic than most of the genre. And there are more explicit external reference points in *Trainspotting* than in the generality of IYFT theatre.

Further, it is not the work of one person. The book is by Irvine Welsh and the play is by Harry Gibson, with permission from Welsh and his publisher, Random House. Welsh and Gibson were not as young as the other playwriters, and they are not listed among the big beasts of the genre.

We will bear in mind that a play is not a script, it is a theatrical production. Unlike a book or a film, which can be brought to a final cut to be delivered to the paying customers, one copy exactly the same as another, a theatrical production is a dynamic event. Many things can affect a performance, and, of course, experiential theatre depends on performance even more crucially than conventional theatre. Theatre has its own momentum, its own potential, and its own limits.

CHAPTER 20

Origins and First Year

IN 1993 HARRY Gibson, play reader at Glasgow Citizen's theatre, was looking for a new idea in a bookshop in Hillhead, the university area of Glasgow. In an oft-repeated story a bookshop assistant, when asked what was a hot read, got a well-thumbed copy of Welsh's *Trainspotting* out of the staff toilet, the only one left on the premises. On the front cover was the boast of Rebel Inc, first publisher of some of the book's episodes: 'The best book ever written by man or woman... deserves to sell more copies than the Bible', while the back cover contained the review of *The Herald* (Glasgow): '... if you haven't heard of Irvine Welsh... don't worry, you will.' Gibson sensed that it strongly caught the mood of the moment and he wanted it on stage 'small and quick'.

He knocked up an adaptation which he took to Giles Havergal, a director at the Citz (as it is universally known). Havergal knew the very man he wanted to put it on stage – Ian Brown, then working at the Traverse in Edinburgh, who had a taste for and a record of putting on new, edgy material. Brown was flattered. Reading the book, he saw the enormous potential for a stage adaptation, with the overblown characters and larger-than-life scenes. Quite specifically, taking the spotlight away from Glasgow, seemingly the impregnable capital and only source of Scottish working class and popular culture, and having a close look at Edinburgh's underbelly, appealed to him.

There was a read-through of Gibson's script in a studio in the Filmhouse, just over Lothian Road from the present Traverse, so it can be said that its first outing was on home territory, near enough. It felt good. But in what some called a travesty, and others one of the many ironies around *Trainspotting*, Brown took it to Glasgow, and maybe that was for the best. The sharpest critique can often be delivered with a little historical or in this case geographical perspective. It certainly worked well for the Citz, where they had recently set up two 50-seat studios in addition to the main theatre. *Trainspotting* played in one of them, with the stage between two ranks of seating.

Brown wanted Ewen Bremner to play Mark, having known some of his previous work. Susan Vidler played Alison, Malcolm Shields played Begbie, and James Cunningham played Sick Boy and Tommy. Bremner employed his genuine street level Leith accent and the others made passable efforts. They were all required to read the book as source material, and Brown said they had a ready feel for the depth and texture of the play's origins. Brown was reading it as a storytelling morality play in its celebration of heroin and its honesty in sharing the big regrets and heavy price to be paid.

Welsh came to rehearsals, and he and Brown worked together with mutual respect, combining well with the small, intimate team at the Citz, and the cast. The importance of these relationships in the early days of translating *Trainspotting* from page to stage and later to screen should not be underestimated. Brown found Welsh 'inspirational'. In keeping with his penchant for a DJ's trade, Welsh could see that his material could be remixed and creatively transformed to another medium. But he was new to this and still had his day job. He had only written what he called 'a scabby wee book'. As he writes on his web site: 'It was when I saw them doing their lines, the whole thing was removed from my head into the world, and I saw it for the first time how others were experiencing it. I felt the power of it for the first time. I walked out there believing that I had actually done something special. I knew it would be a great play.'[52]

Made on a very small budget, Brown wanted it edgy, free-wheeling, fast-moving and bare-boned. It wasn't well made, said Gibson. It was 'a rough sketch of a rough lifestyle, not a full blown drug abuse drama...'[53] The book's cult status led people to expect too much of the play, he went on. Maybe so, but it sold out its four week run after the first night, one of the highlights of that year's Mayfest, Glasgow's cultural party sponsored by the city council and the trade unions. With the actors exposed by a minimum of props, and the simplest of lighting, the production had the spare intensity of a punk gig.

They say that the ushers had to go out into the car park to ring the end of interval bell for the numerous clientele who were enjoying a spliff. It had a mixed but generally enthusiastic reception from the critics: there was an objection to nattily-clad members of the audience and their self-gratifying laughter; one critic noticed an audience member 'with pierced nostrils' who cried when Tommy acquired the virus; the play contained 'incipient anarchy... desperate degradation... and dramatic urgency'; it was 'a dynamic production full of dangerous, deranged performances that articulate the fearful nihilism of the dispossessed'. All members of the cast attracted praise,

Ewen Bremner in particular as 'an angular, fidgety youth, nervous and loud by turns'[54] and for his facial expressions catching every nuance in the action. 'Welsh's bleakly accurate account of the tragic lives of blank generation Edinburgh is comedy at its blackest... if you consider yourself unshockable (as some of the more persistent chucklers in this audience clearly thought themselves), prepare to be educated – especially if the darker side of the capital city with its smack culture, HIV epidemic, and distinctive vocabulary is unfamiliar to you...'[55] wrote Ian Bruce in *The Herald*. It seems, sadly, that no visual or audio recording and no written script of this production is in the public domain.

From Glasgow the show went on to do short runs in a 250-seat theatre at the Traverse, Edinburgh, and in a 100-seat studio at the Bush, London, which Brown found to be a terrific venue. The programme claimed the show as 'the English premier' over the two laughing skulls from the prefilm editions of the book. Clearly it came with reputation – edgy though it was, there was a brand to help sell it. *The Times* headlined its review 'West End gets smack in the mouth'. Aleks Sierz saw it at the Bush, April 1995, and he describes the seedy set with a stained mattress, a crusty toilet bowl, and flickering candlelight as the action trawled through a nightmarish vision of hell with unexpected tender moments. He picks out one moment of 'masterly theatricality... Mark describes a heroin party, saying "Alison wis thair." He looks over to her; she doesn't move. "Ye were thair," he insists, and sulkily she joins in as Mark carries on: "Alison wis cookin."'[56]

One enthusiast recorded online his view of the Bush production: 'I saw this production [earlier] at the Traverse theatre and it was fantastic – pretty much changed my view of theatre. Ewen Bremner was brilliant'.[57] Naturally enough, perhaps, the critics were divided. Michael Billington complained that the play never gets to grips with why the characters succumbed to the drugs in the first place. One reviewer accused it of moral tourism: hell's a popular place if you have a return ticket.

Brown relinquished his rights in the show, perhaps naively, as he reflected later, leaving it to Gibson to develop its commercial potential. It had caught hold of a new theatre going public as it toured up and down the country, delighting managers who reported that it was filling their theatres as well as generating brisk business at the bars. There is the tale that at the London Ambassador's Theatre performances were delayed because the box office couldn't cope with so many people paying cash. There were seven productions throughout the country within a year, the cast of four going through 23 different line-ups, an indication of just how exhausting and demanding of the actors it was. The play was awarded *The Sunday Times* Best First Play Award, 1995. There is no doubt, as Adrienne Scullion says, that productions in this early period conveyed 'a sense of experiential intimacy, dramaturgical risk, and artistic experimentation'.[58] The BBC asked Gibson for a radio version, but there could be no compromise on the language or the insolence, and the idea was dropped.

By now (1996) *Trainspotting* the film had been released, attracting immediate, noisy and colourful attention. The film was *Trainspotting*'s third manifestation in as many years – quite remarkable for a first book – and the three fed and fed off each other, shooting round the country and the world.

CHAPTER 21

Analysis of the Play

TRAINSPOTTING THE PLAY has nothing to do with Leith, notwithstanding programme notes, effects, and stage instructions connecting it to Leith Central Station. They are tenuous at best, and they are never brought to a full understanding of the reference. Although stage directions and perhaps programme notes indicate that the final scene of the play is placed in Leith Central Station, the meaning (if any) of the title remains enigmatic. Various attempts to work into the play some ghost train effects or Leith references do nothing to help. The David Bowie-inspired upbeat redemptive ending is missing.

Neither is it particularly Scottish. Some of an audience may relish an awareness that Edinburgh's high class, highbrow capital city profile looks very different from Leith, but for those who know little of the play's origins or who can recognise Scottish accents (if there are any on stage), the play is loosely set 'somewhere in Scotland'.

Gibson is quite clear: the play was intended to be relevant universally, not just in Scotland. As the play travels it can be adapted by local producers, with permission, to have local meaning, whereupon its Scottish origins become irrelevant and lost. Gibson says that the play in English language has a reputation which is worth defending, at least as far as major productions are concerned, so higher standards are required than for productions in translation. He has offered to do different cuts through the core material, but he has received little encouragement from producers. He recognises that only the original (the book) is definitive, and that there is plenty of scope for creativity among derivations.

All that can be expected of a derivation is that it takes the title, the central characters, and the main ideas or plot from the original. Some of the complexities can be represented in a different form by various theatrical effects. What is performed in front of the audience is not what readers of the book have created for themselves in their own imagination: if the most vivid theatre in the world is inside one's own head, then a performance by others is either a challenge and enlightenment or a disappointment. The audience has paid to experience *Trainspotting* the play.

Gibson as director did not copy Brown, preferring to paint a social picture with elders like Franco's (renamed from Brown's Begbie) father to show a wider, deeper scene, to telling a junkie story in isolation. The version analysed here is what Gibson calls the New York version, the only version in publication.[59] It should be borne in mind that what follows is an analysis of the script, not an account of being present at a performance, which is the very thing that experiential theatre requires. Gibson says it was not his most successful. He tried to make it cool – that is to say, available for detached consideration by the audience – and hot – that is to say, immediate and in-yer-face. He liked it, but the critics didn't. He turned the whole theatre into a soot-blackened subway tunnel, and several stage effects suggested a subway. The New York version is written to be performed by four actors, doubled up as follows:

Mark, boy;

Drunk, Tommy, Simon, Morag;

Franco, Johnny, mother;

June, Lizzie, Alison, lassie.

The opening scenes are accounts of body waste in the wrong places, sex, and violence, to set the tone. The first two scenes are certainly written for a stand-up style delivery, the second introducing Mark and Tommy as genuine friends; the third scene gets more dramatic. Scenes 4 and 5 contain actual violence, the first in a domestic situation and the second in public; then the play goes on to Franco's brief and brutal denunciation of adult partnership and parenthood. The drug theme, and the lifestyle choices involved, is introduced in Mark's reflection, and heroin makes its first appearance in scene 8. The desperation, squalor and dangers of the druggies' life become apparent, but it descends to foul farce in the toilet scene.

The mood darkens as Tommy asks for a score, complicating a friendship in the world of junkies, in scene 11, and Alison's parody develops the theme. Nevertheless, the characters go on to show youthful fun, irreverence and compassion in the squirrel scene. The outside world comes onstage sharply with the radio news cast announcing the death of Mark's brother, and the occasion of the funeral quickly develops into family feuding and Mark shagging the grieving pregnant girlfriend. More slapstick follows on the train and there is foul female revenge on loutish Englishmen in the restaurant.

A breakdown of the play's script and its relationship to the book.			
Scene number/ name	Characters on stage	CONTENT	RELATIONSHIP TO BOOK
01	Mark	Mark describes waking up in Gail Houston's bed and the accidental spilling of puke and shit in the kitchen.	Based on *Traditional Sunday Breakfast*; omits location details; Davie Mitchell is changed to Mark.
02	Mark, Tommy	Tommy recounts experience with Laura McEwan to take her arse virginity.	Based on part of *There is a Light...*; Spud is changed to Tommy; reference to Laura's previous boyfriend is new material.
03	Mark, Tommy, Franco	Franco recalls incident in a pub when someone he thought of at school as a hard cunt turns out to be capable of compromise – a disappointment.	Based on *A Disappointment* with fragment from *The Glass* to introduce Franco in his own right.
		Mark recalls watching girl watching on school sports day, and Franco's masturbation.	Based on part of *Cock Problems*.
04	Franco, June	Scene of domestic abuse.	From the beginning of *Inter Shitty*.
05	Tommy, Boy, Lassie	Tommy describes violence against the lassie in pub.	Based on *Her Man*; Second Prize is changed to Davie Mitchell; omits reflection on domestic violence.
06	Franco, Mark, Tommy, June	Franco shows sociopathic tendencies.	Based on part of *Inter Shitty...*
07	Mark	Mark's brief reflection: 'Choose life!'	Based on part of *Searching for the Inner Man* plus one line from *Speedy Recruitment* and new material.

08	Mark, Simon	Mark and Simon watching the Jean-Claude Van Damme video; the need to score; the taxi rank and the menace of community violence.	A thought similar to *Junk Dilemma #65*; based on *Skagboys...* Faithful to the book, omitting references to place.
09	Mark, Simon, Johnny, Alison	Arriving at Johnny's; the hit; the change of Johnny Swan from a nice boy to a dealer; Alison as needy as the boys.	Based on *Skagboys...* omitting location and other characters in the flat.
		Baby Dawn dies offstage; anxious discussion re responsibility, paternity.	Based on *It Goes Without Saying...* Mark takes some of Spud's attitudes and lines.
10	Mark	Mark prepares for withdrawal; journey to Muirhouse; scores suppositories from 'the skag merchant'; the toilet scene.	Based on *The First Day...*; faithful to the book but omitting complexities.
11	Mark, Tommy, Lizzie, Alison	Tommy asks Mark for a fix; description of Lizzie and sex; Mark's 'boring and futile' speech, parodied by Alison; Alison as commentator.	Based on *Cock Problems*; Tommy's familiar fuck-the-wind style; critique of heroin is new material.
		In the Meadows; squirrel and women bystanders; reflection from Mark; Alison's nipples.	Based on *Strolling...*; some new material. Alison feeling her nipples and inviting the boys to do so is new material.
12 Requiem Aeternam (Eternal Rest)	Mark	Radio voice; Mark's monologue; memories of childhood; narrative of graveside scene, post-funeral drinking scene, avuncular hostility, shagging Sharon, shared intimacies in his flat.	Based on *Bang to Rites*. The political background behind the death is removed.

13 Dies Irae (Day of Judgement)	Mother Mark (mother transforms into Franco)	Mark in cold turkey; asserting his vegetarianism.	Based on *House Arrest*.
		Mark and Franco on the train to London; reserved seats, American women; Tommy's auntie wanting a house on Princes Street.	Based on *Inter Shitty*.
		'They're never gonna keep me down!'	New material.
14 Offertorium (Offering)	Alison	Alison monologue; female fluids in restaurant dishes.	Based on *Eating Out*; Alison replaces Kelly.
15 Sanctus (Holy)	Alison, Tommy, Franco, Mark	In 'the old pub'; Tommy and Franco describe sex scenes; Tommy asks Mark for junk, Mark (now clean) gives money instead; Franco denies June.	Fragments of *There is a Light...*
		Alison reflects on being the parent of a junkie.	Based on Matty's mum's reflection in *Memories of Matty pt 1*; new material.
16 Agnus Dei (Lamb of God)	Alison, Mark, Tommy, Franco	Alison recites Hail Mary; Tommy (naked) shoots into penis; Alison tells Mark to visit Tommy;	New material. Based on fragment of *Cock Problems*; based on a fragment of *Trainspotting at Leith Central Station*, Alison taking the part of Begbie.
		Discussion between Mark and the sick and dying Tommy; passing mention of inadequacy of housing, public hostility to HIV/AIDS.	Based on part of *Winter in West Granton*.
		Franco changes subject.	New material.

17 Libera Me (*Release Me*)	Alison	Alison's parody of where people she knows are going.	New material.
		With Lizzie, altercation with scaffolders, meets up with New Zealand lesbians and older Edinburgh women.	Based on *Feeling Free*; Mark absent.
18 Requiescant in Pace (*May they rest in peace*)	Alison, Franco, Mark, drunk	Franco: 'let's go for a pish'; drunkard already there; he suggests the boys are spotting trains; clearly identified as Begbie's father.	Based on part of *Trainspotting at Leith Central Station*; some new material.
		Begbie pisses on him, inert on the ground. Ending # 1: How can I keep from singing?	New material.
		Ending # 2: more or less domestic scene, Mark with typewriter, Alison with coffee; Mark repeats opening couple of lines.	New material.

More crude sex is described in the pub, and suddenly Alison is mature. Tommy is now far gone as a druggie, shooting up into his penis, and very quickly he is seen in the public hostility and squalor that was, in the real world, the experience of many a terminally ill HIV/AIDS victim. Alison's account of an incident with Lizzie involving feminist assertions and lesbianism is bound to raise a laugh and a cheer from right-on members of the audience before the final scene in which Mark and Franco piss on the inert body of Franco's father, and the play is brought to an end.

In the book Franco's father is present at Leith Central Station, and indeed he utters the enigmatic word 'trainspotting', but the play's detail of the young men pissing on him is not in the primary source. Gibson intends the old man's appearance here to make the play 'lean outwards', ie to bring the audience out of the self-referring world of the onstage addiction.

Audiences will decide for themselves whether this passive, abused character does that job, or whether he is an object of that very egocentricity.

In a different production the cast finishes the play by reciting together
The Lord's Prayer after Franco has cried out 'ma faither!' The New York
version offers alternative endings. In ending #1 Franco continues pissing
on his father while Mark cries out for Tommy and Alison sings 'How can I
keep from singing'. Originally an 19th century American church hymn, Pete
Seeger revived it in the 1960s in a version which removed all specifically
Christian references but kept and indeed enhanced the song's awareness of
a loving presence in this world and in another world. The song enjoyed
another particularly North American revival in the early 1990s, thus ensur-
ing recognition by a wide age group in the New York theatre. It carries
a reassuring and hopeful message. Arguably, this goes some way towards
serving the same function as the David Bowie-inspired ending of the book
and the film.

Ending #2 has Franco pissing on his father while Mark edges away into
a more or less domestic scene with Alison and a typewriter. He repeats his
own opening lines of the play, which can suggest either that he is reviewing
the whole episode of the play with the detachment of removal from the drug
scene, or that he is starting all over again – it's hard to tell. Either way, there
is sadness.

The script includes content that is not in the book, some of it linking
passages from the book and some creating substantive new material. Pete
Milne, who played Renton in a later production, tells me that the additions
are the hardest lines to play. The religious elements are nowhere in the book:
Alison reciting the Hail Mary is explicit, but naming the scenes of the second half of the show with liturgical Latin seems odd – not that the audience
would be aware of it unless it is contained in programme notes or otherwise
conveyed. Alison's sudden preoccupation with others' and her own nipples
is an opportunity for some onstage bare breasts, which commends the play
for inclusion in the IYFT genre, but it is not in the book. The sexual content
can, however, be seen as stage version of the book's (and the film's) sex scene
between Renton and Dianne.

There is scope for different productions to be original in their script,
and Gibson says almost nothing is not negotiable. The only part of the
play that Gibson is not prepared to omit is Mark's speech to Billy's coffin. Mark is quite specific about the circumstances of the death: he refers
to Crossmaglen, a notorious danger zone on the border between British
Northern Ireland and the Republic of Ireland, where, in history, many a

British soldier died in ambushes during the Troubles which started in 1969. The Army is present at this theatrical military funeral, but Mark calls his brother 'a prick in a uniform' and holds the imperialist culture and intransigent members of the Houses of Parliament responsible for his death. It is a complexity which only British audiences would readily understand, and in New York, a city which traditionally supported the Irish Republican Army, this political analysis might be expected to be uncontroversial. All this and more is in the book, but the background to the issue has nothing to do with the main matters of the play, so we must search for Gibson's reasons to insist on retaining it.

It brings death onto the stage: there is a coffin, which has more dramatic potential than a body. In recalling their childhood, Mark gives his own character depth of history and personality. The occasion offers an opportunity to display irreverence for authority, this time in a sombre and, with the Army present, a State occasion. Even if an audience knows little or nothing of the British/Irish dispute, it will know that the characters live in real time in a real place. Mark's lust for life in the family feuding and in shagging his brother's pregnant girlfriend overrides the formalities and the darkness, asserting again the instinct to survive and enjoy life.

Welsh has said that ending the play at Leith Central Station is 'more honest' (than the endings of the book and the film). Upbeat endings don't happen. This leaves us with the truth that a story of drug addiction is difficult to end. The betrayals, the destruction of relationships, the breakdown of health, the squalor, and the inexorable decline into loss of autonomy and personality, all this is the real story. Dramatically, death is too easy.

The uncertain ending suggests that the play hardly knows what it is about. Even though Leith Central Station is specified, it is not about location. Gibson is fond of highlighting Welsh's sense of friendship and community, but neither element is particularly prominent. We have only fleetingly been shocked by depravity and violence. There has been no great story or moral. The characters, though interesting, fall short of being well developed or fascinating. There are some funny stories and situations, and some good lines. The play contains stand-up humour, slapstick, depravity, heroin and alcohol abuse, violence, feminism, religion, irony, sadness, HIV and death. At several points it is a peek into a junkie world. Gibson points out that no-one could leave the play with the idea that doing heroin is a good thing, but concedes that there is a question of what the play is all about. The main memory is of youthful pain and insolence. Maybe that's what it's all about.

Character

All the characters have a single, soft, personal name, removing the book's complexity of several nicknames. During the course of the play Simon and Franco are each related to the book's Sick Boy and Begbie respectively. The book's Spud Murphy disappears; most of his attributes – the distinctive manner of his speech and the contents of his thoughts – are transferred to Tommy, who is listed as Tommy Murphy, and who is a composite of several other characters from the book as well. Mark also takes some of the book's Spud.

Mark is by some distance the dominant character. In Gibson's last tour (2006) he was on stage for the entire show. In the New York version he has about five scenes off. He begins with the laddish account of body waste in the wrong places and goes on to be a resigned observer of and mate to the impossible Franco. After his famous 'Choose life' reflection he is revealed as a desperate junkie, he's not confident about his relationship with girls, and his preparations for withdrawal end up in farce. Immediately afterwards he gets 'serious' and 'honest', if independent-minded and irreverent towards his family and authority in general. With some sense of adult responsibility, he goes through with visiting Tommy. In the Central Station, however, in ending #1 he returns to immaturity and suggestibility by pissing on Begbie's father. In ending #2 he appears to remove himself from the whole scene. Or, as suggested earlier, is he starting again?

Alison does not convey junkie reality but does show youthful vitality in snapshots. She first appears in scene 09 as the needy drug-ridden girl who is suddenly the grief-stricken mother of the dead baby Dawn. Two scenes later she is fun-loving and playfully bares her breasts. In four consecutive scenes she wreaks foul revenge on her customers in the restaurant; she offers a mature reflection on being a junkie's parent; she gets religious, reciting the Hail Mary, and tells Mark to visit Tommy out of compassion; then she is an assertive, rejoicing feminist. She finishes the play with Mark in reflective mood. The same actress plays the sexy, betrayed Lizzie, the miserable, abused June, and the object of violence in public who defends her abuser in Scene 05.

Tommy is the nice boy, the sympathetic character, who suffers the fate of the Leith junkie of the 1980s – not sudden death by overdose, but slow, public death by the dreaded virus, presumably acquired by sharing needles, while his friends get away with it. He takes over the book's Spud's naivety and good nature. He tells a good-humoured story about sex with Lizzie; he tries to intervene for the best in the violence in the pub, and later he defends the hapless squirrel from the others' cruelty. He accepts the justice of being rejected by Lizzie for going to the concert instead of remembering her birthday and is so upset that he asks for a fix to stay in with his pals. In Tommy's final appearance he is aware of his ill luck and shows just how far gone junkies get in begging for more skag.

Franco is almost the Begbie we know from the book: cynical, brutally violent, vicious, sexist, immature, perverse and irresponsible. He steps out of character briefly in scene 13 when he combines with Mark to assert that you always get up again after being knocked down; new material. Otherwise he is the stage ogre, but completely authentic as the sociopath we all don't want to know. Simon, who we are told is 'one sick cunt' (the opening description of Sick Boy in the book), is only involved in the scenes of scoring at Johnny Swan's and the discussion around the paternity of the dead baby Dawn.

Clearly, depiction of plausible characters is not a priority. In this, the play is entirely in keeping with both the book and the film.

CHAPTER 22

Aftershocks

THERE WAS AN export market for *Trainspotting* the play, just as there was for the book and the film. Over the next decade the play travelled widely, offering problems and opportunities for translation into both languages and cultures around the world. Language translation was an issue in English-speaking countries as much as elsewhere. One of my customers on the tour who saw the New York production vividly recalled for me a tape playing into the auditorium while he was taking his seat. Begbie was saying 'Lit's git some scran, ah'm fuckin Lee Marvin here', followed by a pause before a flat American newscaster's voice translated: 'We should get something to eat, I'm quite hungry'. In French-speaking Quebec, where the vocabulary of expletives derives mostly from the Roman Catholic Mass, there was an irreligious edge, whereas in Japanese there is no great range of obscenity or profanity.

Other cultures raised different issues. The New York version, discussed above, is relatively dark, whereas the production in the Australian tour was funny. In Dresden, the city in eastern Germany that was virtually obliterated by the 'liberators' bombing in 1945 and only recently released from Soviet oppression (the like of which we in the west know nothing), they asked how, emanating from green, pleasant and victorious Britain, theatre could be so violent. This production, says Gibson, was a chaotic mish-mash of bits from the book, the play and the film, acted out in workshop games, and it had 17 curtain calls.

A production in Iceland was placed in a sort of mythical world; Tommy was a simple boy and Mrs Renton a frightening Nordic witch: 'high on epic, low on street credibility' as Gibson puts it. In a polite theatre in Toronto, Canada, that didn't normally attract many young people he did the production in a colourful style with upbeat music, almost like a kids' show. They loved it, but he regretted it. He has said he would have no objection if a Japanese production wants to stage it kabuki style, or if a Balkan production wants to substitute Belgrade for Belfast. If it lost its Leith and Scottish origins, it gained an international currency.

One online reviewer of the show in the Sage Theatre, Calgary, Canada in 2006, wrote:

> ... the onslaught of horrific images that most of us don't ordinarily see... the bombardment of profanity... the audience experiences shock and awe with laughter, and that tends to disguise the lack of any real depth or dimension to the characters. It seems not to matter. We're swept along with the play's sheer audacity, anecdotal storytelling, and great dialogue...

And in an insightful comment that would be more expected in a review of the book than the play, and in answer to Billington's complaint of ten years earlier this article went on:

> ... it's not a play that's delving into how these people individually got to be where we find them. If a finger is pointed, it's pointed at society in general, class and economic distinctions, consumerism.[60]

2006 was a busy year, with a 20-week UK tour, directed by Gibson and presented by Mark Goucher. Gibson says he did it for love – audiences and actors loved it. So by now it was acquiring a nostalgic feel. Evidently the marketing people felt the need to trade on the film: the universal programme cover had a Ewan McGregor lookalike running down a street very similar to the moments in the film before he crashes into the bonnet of the car. Ahead of the tour, Welsh anticipated that it had lost its shock effect.

In an attempt to discover new talent, Gibson advertised widely for applications to join the cast. After much competition Pete Milne, Leith born and bred (well, next door Trinity, and he went to Trinity Academy, where we would expect the book's Mark Renton to attend) and London-trained, was given the coveted, iconic part of Mark. It's like a Scottish James Bond part, he says, passing through a notable roll call of actors. He objects to the way the film makes Mark into the good guy – the play's Mark is more complicated and less nice. Other parts went to experienced actors.

When it came to the 1,350-seater King's Theatre, Tollcross, Edinburgh, just up the road from the Filmhouse where it was first read through, there was a palpable feel that this was the local story that had gone big and had come home. The actors played into this by turning up in Bennett's Bar next door after the show. The whole company enjoyed bonuses for playing to a week of full houses. There were many students in the audiences, who would

be children at the time of the setting of the book in the late 1980s and in
their early teens when the play was first staged. For Welsh's contemporaries
and other veterans of the scene, it was a ten-years-later reunion.

This tour didn't revisit Glasgow, but took in new territory. In Aberdeen
Milne was criticised for not looking enough like a junkie to be in need of a
Paracetomol, whereupon he tried to lose some weight, but it hardly helped.
He was encouraged to splash water from the toilet over the front row of the
audience; he shook hands in congratulatory fashion on his way up a gang-
way through the audience after shagging Billy's pregnant girlfriend at the
funeral; egged on by Gibson, he came onstage on one occasion, and, going
off-script and with the other actors unprepared, called out 'Hey, come on,
this is my show...' These blatantly pantomime moments confirmed Welsh's
expectations, as well as Ian Brown's fears for the future of the show after its
initial run, and they earned the show the soubriquet *Carry On Trainspotting*
– a reference to the 1960s British film series of slapstick nostalgia.

But it was still relevant. The shock had converted into an educational
role. In Birmingham a drugs-awareness element was part of the programme.
One online reviewer of the Oxford show wrote that she was expecting a
'grittier, real, de-commercialised version of the film', and she was not disap-
pointed. It was:

> much grittier and darker than the film, but so much more emo-
> tional and real... I didn't want it to end and when it did there
> were many loose ends which kept our discussions going over the
> post-theatre drinks – always a sign of a job well done. Mark was
> compelling and sexy, Alison was full of damage and sparks and
> energy, Tommy was heartbreaking, Begbie was just an absolute
> git. The drugs references and acts are as real as it gets, so do go if
> you understand and do go if you want to understand, but be pre-
> pared that it ain't pretty – the play doesn't glamorise the life, but
> tells it as it is, and don't expect the liberation of a happy ending –
> after all that only happens in the movies...[61]

Brian Mathey, with two much-acclaimed previous productions to his credit,
directed the play again in 2013, with his Seat of Your Pants company in
Los Angeles, USA. With permission from the holders of the copyright, it was
more of a full blown drama, with a larger cast and more material: Spud's
job interview (given to Tommy) for example, and the scene with the woman
on the bus as Renton goes to score in 'The First Day of the Edinburgh Festival' were included. Mathey went to great lengths to make the whole thing
Scottish, rendering it almost incomprehensible to some. Language wasn't the

only tricky thing to translate. It seems that Begbie's bristling aggression was not as familiar in the USA, where sociopaths, or at least their stereotype, are more on the cold and calculating side. Justin Zachary won almost universal acclaim for his playing of Renton.

But there was still a problem with the ending: 'While Mathey's work overall is very tight, the final moment feels underdeveloped and anticlimactic'[62] wrote one online critic. Unless the play takes the Irvine Welsh / David Bowie / Danny Boyle route of the redemptive ending, this seems always likely to be a problem.

In December 2013 an In Yer Face Theatre production of *Trainspotting* was put on at the excellent Out of the Blue arts and community complex in Dalmeny Street, off Leith Walk, Leith. The advertising used imagery from the film, and the review on the billing followed suit: 'A completely immersive theatre experience that allows the audience to experience what it is like to sit inside a movie.' The audience was warmed up (if that can be said – the heating was left off, for dramatic effect) before the play began with 30 minutes of rave music, a musical pointer to the mid-1990s, not the 1980s of the heroin scene. General opinion seems to be that although several scenes were well done – the one based on 'Feeling Free' was singled out – the play amounted to not much more than a series of fragmented glimpses into drug addiction. True to Gibson's resolve, Tommy's funeral scene was included. Some of the action – shooting up – and some of the dialogue was done off-stage, among the audience. That's what is meant by immersion; it's an extension of In-Yer-Face.

Despite what critics thought was an over-reliance on the film, the local story was not entirely lost: 'This story does not simply stroll through the cobbled streets of Edinburgh; it roars through them, coughing and spluttering on the way. It is a thrill of a ride whichever way you look at it'[63] wrote one reviewer.

A play needs a platform of topicality and public interest to make productions of it viable. In its first blush, the play traded on being Scottish, which was quite edgy at the time. A lot has happened since then. Firstly, following a referendum result resoundingly in favour of devolution, the Scottish parliament came into being after a gap of three centuries. Despite a voting system that was designed to prevent single party power, the separatist Scottish National Party formed the government in 2007 and again in 2011, and in 2014 held a referendum on whether or not to depart the United Kingdom. The Union remains intact, but Scottish identity is no longer clandestine. It is robust and noisy.

Further, the heroin scene, and indeed the whole illicit drugs scene, has moved on. Of course it still exists, it always will, causing problems, hurt, and damage. But these days, although the legal framework remains confusing and dysfunctional, there are some more realistic public attitudes and policies, together with better education and supports. HIV/AIDS is not, in Scotland at least, the menacing ogre that overshadowed the period of the writing of *Trainspotting* the book, and which had to some extent been tamed by the time of the first productions of the play. So the first platforms barely exist any longer.

However, there are some enduring themes for the play to work with. The central premise is that youth has a propensity for experimenting with dangers of various sorts. Drugs is one danger, of which heroin is an example. If the play can tell a compelling story of how it goes wrong, then it remains relevant; there will always be heroin. It creates fractured, desperate communities, in which the laughing and the weeping – which are not at opposite ends of a straight line spectrum but which meet each other on a circle – sharpen the lust for life to the point where outsiders can be jealous of the sense of belonging even if they eschew the drawbacks; a potent dramatic tension.

And although you could hardly leave heroin out of any production, other themes can also be relevant. I saw a much-lauded production at The Citizen's Theatre, Glasgow, in 2017, a welcome return home, this time in the main auditorium. The gauntness of the heroin scene was all there in the bleak scenery and lighting, along with the isolating scattering of the individuals across the large stage. Johnny Swan was some sort of Olympian god, with tight briefs and a flowing transparent cloak. As Tommy asked Renton for his first shot, the young women in front of us said 'Naw, dinnae, Tommy.' So the audience was certainly engaging with the heroin scene.

But 'for me it was the politics of the piece' said Gareth Nicholls, director. 'At the story's heart are these disenfranchised characters who are trying to escape, but who are all trapped in this 1980s Thatcherite landscape. It feels that in the times of austerity and disenfranchisement that we're living in now that we've come full circle, and the play so speaks to now.'[64] 'Nicholls shows *Trainspotting* still speaks loudly, scabrously and irreverently about urban alienation and young lives under pressure' wrote Mark Fisher.[65] Several productions are on the stage in 2018 in Edinburgh, London and New York, and, no doubt, elsewhere, addressing various aspects of the situation locally. Theatre is a flexible, responsive art-form, and, with the script not set in aspic, *Trainspotting* is proving to be very adaptable. Ian Brown's interpretation of it as a morality play is proving to be very prescient.

We can already pose George Bernard Shaw's test of judging a play by what it does in the world. Here is one answer: senior figures from the police, medical, health, education, housing and social work professions, the Scottish Office, and the judiciary, were invited to the dress rehearsal of the 1994 show at the Traverse, Edinburgh. As they gathered there was some muttering among them about the usefulness of the occasion, but the then head of the Drugs Squad, Detective Chief Inspector, Jinty Kerr, told me that attitudes began to shift in the first round of phone calls in the morning. She was clear that what had hitherto been predominantly seen as a policing and law enforcement problem was now refocussing as a health and education issue. As a result of seeing the play, she saw to it that a copy of *Trainspotting* the book was placed in the police resources library and at least one officer soon reported that it had opened his eyes and changed his mind. So it is a matter of record that *Trainspotting* the play, specifically, at least in Edinburgh, had an impact on official policy towards heroin and, by judicious transference, into other drug policies as well.

SECTION VII
Trainspotting the Film

CHAPTER 23

The Making of the Film

ON 23 FEBRUARY 1996, *Trainspotting* the film was premiered. The speed of developments since the launch and that daring, insolent reading of the episode 'Traditional Sunday Breakfast' at the Edinburgh Book Festival by Irvine Welsh a mere 30 months previously, was truly astonishing. The book was being translated into several languages and *Trainspotting* the play was filling theatres and making headlines. On that evening in Glasgow the explosive *Trainspotting* phenomenon turned into a cultural and box office fireball.

It is reckoned that over 90 per cent of films showing in British cinemas in the early to mid-1990s came from Hollywood. Many mainstream British films were from the Merchant Ivory stable, with such titles as *A Room With A View* (Ivory, 1985), *Howard's End* (Ivory, 1992), and *Remains of the Day* (Ivory, 1993); plush, polished, intelligent, expensive, and good earners in the export market. What was missing in the British output was anything in which people, particularly young people, could see themselves. Multiplexes, the new style meeting places for culturally conscious young people, were cinema's answer to the onslaught of television. There was an open door for a new type of film.

Trainspotting the film has three deep roots. First, of course, is Irvine Welsh and his book and subsequently the play of that name. Second is Film Four, a branch of Channel 4, which developed a commitment to innovative filmmaking on tight budgets. They were pleased with their investment in *Shallow Grave* (Boyle, 1994). The third root was *Shallow Grave*'s team of John Hodge, hospital doctor and budding screenwriter; Andrew MacDonald, budding producer with a family history in the industry, both self-consciously Scottish; and Danny Boyle, director. They all worked well with the production team of Brian Tufano, photography; Masahiro Hirakubo, editor; and Kave Quinn, production designer.

Their next project was going to be *A Life Less Ordinary* (Boyle, 1997), which turned out to be disappointing, but at the time the production team genuinely believed that if *Trainspotting* broke even that would be a good outcome, and they could restore their nascent reputation with *A Life Less Ordinary*. We know now that they were collectively at the top of their game. The success of *Shallow Grave*, the good relations within the team, and the fact that the team could be reassembled quickly for *Trainspotting* meant that they were ready to go again with good levels of creative energy and mutual confidence. With the next job in the bag, they could relax and enjoy themselves. It all generated and released a creativity that is not easy to contrive.

The story is that MacDonald fell for *Trainspotting* the book and showed it to Hodge, who agreed about how good it was but couldn't envisage the journey from page to screen. Furthermore, it was a book, and, worse, a brand, adaptations of which they had forsworn because they wanted to make cinematic films out of original material. The political edge and implicit satire of *Trainspotting* worked well with Hodge. The humour and style worked well with Boyle. They went to see the play at the Citizen's Theatre, Glasgow. It was a dramatisation of parts of the book. They found the energy, the freshness, and the Scottishness irresistible; but a film would have to be very different.

They arranged to meet Welsh in Glasgow Film Theatre. He had already said and demonstrated that artistic endeavour and output isn't easily compartmentalised into defining genres, and they found him very willing to explore their ideas creatively. No doubt he could also sense the marketing value of a crossover product (literature, theatre, cinema, music). The film rights had already been sold, and this took some time to resolve.

In converting from page to screen, Hodge was faced with far too much material, a pretty chaotic narrative progress, a wide variety of points of view and voices, and a very close relationship with location. It seems he took to heart Alfred Hitchcock's famous remark: 'What I do is to read a story only once, and if I like the basic idea, I just forget all about the book and start to create cinema...'. Typically, film adaptations of books simplify the plot, reduce the number of characters, and concentrate on the action. Hodge resolved the problems by ignoring a lot of material, he created some of his own, he centralised Renton, and he brought the chaos into the framework of a Basic Plot (more on this in the next chapter).

Lots of things are transformed in the journey from page to screen. Perhaps we can say that Welsh's explosive, insolent, demotic use of language is replaced by Boyle's unusual, characterful use of the camera and the sound track. In both cases it's difficult to pick up the full meaning at the first exposure. But it's not a precise trade-off. Different medium, different story, different reader/audience experience. And while it was one thing for Welsh to invest his time speculatively in writing the book, Boyle had to be a whole lot more professional and commercial. Films are not cheap to make. As with any art form, there is a tension between what is good and what pays. But people care about adaptations because adaptation matters.

A recurring theme through several of the films made by the trio of Hodge, MacDonald and Boyle was friendship: its development and breakdown. This was maintained while setting it in the junkie scene where it collided with HIV/AIDS. Although this is a dark, difficult subject, the film was to be entertaining and upbeat, something quite different from social realism. There was to be no explanation of or apology for the use of drugs. Out went any explicit reference to economic, social or political issues of the day that are found in the book, and Leith Central Station disappears; various cinematic railway effects make use of the title rather than do anything to explain it.

And there had to be a decision about location. Edinburgh is a fine location indeed for a film. Coastal and north-facing, many artists and photographers have said how good the natural light is. It has plenty of contours permitting interesting angles, a real castle, a real palace, and a dramatic High Street. Down the hill is the work-a-day port town of Leith, and all surrounded by suburban sprawl, some of it distinctive to Edinburgh (tall, comfortable middle class tenement stairs, detached bungalows), and much of it characteristic of the drabness and anomie of British post-war municipal schemes, which is home to the *Trainspotting* story. Widely regarded as an attractive provincial capital with a long established summer festival, wasn't a story of transgressional, counter-cultural heroin abusers actually set in the city, the perfect opportunity to portray another side of the Scottish capital?

As an alternative, Glasgow could have been considered, with its 'hard place for hard men' tag, fed by legendary hard poverty, hard drinking, hard work, hard bigotry, hard humour, hard criminality and hard Barlinnie prison. Indeed, because this was a widespread perception, many in the non-Scottish audiences lazily assumed *Trainspotting* was a Glasgow story.

What was the problem? The problem was all of the above. Or, more to the point, all of the above was irrelevant. The surreality of the heroin experience was more important than the reality of location. The makers of *Trainspotting* started from their own position. The basic premise of their film is this: young man gets into heroin, experiences the highs and lows, has some good laughs, lives dangerously, is introduced to death, tries to get out of heroin and eventually decides that his future lies in leaving his friends and everything else behind. You can tell that story anywhere. But they needed a setting.

It's worth having a look to see how Scotland is used in two contemporaneous films. *Four Weddings and a Funeral* (Newell, 1994), set and mostly shot in London, feels like a Hollywood set of London, with the beautiful, sexy Andie McDowell there to give it the Hollywood seal of approval. It contains an element of Scotophilia in the sympathetic Scottish character Matthew (John Hannah) and, more obviously, in setting one of the weddings in Brigadoon Scotland. It's not that there aren't any weddings held in expensively restored castles, replete with pipers, a dance band, and plenty of kilts. It's just that not many of us have invitations to them.

Then there is *Braveheart* (Gibson, 1996), with a budget of $70m and ten Academy Award nominations and five Oscars to show for it. Shot mostly in Ireland, it tells the story of William Wallace, Scottish nationalist hero of the 14th century Wars of Independence (with England the aggressor against the Celtic countries of Ireland, Wales and Scotland), and Anglophobia is an integral part of the plot. The political establishment and the box office loved it. Cultural and historical distortions were overlooked, as it put a welcome bit of colour and texture into an Anglicised Britain without, since the story is a safe seven centuries old, any obvious threat to the existing constitutional status quo. It was remarked at the time that if there had been an Oscar nomination for 'best supporting country', Scotland would have been a runaway winner.

For the makers of *Trainspotting*, it was important to preserve the Scottish element. All accents are modified to gently accented standard English, even though they retain their distinctive regional inflexions (nevertheless, Renton's articulation of Saughton [prison, Edinburgh] as 'Sawton' on the bus to London is unforgivable. The 'augh' is pronounced as 'och' as in 'loch'). Scots objected to the smorgasbord of such disparate accents among the central characters who purport to be childhood friends, but the filmmakers knew it didn't matter; their market was England, where they can't tell one Scottish accent from another. There is a bigger cinema going public in London than in Scotland. This was to be a Scottish film and its main market was England, its own capital city shown as a tourist destination and the setting for a dodgy deal.

So, like any good pantomime, *Trainspotting* is set 'somewhere in Scotland'. But it deliberately, explicitly, subverted the authorities' image of Scotland in two scenes. In picture postcard Scotland, with a snow capped mountain in the distance, Renton denounces his countrymen as 'the lowest of the fucking low, the scum of the earth, the most wretched, servile, miserable pathetic trash that was ever shat into creation'; Englishmen are 'wankers' (p.46).[66] It's edgy to insult your target audience. And in the sequence gratuitously captioned 'The First Day of the Edinburgh Festival' an American tourist is mugged and robbed. You can see why the Scottish authorities didn't like it.

More than that, the film would pick up a broader cultural mood of the moment. The Conservative party had broken the political cycle, giving Thatcherism a five-year term from May 1992, but under John Major as prime minister it was chaotic and ideologically clapped-out. There was a widespread frustration at the political high-handedness and inertia, particularly in Scotland, where the Conservative party had been virtually wiped out in 1992. The 'democratic deficit' was openly discussed in the Constitutional Convention, hosted by the Church of Scotland with contributions from a wide variety of civic and business interests and most political parties (not the Conservatives). Scotland was the ideal base for a piece of assertive insolence.

Furthermore, arts funding had dried up; to produce the insult on a pretty limited budget (none of it public, and Channel 4 was a free market child of Thatcherism) made it all the more delicious. It was to be a film of considerable ambition. *Trainspotting* became part of a change in British political and public life.

Welsh was keen on Ewen Bremner to play Renton, following his widely acclaimed stage performances. Many people agreed that he would play the part with great verve. But the production team was insistent on casting Ewan McGregor, on the strength of his performance in *Shallow Grave*. The rest of the casting was 'ludicrously easy' says Boyle. For the part of Johnny Swan they took Peter Mullan who had enjoyed success in the all-Glasgow *The Steamie* (Haldane Duncan, 1988). Similarly, for the part of Begbie they went straight to Robert Carlyle with his bristling aggression and Weedgie accent.

The shoot was scheduled for seven weeks from late May, 1995. Around 70 per cent of the shooting was done in a disused cigarette factory in Glasgow, which gave the scene makers full scope to do what they wanted with space, shapes and lighting. Boyle said later that if he were making the film again he would shoot a greater percentage in this 'studio'. They adapted what had been the social area for The First Day of Edinburgh Festival scene.

The Volcano club, formerly in Benalder Street, Glasgow, is no more. The football match was filmed at the Firrhill Health Complex, Renton shoots the dog in Rouken Glen, Begbie throws the beer mug over his shoulder in a club in Queen Margaret Drive, and Renton and Spud share the milkshake in a little café in Maryhill Road, all in Glasgow. Trains no longer stop at Corrour on their journeys between Glasgow and Fort William, and of course the crew was lucky to catch a nice day, complete with some photogenic patches of snow in the distance. Renton's London flat was in Taigarth Road, West Kensington, and the hotel entrance and scene of the sale was in The Royal Eagle Hotel, Bayswater, both in London.

At no. 124 Princes Street, Edinburgh, then a branch of stationers John Menzies, you can find the exterior shots preceding the second flight and rap, with its memorably distinctive mirror over the doorway. The mirror has long gone, but the lintel at 45 degrees is still there. Look down Hanover Street from George Street to see the galleries which are behind Renton and Spud as they run up the hill. The most easily accessible and recognisable film location in Edinburgh is the Black Bull steps, Leith Street, and the Calton Arch with Waterloo Place above. Among other factors that commended this location was almost certainly the small, narrow dead-end opening, St Bernard's Row, from which the car emerges in front of Renton, where the scene could be prepared without holding up any traffic. The best guess is that the man who can be seen, smiling, standing against the opposite wall as Renton bounces off the bonnet and picks himself up (in the second showing of the sequence) was given the job of signalling to the car to move as McGregor approached.

The major decision had been made that the running time for the finished film was a very tight 90 minutes. This is short for an aspiring feature film, but it was a very carefully considered strategy. Several scenes hit the cutting-room floor, which aficionados might wish had been included in the final cut. For example, immediately ahead of the scene where the train departs the platform and Tommy strides out towards the mountains, the following is missing:

EXT. RAIL BRIDGE. DAY

A train speeds across.

INT. TRAIN. DAY

Sick Boy, Tommy, Spud and Renton sit drinking from an extensive carry-out.

SICK BOY

This had better be good.

TOMMY

It will be. It'll make a change for three miserable junkies who don't know what they want to do with themselves since they stopped doing smack.

SICK BOY

If I'm giving up a whole day and the price of a ticket, I'm just saying it had better be good. There's plenty other things I could be doing.

TOMMY

Such as?

SICK BOY

Sitting in a darkened room, watching videos, drinking, smoking dope and wanking. Does that answer your question?

They sit in silence (p.44).

It would have been a fine introduction to the scene on the platform. Other casualties include a shot of Diane, in school, writing her letter to Renton in London. Renton and Diane meet before they take the skag to London; in a good humoured conversation he suggests they might 'go somewhere together' on the proceeds, but she replies that she has a young and healthy boyfriend and Renton is 'such a deadbeat' (p.93). Ahead of Spud's masterful sabotage of his job interview, Renton is before the same panel and getting on dangerously well until he is invited to explain the gaps in his cv. With unimpeachable honesty he explains that he has had a long-standing problem with heroin addiction. He has been known to 'sniff it, smoke it, swallow it, stick it up my arse and inject it into my veins. I've been trying to combat this addiction, but unless you count social security scams and shoplifting, I haven't had a regular job in years. I feel it is important to mention this' (pp.21, 22).

This hard cutting left some of the storylines unfinished, which turned out not to be the problem the production team was anticipating. The story started in the shot of Alison shooting up somewhere in Johnny Swan's groin was intended to be finished in a hospital ward where Mark visits Swanny recovering from the amputation of his leg, where he is planning an extended trip to Thailand as a sex tourist. This scene was one of the last to be edited out. Including any of these scenes, the thinking went, would make the film slower, more complete and perhaps even 'better' in some respects. But they had to go, not only in the interests of adhering to their 90-minute rule but also keeping the plot simple and, in the final 20 minutes, focussing almost entirely on Renton.

For all the clever editing, continuity is not perfect. Eagle-eyed fans have spotted some slip-ups. Renton uses his belt as a tourniquet when he shoots up in Johnny Swan's gaff, but it is next seen safely holding up his trousers as he is dragged out into the street. Renton doesn't change the direction of the binoculars to follow the fast-moving group of runners when he views them a second time almost a full minute of screen time later, as he and Sick Boy are about to shoot the dog. Such things in no way spoil the thrust of the film, and they do give material for fans to pore over.

Things happen during the course of a seven-week shoot, and there wasn't enough of a budget to plan every single detail in advance, nor the time to do again things that didn't work out. For example, the original plan was to have Renton swimming through 'turds' on his way to recovering his suppositories, but it would have been prohibitively expensive. So he swims through clear water with a nice light, and now the sequence works as a metaphor for how squalid is the search for drugs and how beautiful it is when you find them. Renton and Sick Boy were going to be meeting in an 'arid place', for shooting the dog, but it was one of the nicest days of the year. And the actors turned up with hangovers, having had a hard day the day before running away from security guards in the chase down Princes Street, and McGregor was sore from tumbling over the car bonnet, more than once. Now we know this, they do look a bit rough, handling the binoculars and the airgun.

On realising that Spud is not going to have sex with her, Gail looks to see what she is missing. Her line, 'Not much!' (p.36) doesn't fit, as everyone sees a fine big penis lying on Spud's thigh. Maybe they should have hired a stunt man for that shot. Diane was supposed to sing David Bowie's *The Golden Years* to Renton in his cold turkey, but Macdonald didn't know it so she sings New Order's *Temptation*, much more appropriate for her screen age.

CHAPTER 24

This Film is About Heroin

THIS CHAPTER EXPLORES aspects of the film that are strongly related to each other and are not fully discussed elsewhere. The film's structures, shapes, and music combine to make it a film about heroin.

For some, the title of this chapter is not true, or not particularly true. The film is about a small group of young men (mostly) who try to have a good time that goes wrong. They are delinquent, they dabble with heroin, they eventually undertake a criminal enterprise and one of them clears off with the proceeds. Others see that heroin is more than a distracting presence as an unlikely friendship group laughs and stumbles its way towards a Western-style ending. It is worth expanding Mark Browning's observation when he says the film is 'a celebration of youthful energy against the background of heroin addiction that warps everything with which it comes into contact'.[67]

Narrative

The progression of *Trainspotting*'s storyline is familiar and predictable. It is the same as in three roughly contemporaneous comparators which all have heroin at their core: *Christiane F.* (Edel, 1981) based on the book *Wir Kinder vom Bahnhof Zoo*[68]; *Candy* (Armfield, 2006), based on the book *Candy: A Novel of Love and Addiction*[69]; and *Requiem for a Dream* (Aronofsky, 2000) based on the book *Requiem for a Dream*[70]. Straddling three continents, illustrating the universality of the heroin experience, a collective title for them could be *Studies in Heroin* or *A Junkie's Progress*. It goes like this.

Young people are under stimulated and bored. It's easy to reject and ridicule conventional life. Heroin is there, readily available. A first shot is taken, experimentally, in a peer setting. The hit, the rush, is sublime, and the temptation is strong to take another. It is all deliciously delinquent and there are no early warning signs of danger ahead. Some people do see the dangers and get out of it before much damage is done, whereupon normal youthful activities can be resumed – sex is among the possibilities, since, without heroin, the libido returns to normal.

But solo efforts to quit are not likely to be successful; many people get to the stage where they think that because they have successfully quit once, they can do it again, so they take another shot. But it's less easy to quit a second time. They become unemployable, but they need money. Prostitution (not evident in *Trainspotting*) is a lucrative possibility, otherwise they are down to straightforward thieving. Previous morality is forgotten. It all gets increasingly desperate, and it's only a matter of time before the bubble is burst by a death, or an overdose, or an appearance in court. Few recovering junkies have a loving family they have not alienated, and that is willing and able to provide the real help and support needed. Cold turkey is frightening, and rehab (again, not present in *Trainspotting*) is long and difficult. No-one emerges from heroin addiction as a train emerges from a tunnel; an ex-junkie is more like a moth that has flown too close to the candle.

Assuming a good recovery, a job, somewhere reasonable to live, and a degree of autonomy would be ideal. Old associates will be unhelpful. It's a classic mistake to go back to the scene, even if there is a funeral you want to go to. Once again, good progress can easily be brought to a halt with one more shot. The outcome is quite likely to be terminal, either by death or in the sense of losing the prospect of ever again getting so close to full recovery. Whether by voluntary separation or by prison or by death, successfully kicking the habit necessarily involves permanent departure from previous associates. By the end of all four of these films, the protagonists are separated from their erstwhile friends from the heroin scene.

Trainspotting conveys this breakout in upbeat fashion; but if we have been tracking the junkie experience in a mode of realism, Renton's glad confident smile as he crosses the bridge at the end is magical and fanciful. The other three films convey the full sadness.

None of this cuts any ice with the critics and commentators who do not accept the heading of this chapter. It is no defence for Boyle to say (correctly) that the acquisition of the heroin, the trip to London, the sale and the heist, is all one of the more faithful adaptations of his source material, *Trainspotting* the book. We have already noted that the episode on which it is based, *Station to Station*, poses major problems in the book. Boyle is making a film. He has been pretty creative with his source material elsewhere. Why does he burden himself with a problem ending? The final 20 minutes or so, almost the last quarter of the running time of the film, is not convincingly connected to what has gone before as far as character and theme are concerned, and it seriously parts company from the reality of heroin use as told in a narrative.

Trainspotting could well have ended at Tommy's funeral, and from Sick Boy's description of Mikey Forrester acquiring the heroin to the end could easily be expanded into a full length film on its own. Or, better still, and more to the point in this case, the trip to London and beyond would serve very well as the launch pad for the sequel. As it is, from Tommy's funeral onwards the film is not about heroin. It's about a criminal undertaking and a piece of treachery. Renton heading off with the swag reduces the whole thing to a Western, along the lines of Blondie departing the graveyard at the end of *The Good, The Bad, and The Ugly* (Leone, 1966).

Renton's rap as he crosses the bridge (don't miss the symbolism) at the end is not far from Louie the Ape's memorably entertaining and over-ambitious song: *I wanna be a man, mancub / And stroll right into town / And be just like the other men / I'm tired of monkeyin' around... / I wanna be like you / I wanna talk like you / Walk like you, too / You'll see it's true / Someone like me / Can learn to be ... / Like someone like you...*[71]. But Louie remains an ape, the loser, and is left behind; the hero is Mowgli, who accomplishes his quest when he finds a human girl. Giving Louie's attitude and Mowgli's outcome to Renton doesn't work. Any clever analysis that derives sound, coherent meaning from this poorly connected and over-long and contradictory epilogue is no more than a fortunate by-product of some poor directing.

These problems with the final sequence are, in a formal sense, real. However, in the onward rush of the film, we don't notice the change of gear, and there isn't even the decency of a clutch movement. And the entire film is about heroin. The recovering junkie realises that he can no longer negotiate with heroin, or with his associates. They won't go away. He needs to depart. Diane's letter is a reminder of what he is leaving behind: nice girls (like her) are all too easily suckered into 'working for' exploiters (like Sick Boy), while fellow junkies who don't kick the habit end up metaphorically, or in Spud's case, literally, in the gutter.

From Tommy's funeral onwards the heroin story is not contained in the surface narrative; it is contained within Renton. Notice how Renton is almost the sole focus of attention. The verbalised voiceovers to which we have become so accustomed are augmented by subtle, silent discussions. We are somewhere inside his head for the long moment as he and Spud are left with the bag of cash; we are with Renton as Begbie, now personifying everything Renton must leave behind, expends his dying hold as he blows smoke over him; and as the others lie sleeping off the events of the day we see Renton as he sees himself in the mirror. He has come to the point of departure out of his own resources and motivation. That's the way it is for junkies. It's a lonely road. For sure, it's foreshortened. Missing is the long, hard rehab process, and no-one – no-one – walks confidently over a bridge to a new life on a glad sunny morning within a day or so of shooting up (twice). Cheesy and Western-like though the final part of the film may seem, for those familiar with heroin there is plenty in it to identify with. It asserts everyone's right to move on, achieved by whatever means.

Everyone wants to agree with the proposition that we should live life to the full, that there is everything to hope for, however oppressive the circumstances. Put as a proposition, people will use facts and experience to argue against it. The upbeat, swaggering finale of the film carries it off in narrative form. It is imbued with a quasi-religious quality: don't try to understand – hope and believe! In other words, this is a resurrection story. We need not find the fault that it is not lifelike – we can celebrate that it is life-ful.

The production team knew there was no place in the market for another true-to-life social-realism style junkie film in which the protagonists, if they survive, have nowhere to go. Breaking the laws of history and nature, fiction has the power to uplift spirits and create communities. Boyle knows this; any film that sets out to entertain, particularly one that is consciously seeking to avoid social realism, needs a happy ending more than a book needs one. If Welsh had not provided one, Boyle would have had to invent it.

Structure

Firstly, *Trainspotting* falls into the framework of three of the seven Basic Plots of all narratives, alternating between periods of constriction and expansion. It fits most easily into the model of the five-phase 'Overcoming the Monster' plot. To begin, in Renton's opening rap we are made aware of the monster (heroin): this is phase one: constriction. Some effort is required to shake off the monster. The means is an opium suppository which, as Mikey Forrester says, will bring him down gradually. With this, in phase two, the dream stage, normal life (sex and various youthful escapades) is resumed; expansion. But the monster returns in the confrontation and frustration stage. Tommy ominously asks for a shot, the baby dies, our hero is hauled before a court of law, he overdoses and undergoes a dreadful cold turkey experience: phase three, constriction again. The secret of how to overcome the monster comes from an unexpected source: 'The point is, you've got to find something new' (p.76), says the schoolkid Diane, the young oracle of a healthy future.

Although it starts well, with Renton getting a job and somewhere to stay in London, phase four, the second expansion stage, is darker than the first. His very identity is undermined, and he makes the mistake of attending Tommy's funeral, where he revisits the junk scene he has been trying to leave behind. In phase five, a make-or-break opportunity to rid himself forever of the monster is presented: the nightmare stage, the last constriction before the resolution, always the most tense. In a miraculous escape he crosses a bridge in the dawn of a new day; the final release and expansion.

To be sure, the monster is not slain, so the world is not saved; this element is a variant of the classic 'Overcoming the Monster' model. Renton is clearly cast on the side of 'light' (he is the hero, after all) in opposition to the 'dark' of the monster. As Christopher Booker puts it,

> ...the whole underlying purpose of the action [of all of these Basic Plots] is to show us the hero or heroine maturing to the state where they are finally ready for that decisive confrontation with the archetypal power of darkness which can bring their complete liberation.[72]

It is surely this framework that guided Hodge and Boyle as they sifted through the chaotic material of their primary source, *Trainspotting* the book. This basic shape has enthralled and satisfied readers and listeners since storytelling began.

Trainspotting the film can also be seen as a weak form of Comedy. This is not a reference to the many moments that raise a laugh but to the way that a very serious topic – heroin abuse in collision with HIV/AIDS – is dealt with lightly and with humour. Identity and marriage are not matters for fooling around, but *The Marriage of Figaro* is very funny. Indeed, Aristophanes, Shakespeare and Mozart all 'while constantly provoking their audiences to laughter, [...] manage to explore some of the deepest issues of human life'.[73]

The central point of Comedy is that the hero comes to a moment of illumination, reverses what he has done before, and is projected on course for a happy ending. Having been in the dark about the true state of affairs, he moves into knowledge and light. In the final scenes of *Trainspotting* darkness is personified in Begbie who, in his rage at being defeated, smashes up the hotel room. The approaching policemen are his just deserts. Darkness has become the pantomime villain. A comedy normally requires all the main protagonists to share in the happy ending, but in this case only Renton enjoys it. We will see in the next chapter just how emphatically Renton is the central figure in the film, which helps the case for putting *Trainspotting* into the category of Comedy.

Without any changes in the earlier part of the film, if there were no moment of enlightenment – if the hero fails to resolve his opening problem – the story would be a Tragedy. He would be a victim of his own weaknesses and inadequacies. It would be a Tragedy also if something were to go wrong in the last part – if Renton was arrested for carrying the heroin, for example, or if he lapsed again into hopeless addiction. This would be the proper outcome of Renton's hubris in not knowing his limits, and taking a risk too many.

The second construction of the film is as an entirely conventional three-act drama. The programme notes look like this:

	summary of theme	scene / action
ACT I Scene I (also serves as Prologue)	Introductions: rejection of conventional life; manifesto for heroin; characters on display.	Flight with 'choose life' rap; football game; shooting gallery; counter-advice; Renton decides to reject heroin.
Scene 2	Preparations for not using.	Renton barricades himself into his room; Mikey Forrester; worst toilet.
Scene 3	Escapades and character studies while not using.	Shooting the dog; Spud's job interview; Begbie's pool game; Renton swaps Tommy's videos; the glass in the pub; rave scene; Diane; Tommy/Spud/Renton sex scenes; three morning-afters; abortive walk in the hills.
ACT II Scene I	Using again, and surrounding delinquency.	Shooting gallery; Sick Boy pontificates; Tommy asks for a shot; thefts from old people's home, Renton's mother, car, doctor's surgery, American tourist.
Scene 2	Serious downsides of using heroin; real life and conventional society intrude; failure to quit.	Death of baby in shooting gallery; re-play of opening flight with changed rap; in court; overdose with Johnny Swan.
Scene 3	Cold reality cannot be avoided; HIV a serious concern.	Cold turkey at home; bingo club with parents; Renton is not HIV+; Tommy has HIV.
Scene 4	'You've got to find something new.'	Diane visits Renton.

ACT III Scene 1	A new start.	Renton has a job in London.
Scene 2	Things go wrong, again.	Begbie arrives; Sick Boy arrives; ownership of Renton's identity (passport) is questioned.
Scene 3	Final warning.	Tommy's funeral; return to the junkie scene.
Scene 4	Tempting, dangerous opportunity to break out.	Renton gets involved in the heroin scene again; Renton tests gear; on the bus; the deal; tensions in the pub; Begbie's violence; Renton's heist.
Scene 5	Resolution.	On his way out, Renton reverses early raps.
Reprise	Sanitising Renton's character? Anticipating the sequel?	Spud finds his share.

The play is dominated by the central Act ii, phase three of the plot structure, which is a full blown crisis in a mid-career in heroin. Act I acts out the early stages, the approach to the crisis, and Act III takes us through the departure via a mistake that shouldn't have been made but which turns out to contain the seed of the resolution.

In the third construction of the film we may say that its intellectual progression is contained in the three variations of the 'choose life' rap. They top and tail the film, and make an emphatic punctuation point at more or less its mid-point.

The first is a scornful rejection of conventional life: 'Choose life. Choose a job... Choose a fucking big television, choose washing machines... Choose good health, low cholesterol and dental insurance...' (p.3). In the same vein, Renton makes a defiant manifesto for heroin as a consumer choice: 'I chose not to choose life'. Heroin trumps any other consideration: 'Who needs reasons when you've got heroin?' (p.5). He explicitly acknowledges that there are dangers and downsides, which are not to be ignored, but which are easily outweighed by the pleasures.

After the death of the baby, and having undertaken a thieving spree for which they are finally being chased, the rap – delivered in voice-over as Renton and Spud are being chased down Princes Street for the second time, thus clearly identifying it as a new version of the same rap – has to face the fact that the downsides cannot be ignored: 'Pile misery on misery... keep on going, robbing, stealing, fucking people over... no matter how much you steal, you never have enough' (p.56). Renton explicitly recognises that other people, non-heroin users, are caught up in the downsides. The joke is over, the pleasures have to be put into context, other people are paying a price. This is the beginnings of subscribing to conventional morality.

On his way out at the end of the film, Renton reverses his opening remarks and, building upon the mid-point, fully embraces conventional life: 'I'm moving on, going straight and choosing life... I'm going to be just like you: the job, the family, the fucking big television... junk food, children, walks in the park... choice of sweaters, family Christmas...' (p.106). Without any ambiguity, and without moralising, the intellectual thrust of the film comes down against the use of heroin, and it does so in good, realistic, well-argued order: heroin is available as a choice; it is seductive and very dangerous; it leads to personal and social behaviour which cannot, under any circumstances, be described as positive or healthy; and if you are lucky enough to escape its clutches, conventional life is a much better option.

If ever there was a subject matter that lent itself to some trickery with time and space, it is heroin. The central rap is the two-way tipping-point in the cinematics of the film. In the first part, rapid cutting between scenes and storylines creates some sort of hyper-reality, and you can't be sure about the chronological order of some of the sequences of events. Indeed, can you be sure that the entire first part of the film up to the death of the baby isn't a flashback, recalled from the second flight down Princes Street? The second part is shown in a fairly straightforward narrative sequence.

The only securely told junkie narrative is Tommy's story. He is the nice boy, who keeps healthy, has a nice girlfriend and a healthy sex life, and is proud to be Scottish. Temporarily destabilised because Lizzie has dumped him, he asks for a shot, the classic first use of heroin. 'I want to try it, Mark,' he says. 'You're always going on about how it's the ultimate hit and that. Better than sex. Come on, I'm a fucking adult. I want to find out for myself... I've got the money' (p.48). He quickly becomes addicted, quickly picks up HIV, and quickly dies.

Music

The musical soundtrack is a significant vehicle for the film's depiction of a junkie's relationship with heroin. It announces its presence from the out-set. To the thumping, dustbin lid clatter of Iggy Pop / David Bowie's *Lust for Life*, Renton offers his opening rap with its defiant upbeat manifesto not only for heroin but for the right of junkies to live as they choose to live: 'Cause we're the masters of our own fate / We're the captains of our own souls'.[74] Iggy Pop's well-known reputation as a drug-fuelled hell raiser, together with Bowie's part in the film *Christiane F.* leave no doubt about the film's subject-matter.

The musical accompaniment to the second rap, Blur's *Sing*, melancholy, repetitive, and somehow hopelessly and sadly faraway, reflects Renton's growing awareness that heroin is doing great damage to himself and others, while he has lost control of his destiny. The final rap is delivered to the strong, exciting rhythm of Underworld's *Born Slippy (Nuxx)*, which has nothing to do with heroin and was bang up-to-date for the 1996 audiences. Its explicit meaning, if there is any, is pretty enigmatic; techno and lyrics don't go well together. Its effect is mostly with the strong, pulsating, confident music. The intellectual progression, so important to the film, could almost be conveyed by the music alone.

When, in what at first sight is simply a moment of pure entertainment, Sick Boy opens the false heel on his shoe to reveal a hidden injecting set saying that heroin has 'personality', he also introduces a further depiction of heroin: as a character. We have already met Heroin the character, introduced musically. Directly after the prologue, the film title has at last appeared on the screen, and the narrative proper starts. Mark has just asserted his intention to quit, and he prepares to stop using. Although there are no lyrics in this playing of Bizet's *Carmen – Habanera*, the aria is easily and widely recognised as being in the mouth of that great seductress Carmen: 'You don't love me, maybe, but I love you... be careful!' She mocks and undermines Mark as he stocks up the essentials for an uncomfortable few days and barricades himself into the room. We are carried swiftly from a view of Renton in the mirror reassessing his situation ('All I need is one final hit'); we see the barricades in a chaotic heap on the floor; he calls Mikey Forrester ('Can you help me out?'); and he holds the opium suppositories ('What the fuck are these?') (pp.9,10). Round One to Carmen.

Carmen does not aim to win Round Two. The final chord of the music plays, beautifully timed, as Renton's foot disappears, ballet-like, with a final twist, down the toilet. She makes her point – 'it's not so easy to get rid of me' she implies – and, departing, she has set up the film dramatically.

The second personification is no less explicit. Lou Reed's song *Perfect Day* starts as Mark injects his overdose in Johnny Swan's flat. Ostensibly this is a love ballad sung by one who has had a perfect day with his sweetheart in the park and the zoo, even though he knows his love is not requited:

'You just keep me hanging on, you just keep me hanging on...'. But, coming from Lou Reed, the song cannot escape close associations with heroin. This is non-diegetic music, conveying the inner thoughts of the main character and direction of the sequence. 'Just a perfect day...' plays as we see Renton flat on his back in a bleak street on a dull day. He is in a quiet, restful place. Oblivion is a perfect day. Ordinary life is too difficult. Renton is singing to Heroin: 'You made me forget myself / I thought I was someone else / Someone good.' A relationship with Heroin can be likened to an unbalanced love affair: one is irresistibly seductive while the other risks becoming a slave. 'You just keep me hanging on, you just keep me hanging on.'[75]

Or maybe Heroin is singing to Renton. The ambiguities work well in music. The punchline, applicable to both the lover and the junkie, is a musical rendering of the Biblical verse: 'You're going to reap just what you sow' (Galations 6.7). If you sow wheat, you will reap wheat. It is repeated four times as Mark is slapped by an authoritative doctor, comes out of his stupor, and, looking unwell and vulnerable, sits between his parents in a taxi going home. If you do heroin, you will do cold turkey. That's where he is heading.

Previewing the film, NME Monthly wrote: 'The overdose is the most powerful scene in... *Trainspotting*... It's just sort of calm, dreamy, like it's not really happening. Like the feeling addicts get when they really *are* overdosing.'[76]

Mise En Scene

A good deal of *Trainspotting*'s heroin story is conveyed by the artful use of camera work and set. At its best, heroin is wonderful – look at the bright cheerful colours on the flats behind Renton as he walks away from Mikey Forrester with a nice, comfortable low level opiate fix up his bum. It's a great life – but it can't last like that, and it doesn't. Perhaps the most fantastical scene is the foul, dank, filthy approach to the toilet and the toilet itself, such a powerful image we can almost smell it. It tells us that nothing is more demeaning than living with heroin. But we can read Renton's swim through clear bright water as a visual metaphor for pleasure and satisfaction in searching for and securing a fix: 'Ya dancer!' he shouts out, audible through the water. Nevertheless, he returns through the foul toilet bowl, and that fantasy is over. Or is it? The film playfully mixes fantasy with reality as Renton returns to his real flat, still dripping wet from his 'fantasy'.

On the whole, for heroin-associated scenes production designer Kave Quinn wanted lurid, livid colours and suggestions of human distress. The shooting gallery scenes were shot in cavernous, almost open plan areas with

few and incomplete divisions, very different from the reality of most shooting galleries in poky flats. She wanted a sense of depth and easy movement.
Floor level cameras produce an impression of chaos and squalor, exaggerated by holes in walls. Where Tommy is ill and dies is no living accommodation at all, but a bleak space in a warehouse. The ball Renton kicks around
is lifeless and the poster of Iggy Pop is ever more raggy and askew.

Heroin is only ever used in these worse-than-reality surroundings which
scream dereliction and damage. Mikey Forrester's flat is nothing but bare
walls and a mattress on the floor. Renton's movement through the floor as
he overdoses is repeated as Tommy's coffin is lowered at his funeral, with
rectangular shapes in both scenes. Spud lies, folded, distressed, Salvador
Dali-like, in the gutter.

There is a terrible awfulness about the hallucinations in the cold turkey
scene. It culminates in the dead baby crawling on the ceiling and screwing
its head round to look blankly at Renton below. It would have been easy
to make the puppet of the dead baby move across the top of a surface and
flip the shot, but Boyle insisted that he wanted the puppet on the ceiling and
Renton in his bed in the same frame, so the production team went to some
trouble to move the puppet from above. The effort was worth it – there is
widespread agreement that this is the most gruesomely memorable image of
the film, surpassing the toilet scene in its sheer grimness.

There are other pleasing visual associations with the junkie narrative.
The roughness of the planks of wood across Renton's door as he barricades
himself in for his difficult week, and which are very shortly reduced to a
formless pile on the floor, speak of the chaos of his life. Balancing on the wall
for a moment before making the leap into Johnny Swan's flat suggests a level
of ambiguity about his mission – he knows very well that this is a dangerous
step, taken in desperation.

Soft on Drugs?

If the case is made that *Trainspotting* is indeed about heroin, some still insist
that it is somehow 'soft on drugs', apparently meaning that it doesn't give
an explicitly moralising stand against the use of heroin (or any other illicit
mind-altering drug). In addition to the absence of attempts at rehabilitation
and the implausible ending so soon after shooting up on the bus, it is Act II
Scenes 1 and 2 that gives most scope for this charge. Act II Scene 1 is full of
scamming and thieving, a genuine enough portrayal of the life of a junkie;
the only thing on their minds is their next fix. They are reckless and brazen.

Often the stolen goods have little value, and even if something valuable is stolen, the true worth isn't realised. The priority is a quick sale and a visit to the dealer. For the junkies, normal morality is suspended – thieving is all in a day's work, it is what has to be done. As described elsewhere in this book, low level thieving caused a great deal of heartbreak and outrage among the general public. To see the film's characters set about their business without any reference to conventional sensibilities and normal law abiding standards, gives easy ammunition to say the film is delinquent. It is delinquent. It is junkie thieving from the junkie's point of view. To include 'society's' reaction to it would involve a change of genre, presumably to some form of social realism.

This is followed in Act II scene two with Renton's reaction to the death of the baby with 'I'm cookin' up'; and later, within 12 hours of asserting to the sheriff that 'with God's help I'll conquer this terrible affliction', he is shooting up with Johnny Swan. The charge that the film is 'soft on drugs' is misdirected. The film is amoral, unconcerned with the rights and wrongs of taking heroin and surrounding behaviour.

However, there is nothing that is feel-good about heroin in the film. The feel-good factor is all to do with life without heroin. And there is a good deal of educational content in the film, delivered in voiceovers. The voice-over device is itself part of the film's depiction of addiction; junkies are well aware of how their habit looks to others, of the damage it is doing to themselves, even as they hang around for dealers, go stealing, and shoot up. We are told that if you want to quit, being with friends from the scene is a problem; that heroin makes you constipated; that heroin suppresses your libido; that, even in the thick of addiction, you know things will only get worse; that methadone can seem like 'state-sponsored addiction', and 'it's never enough' (p.60); that cold turkey is a truly dreadful experience; that HIV lowers resistance to opportunistic infections; that after the pain of cold turkey 'the real battle starts.' (p.69) and that a junkie can never be sure he has quit until his last fix is a long, long way behind him. If we are open to it, the film enlightens as effortlessly as it entertains. Indeed, some of it is entertainingly put. Taking the first lesson from the list above, having come off heroin gradually as Mikey Forrester said he would, Renton says, 'The downside of coming off junk was that I knew I would need to mix with my friends again in a state of full consciousness. It was awful: they reminded me so much of myself I could hardly bear to look at them' (p.16). Any junkie will attest to the sober truth of it.

And then there is Ecstasy (MDMA). Here the film uses a sleight of hand. By the mid-1990s the worst of the heroin epidemic was over and the closely associated HIV/AIDS epidemic was coming under some level of control. The two drugs produced profoundly different scenes: the heroin scene is clandestine and isolating, while ecstasy is vibrant and inclusive. Ecstasy is not as dangerous as heroin and it is not addictive. The misconceived and poorly aimed Drug Trafficking Act (1994) had come into force, an expression of public and official hostility to drugs in general. But many in *Trainspotting*'s early audiences had an intelligent awareness, if not direct experience of the rave scene.

If the film suggests heroin users were also ravers, this would be dishonest. We should not overlook the detail that neither Renton nor Spud, the two characters who certainly go on to use heroin later, are seen actually taking ecstasy in the Volcano club; but even so, it stretches credulity somewhat even to have them at a rave scene, and we should resist the suggestion that for any individual the two drugs were interchangeable or continuous. For the knowing 1996 audiences, however, their own familiarity with the situation enabled them to easily work through all this, and it gave them an insider's insight, adding to their identification with the film and their sense of belonging to their own generation simply by being there.

Relationship with Reality

This playful, multi-sensational, entertaining film relates to a much broader range of realities than the heroin scene. The junkie world does not play out in some mythical abstraction. John Hodge takes us straight to an example that may not be immediately obvious: he says he overheard a young man on Edinburgh High Street saying, 'It was fuckin obvious that that cunt wis gonnae fuck some cunt'. As far as he could make out, it was precisely the context in which his fictional characters find themselves after the court appearance in which Spud is sent to prison, and here was Hodge's perfect opportunity to work such an authentic and colourful remark into the script.

Sick Boy's explanation of how he had come by 2kg of heroin is that Mikey Forrester bought it from two Russian sailors (p.90). This detail is not in the book, and its inclusion in the film stands out as a piece of authenticity that is local to Leith. Possibly the production team, seeing that the plot needed some context for the acquisition of the heroin, asked Welsh for something plausible. Equally possibly, Hodge simply referenced the Russians from readily accessible Scottish folklore that involves Russians and Scandinavians coming from over the sea.

The shot of the bingo carousel is almost a replica of the newly-launched National Lottery televised Saturday night draw, instantly recognisable beyond the bingo-going community. Dale Winton's contribution in which he plays himself in a game show also carries a large dose of mid-1990s British culture. Welsh's beloved Hibernian Football Club, together with his real life hero Pat Stanton, is on display in Mark's bedroom, and there is real footage of Archie Gemmill's famous, wonderful goal for Scotland in the World Cup finals in Argentina in 1978. Repeated references to Sean Connery's output, and the discussion about several musicians and other public figures while Mark and Sick Boy are lying in the park ahead of shooting the dog, all tie the film in to the real world.

With the exception of the Volcano club, well known in Glasgow, the camera does not show readily identifiable locations, although you would easily recognise Princes Street, Hanover Street and Calton Road in Edinburgh if you are already familiar with them. The arrival in London with a quick-cutting sequence showing the street names familiar from the Monopoly board is clever; Monopoly, the ultimate game of ruthless boom and bust using pretend money, the very epitome of Thatcherite ideology. There are even a couple of updates: Bishopgate and No. 1 Lloyds' Building, complete with smiling, red-coated doorman, physical manifestations of new money and the Thatcher revolution.

The film has to work against something it can't do anything about: not one of the screen heroin users looks like anything other than in the pink of health. A drawn face, a pallid complexion, poor teeth, and pained movements are what we would be seeing if they were real life junkies. But other images have to speak for themselves, and we can't let ourselves be distracted by this departure from real life.

And – this is central to the film – the production team went to great lengths to represent the realities of the drug scene in convincingly accurate detail. The squalor of the shooting galleries, the prostrate bodies, the quiet conversations between those who were capable of talking interspersed with outbursts of anxiety or anger, are all recognisable.

Close-ups of the powder being mixed with water and heated on the teaspoon, and the liquid being drawn up into the syringe, were shot under the knowledgeable guidance of the Calton Athletic Recovery Group. It was important to show the junkie habit of drawing up a little blood into the chamber, to check the needle is in a vein, and the team went to a great deal of trouble to make a life-like prosthetic elbow. The shot of the contaminants left in the bottom of the chamber after Renton has injected contains a wealth of truth. Calton Athletic – playing football in the blue strip in the opening sequence – were well rewarded for their troubles in the form of considerable funds from the proceeds of the film as it shot round the world. There is enough good, straightforward knowledge included in Gav's account of Tommy's death by toxoplasmosis, soberly told at the funeral, for an Edinburgh academic parasitologist to show the clip ahead of her series of lectures on HIV.

Trainspotting is often criticised for dealing lightly with death, but is this fair? The death of the baby has the effect of inspiring both Sick Boy and Renton to try to kick their habit. Life goes on, but differently. Films that contain much violence and murder rarely show bodies, or screen mute ghosts, or attend funerals; they are not usually accused of treating death lightly. Spud's simple, unaccompanied singing a poignant little song at Tommy's wake, in which everybody is sober and serious, is the still heart of the whole film.

And there is a little moralising message, deftly delivered: even transgressional young men must wear a condom for safe sex, and must respect a woman enough to vacate her bed at her request. There is a body of Marxist theory saying that education is very effectively carried in association with entertainment.

CHAPTER 25

Character

WE HAVE SEEN that in fitting *Trainspotting* into the structure of a Basic Plot a good deal of narrative plausibility is lost; in other words, this isn't social realism. If *Trainspotting* the film is a dramatic study in heroin, the drama is contained principally in the relationship between Heroin and Mark Renton, supported by Tommy, Diane, and Johnny Swan.

Mark Renton (Ewan McGregor)

To point out that Renton is the central character of this film seems to be no more than a statement of the obvious. Yet it may not be easily and at first realised just how emphatically he has been made central, and how many devices are used to achieve this. Simply visually he has all the box office requirements (not a small consideration): hunky, sexy, good-looking, with a gentle Scottish accent. His dress is conventionally scruffy, although he scrubs up nice when required. Although he can easily use foul language like the others, he has a wider register available, even if it is here somewhat exaggerated: 'Relinquishing junk. Stage one: preparation. For this you will need: one room which you will not leave... one bucket for urine, one for faeces, one for vomitus' (p.9). Already the disparate youthful 1996 audiences can identify with some part of him.

He is usually foregrounded on the screen – the opening shots of him at the front of the pack being chased down Princes Street tell us what to expect. He spends a good deal of time on screen apparently doing nothing, which not only reinforces the focus on him but, in some cases, actually progresses the storyline. For example, in the pub at the end we are somewhere in his head as Begbie's violence spirals out of control behind him and Renton considers the situation. Only fleetingly is he a character in someone else's story. We feel his mother's pain as she, out of focus, knows he is going into her bedroom to steal from her. The driver of the car with which he collides, in the second flight, gives our reaction: shocked at the collision, as any driver would be, but also offended at Renton's casual, unapologetic assertiveness.

The sheriff addresses him in a relatively long speech, giving conventional society's view and the court's judgement on his behaviour, but the focus is all on Renton.

Almost everything in the film is mediated through Renton. With the exception of Tommy's and Spud's sexual encounters, which, the audience senses are rightly private, the audience knows nothing that Renton doesn't know. He knows mostly because he is there and part of the action, and otherwise because he is told in voiceover from Tommy (the truth about Begbie at the pool table), Diane (what's happening in Leith when he is in London), or Gav (the circumstances of Tommy's death). On the face of it, Begbie's experience with the 'tall girl' in the London club is purely a Begbie story – but we notice that Begbie is acting out Renton's musings on sexuality. He has something to say by way of interpretation for our benefit about each of the other three: after Spud's job interview he is 'proud' (p.23) of Spud, out of friendship, without any idea of self-serving or gaining advantage. After the death of the baby he remarks: 'Something inside Sick Boy died and never returned. It seemed he had no theory with which to explain a moment like this' (p.55); and 'Begbie was hard, but not so hard he didn't shite it off twenty years in Saughton' (p.95). There is no comparable view of Renton from any of the others.

We hear much more of Renton in the voiceovers than in the dialogue. And the voiceovers are complex. Broadly, we hear from him as a commentator, in which he uses the first person and the present continuous tense, and as narrator in which he is more objective, using the third person and the past tense. But sometimes Renton as commentator and Renton as narrator are impossible to distinguish; for example, he speaks of himself in voiceover in the Volcano. Having seen both Begbie and Sick Boy getting on well with women, and having noticed Diane, he says 'The situation was becoming serious. Young Renton noticed the haste with which the successful, in the sexual sphere as in all others, segregated themselves from the failures... [*Diane takes two drinks from the man and walks away*] ...And with that, Mark Renton had fallen in love' (pp.31, 32). He has spoken of himself in character, giving himself a powerful position in the film.

There is a nice humour in the opening character sketches in the football game, seeing Renton being felled by a football he should have seen coming. This honesty, and a line in self-deprecation, is a feature of the character in the first half of the film. He goes in for comic irony: he says in voiceover that he is attempting 'to lead a useful and fulfilling life as a good citizen' (p.18) even as he primes the airgun after shooting the dog. Yes, he's a bit mischievous in stealing Tommy and Lizzie's sex tape, but he means no harm. In the chat-up sequence with Diane he shows an attractive mixture of male assertiveness and youthful uncertainty. He wears a condom, and allows himself to be put in the hallway on her instruction. Later, apparently caringly, he asks if she might be pregnant. He offers genuine condolences to Spud's mum after the court case.

His ongoing honesty extends to enduring the reproaches, in his cold turkey hallucinations, of those whom he has affected or hurt: Begbie mocks and threatens him; Diane cares for him; Sick Boy is supercilious; Tommy and Spud reproach him for their ill luck compared with his good luck; and the dead baby is speechless. In comparison to Tommy he recognises (to himself) that it's easy to say there's no problem 'when it's some other poor cunt with shite for blood' (p.71). Although it is he who gave Tommy his first shot, he continues to be concerned about him, even making a difficult visit to him when the contrasts between their fates is all too apparent.

He vocalises the film's subversive take on Scotland: 'We're the lowest of the fucking low...the English... [are] just wankers... We are ruled by effete arseholes' (p.46). It's intelligent and funny. But, bored and unfulfilled, he reverts to heroin. This basically nice young man is not resistant to a seductive drug and a delinquent lifestyle. He is all too recognisable. What's not to like about him?

But there is a twist when Renton goes to London. Our hero becomes a child of Thatcher. Any fool could make money here, he observes, and he enjoys the 'sound of it all. Profit, loss, margins, takeovers, letting, subletting, subdividing, cheating, scamming, fragmenting, breaking away' (pp.77, 78). And he repeats Margaret Thatcher's infamous remark that there was no such thing as society, and in any case he stands outside it. This is exactly the ideology that most in the audiences would reject, but Renton is probably the first attractive identifier of it they had ever come across. Then, having stolen the money, on his way out he puts himself at Sick Boy's level: '[he] would have done the same to me if only he'd thought of it first' (pp.105, 106). Thatcherite ideology and the route out of addiction combine in the doctrine of looking after no. 1. This is edgy; it's not easy at first to appreciate all that is going on and sort out which part of his attitude you approve of. It left audiences uncertain how they felt about this otherwise sympathetic character.

Going to London – depicted here as the gateway to the rest of the world and, by implication, an alternative life – for a second time, Renton tells us he has a plan that it is best not to discuss; a device that both generates some drama for the climax and puts him in charge, again. He makes himself no different, morally, from Swanney. We are presented with the good guy who has had a tough time, got lucky, and is organising his own redemption without a care for the trail of dealers through whose hands his heroin will pass, and bringing to many users at the end of the line the very misery from which he is escaping. Does 'looking after no. 1' go this far? We're supposed to like this guy! The Plot is requiring too much from one character. But it's fun!

Does he save his reputation in his last act, by leaving Spud's share of the heist in the locker? For the audience it's a last chuckle before the credits roll and the lights go up, adding to the happy ending and the feel-good factor of the film overall. Accounts of the making of the film say that Danny Boyle insisted at the last moment that Renton should leave the money for Spud. John Hodge worried that this sanitises Renton. Not at all. It is the meanest, most ill-considered thing he does in the whole of the film, and this in his most composed self. He doesn't get away with it on the grounds of looking after no. 1. The newly mature and responsible young man who opened Act III should go through with his plan by not implicating his friend. The safest outcome for Spud would be that he becomes a victim of Renton's disloyalty just like Sick Boy and Begbie. As it is, Renton sows the seed of enduring enmity between Spud and the other two. From the beginning there was little doubt that in this detail Boyle was paving the way to a sequel; and indeed, in *T2 Trainspotting* (Boyle, 2017) it comes up as part of the plot. Renton claims it to his credit, but Spud says it's very dangerous to give that much money to a junkie – he nearly killed himself!

Tommy (Kevin McKidd)

When Renton says about Tommy – 'I got the truth from Tommy' (p.25) – he speaks for the film and for all of us. Through Tommy some truths about the heroin scene are told. In contrast to the others, he keeps fit, he enjoys the great outdoors, he is proud of being Scottish, and he has a healthy sex life with a nice girlfriend. Temporarily disoriented because Lizzie dumps him, he asks for a shot of heroin from his friend, Renton. There is no predatory, exploitative dealer on the scene here. This is a combination of youthful experimentation among peers and the ready availability of heroin, an easily recognisable situation. He quickly develops a habit (though we never see him using) and, in the lottery of these things, quickly acquires HIV, whereupon his relationships deteriorate and melt away, leaving him to face death alone, derided and ostracised by the neighbours.

The decent lad who you could take home to meet your mum is the film's only casualty of the collision between intravenous drug abuse and HIV. His opening character cameo, which has him in a corner of the football pitch and calling for help, to no avail, is acted out in the narrative. It is Tommy's function in the film to carry a clear-cut example of how random, cruel, and quick the descent to heroin and death could be, 1980s-style, in Leith. He makes only relatively brief appearances and he doesn't survive to the end of the film. Tommy's character and trajectory are firm roots in authenticity, permitting the others to act out a more discursive description of the heroin scene, taking liberties with narrative and taking advantage of cinematic licence. Tommy's part is brief and to the point. He is the only entirely convincing character in the film.

Diane (Kelly Macdonald)

Almost the first thing we hear from Diane is delivered in the style of a man-savvy gallus young Glasgow woman: 'The truth is that you're the quiet, sensitive type, but if I'm prepared to take a chance I might just get to know the inner you: witty, adventurous, passionate, loving, loyal, a little bit crazy, a little bit bad, but, hey, don't us girls just love that?' (p.34). Thereafter her register of speech changes, but we don't know her screen age until after she has had sex with Renton. This leaves Renton with absolutely no defence against the charge that he is a sex offender, a real concern in real life, and he remains tense about it. It's all passed off lightly, and it becomes a running joke: 'Too young for what?' (p.75) she asks scornfully as she invites herself in to Renton's flat where she can smell hash.

The character who provides the key to overcoming the Monster needs to be younger than Renton – his contemporaries and elders have had no success. In 1996 the *Independent on Sunday* reported that almost 70 per cent of young people with an average age of 19 years had experimented with an illegal drug in the previous six months, and a shade over 50 per cent of school leavers had experience of recreational drugs. Furthermore, whereas heroin in the previous decade had been predominantly a drug of the poor inner city areas, the new recreational drugs – ecstasy chief among them – had spread throughout society both economically and geographically. The government's 'Don't Die of Ignorance' campaign was by now well established; Diane shows she has been paying attention in her sex and health education classes when she throws a condom on the bed.

So we have this middle class school kid, (her school uniform, her parents' flat and the view from the window, are all clearly middle class) an attractive identifier for the core target audience of the film who had come to the realisation that heroin is dangerous some time earlier, maybe at around Diane's screen age. She and her 1996 audiences are comfortable in the rave scene while the sometime junkies are ill at ease.

The significant difference between Diane and Tommy is their age: if he had been, say, ten years younger, he, too, would have had health education at school, and the drug scene would have moved on. For the 1996 audience Tommy is the film's identifier with the unready, unfortunate generation of Leithers who found heroin so easily available and who were drawn to it with such catastrophic consequences. This is part of *Trainspotting*'s cachet; in addition to being entertained the audiences were expecting real history and grim reality. He tells a story of the 1980s, and she of the 1990s.

The plot doesn't require the one who gives the secret of overcoming the Monster to be a girl, but she is, and therein lies Diane's second important function. A film with an all-male cast of principal actors would have been a very different film. She brings nudity and a sex scene, pretty much a requirement for a film aimed at a young sexually active audience.

There isn't any space in this fast moving film for the lengthy professionalised rehab process for junkies. Diane fills the gap, with her simple unstated message that heroin is history, that junkies have nothing to offer and, stated, that Renton has to 'find something new' (p.76). Although it is she who persuades Renton that his choice is not between life with heroin and boring conventional life, but between heroin and a sporting chance of seeing the age of 30, it's important that she is not there at the end as he strides across the bridge to his bright new future. He couldn't be sharing it with her. She's young enough and wise enough to look after herself. This isn't a love story.

Johnny Swan (Peter Mullan)

The film needs a dealer. The problem for the film is that it needs two functions out of one character; does he fulfil either of them accurately or adequately?

The first is as the character, Mother Superior as the others like to call him. His nickname itself is a problem. He doesn't seem to be any older than the others; is he really old enough to have earned it? Besides, does he have a habit? He is in the shooting gallery the first time we meet him, but the only moment he is clearly reduced to the level of the others is when we see him and Alison shooting up. Otherwise he is always in charge, never out of control.

The other function is as a dealer. We only ever see him as a dealer in his squalid, semi-derelict but luridly lit 'flat', which is a cinematic depiction of the archetypal populist image of the dealer as wicked, subterranean and serpent-like. In the overdose scene he is completely professional: he insists on cash payment before providing Renton with the shot. But of course, this is contradicted by having allowed Renton credit in the past. No dealer ever allowed credit to a user.

Someone is needed by the requirements of the Plot to save the hero from death, by the narrowest of margins. This needs altruism and compassion. In the course of friendship, in the overdose scene, Swanney not only permits Renton to use in his flat, he even has the fix made up in a hypodermic syringe. But in historical reality the nearest a professional dealer ever got to his clients was through the letter box in a reinforced door. To the dealer, the user was just as much a risk and a liability as a paying customer. As far as the dealer was concerned, the user had to clear off immediately after the transaction.

Then, to make matters worse, after the overdose Swanney, now clearly acting as Renton's friend, pulls the comatose body into the street, waiting there for some time and clearly putting himself at high risk of being identified by the neighbours and then the taxi driver. There never was a nice-guy dealer. In addition to this departure from historical verisimilitude, the film wants us to believe that the Monster's salesman can also be the customer's saviour from the inevitable effects of the Monster's wares. It is against the Monster's instincts and interests to 'save' Renton. Would a dragon spare a village from his fire on compassionate grounds? It's not what dragons do.

These different functions are not compatible within one character. It doesn't work. In the fissures between the dealer and nice guy, the dispenser of heroin and the saving angel, there is too much space for critics to say that the film is somehow 'soft on drugs'. Although other scenes depict the squalor and dangers of the heroin scene, the dialogue and the onscreen action of the overdose sequence fail to depict how squalid and dangerous both the deal and shooting up really is.

The better known characters of Begbie, Sick Boy and Spud, who all enjoy far more exposure than these three, provide context and help the narrative outside the heroin drama.

Frank Begbie (Robert Carlyle)

Contingent on the centrality of Renton, the film needs a clear cut counter-point, an anti-hero. Outside the heroin drama, as far as the balance of dramatis personae is concerned, Begbie's character is the second most important. If Renton is the subversive, counter cultural figure who experiments with not only non-traditional drugs but also a new class of attitude and morality, we need someone rooted in conventional life. For all his abhorrent behaviour and attitudes, Begbie plays that role. His drugs – alcohol and tobacco – are traditional. His clothes – Pringles jumpers, rolled-up jeans and white socks – are traditional. His criminality – pub brawls, theft from a tourist, and 'armed' robbery – are traditional. His sexuality is traditional: 'I'm no a fucking buftie...' (p.83). And he demands traditional respect for a departed mate: no talking at Tommy's funeral. He takes time out from serious character-profiling for a moment of entertainment as he and Sick Boy jump from the top cupboard while would-be tenants are being shown round the flat.

His character is caught in the cameo in the opening football game: he commits a clear, outrageous foul and exults in his triumph. He goes on to commit fouls throughout the film, perhaps none more unpleasant than his gratuitous denouncement of Spud's mum after her son has been sent down: '... your boy went down because he was a fucking smack head, and if that's not your fault, I don't know what is' (p.59). He enjoys self-aggrandising: the nervous, sycophantic smiles and deferential glances among his listeners in the pub as he tells his version of the game of pool, and the air of childish wonder as they watch him in the fight below, seem to exist only in his own imagination. Begbie's function in the film is to be the totally unsympathetic character.

Although his character is reasonably plausible, and it plays an essential part in the structure of the film, there remain several problems around Begbie. Despite Tommy's remark: 'The Beggar is a fucking psycho, but he's a mate, you know, so what can you do?' (p.26) it is far from clear what is the basis for his friendship with and involvement in the group. He is not involved in the heroin scene at all, or the sex scenes, or the trip to the mountains. He takes no part in the opportunist thieving, except in the case of the American tourist. He puts himself in charge of divvying up the money afterwards.

Although his criminal tendencies and experience may commend him for the biggest project of all – taking the 2kg of heroin to London – it is this that is the most implausible of his criminal enterprises. His style is violence, not negotiation. He should know that drug-dealing is specialist business. He breaks a golden rule: never trust a junkie, and the distrust should be mutual. He is out of his depth when it comes to negotiating with Andreas, but in the aftermath he recovers his position as cock of the roost – until, that is, he is outwitted by Renton. In our final view of him he is reduced to the pantomime villain, an object of ridicule now our main man has got clean away as, in his rage at being ripped off, he smashes up the room. The approaching police are his just deserts. For all his threat and bombast, he can be forgotten. We can join Renton who, on his way out, 'couldn't give a shit about him' (p.105). This disappearance serves to centralise Renton, again.

Sick Boy (Jonny Lee Miller)

If we have identified Begbie as the out-and-out antagonist, we have no grounds for saying that Sick Boy is not an equally 'bad guy'. His opening cameo on the football field is no nicer than Begbie's as he commits a sneaky foul and denies it. For the first part of the film he is fully engaged in the heroin scene, at one point so much so that he falls back with the needle still in his arm. His faux-formal speech and pretentious ideas about Sean Connery make him seem somewhat apart and superior from the others, at least in his own eyes. We notice that Sick Boy is not involved in any of the sex scenes (it would be pornographic – there wouldn't be much fun or satisfaction about it). Up to the death of the baby – his baby, it seems – his character is presented with a light touch. The worst you can say of him is that he is a pretty boy and a bit of a smart-arse.

Afterwards, with the self-discipline to stop using heroin, he becomes infuriating: 'There's better things than the needle, Rents. Choose life!' (p.59). And: 'It's a mug's game, Mrs Renton... there comes a time when you have to turn your back on that nonsense and just say no' (p.66). Then he gets nasty. He turns to pimping, stealing from Renton, even offering to sell his very identity (his passport). Although he is intimidated by Begbie in the bus to London, the whole scam is his operation – look at the way he leads the troupe of four to the hotel – and he makes it clear that he would have, and will if his chance comes, make off with the proceeds of the sale. For sheer unpleasantness, you couldn't get a cigarette paper between Begbie and Sick Boy, but for the functionality of the film, Sick Boy has been aligned as Renton's problem friend. Their trajectories diverge, again serving to mark out Renton as the central character.

Spud (Ewen Bremner)

And what of everyone's favourite, Spud? Renton makes it clear that Spud is the favoured one: early on he is 'proud' (p.23) of Spud, and his final words about him tell us he feels 'sorry for him. He never hurt anybody' (p.106).

Lanky and poorly co-ordinated, he is the fall guy, the Charlie Chaplin of the film, the oversized glasses being the equivalent of the toothbrush moustache and the bowler hat. He is a masterful comic as he screws up his job interview; his tussle with Gail's mum over the soiled sheets is pure slapstick; and his opportunity for 'casual sex' (p.36), as Gail puts it, is missed in disappointing circumstances. Just as in his opening cameo on the football field he is hopelessly out of position and ill-equipped to deal with the oncoming opposition, he is defenceless against the sheriff's judgement: 'Mr Murphy, you are a habitual thief, devoid of regret or remorse' (p.57). In a touch of historical verisimilitude, he is the sap who goes to prison.

He starts out an enthusiastic heroin user and opportunist thief. He has to be contradicted when he says 'it's going to be alright' (p.54) as the baby is found dead, but there are no hard feelings or recriminations. Although in Renton's cold turkey nightmarish hallucinations he appears to resent having been imprisoned, there is no sign of grievance in the real Spud later. He recovers, miraculously, from being in the gutter (clearly prison didn't change his lifestyle) as Diane passes by, to lead the quiet tribute to Tommy after the funeral. Although he has very recently – on the bus – been a needy junkie, again, with the money on the table in front of them in the pub in London, he says he would like to 'get a girl... and treat her – properly' (p.100). So he really is a nice guy – we were assuming he wanted it for more drugs. He knows at the end that Renton is making off with the money (his money), and is passive enough to let him go ahead without raising the alarm. Once again, Renton is prioritised.

We have already established that this film does not tell a plausible narrative. This analysis shows that neither is it primarily concerned with depicting fully coherent character. But this is hardly the point. As Xan Brooks points out, Boyle succeeds in making his characters neither 'monsters nor pathetic case studies'.[78] They are interesting, different and memorable.

CHAPTER 26

Broader Appeals

Trainspotting the Music Fest

BEFORE EVER SEEING the film, to the early audiences the *Trainspotting* cachet spelled heroin, counter-culture, and Scotland. They discovered, to their great delight, that there was more: the musical score is an intelligent compilation of heroin-related and counter-cultural tracks. *Trainspotting* is one of very few films to be reviewed in *New Musical Express*, a clear indication of its merit in purely musical terms. It won the 1997 Brit Award for best soundtrack. If British music had asserted itself since the Beatles in the 1960s, British cinema had not kept pace, and this is an example of one art form using another for its own purposes. The only prominent element in the film that is not represented musically is Scotland – there are no bagpipes, fiddles or accordions.

Tastes within a generation are diverse and eclectic. Comprehensive the playlist could never be. Inclusive and ambitious it certainly is. Thrown in for good measure are Bizet's *Carmen-Habanera*, a passage from J S Bach's *Hertzlich tut mich verlangen*, and a verse from a simple Australian folk song. The film even works in a blatant non-audial Beatles moment in the four figures crossing the street in London in the same fashion as the quartet from Liverpool on the front of their famous 1969 *Abbey Road* album. That's our braw lads from Scotland hitting town like the big boys. Heaven 17's *Temptation* playing in the Volcano club, combined with the writing on the wall behind Tommy and Spud, is a clear reference to *A Clockwork Orange* (Kubrick, 1971). It all does a lot towards broadening the film's appeal.

The music is certainly not only British: key parts of the action, especially the heroin-related moments, are strongly associated with USA output. The net effect was to appeal to a wide spectrum of culturally aware people in their 20s and 30s and beyond. Recognising the quality of the musical compilation, the promoters Polygram released the musical sound track as a freestanding item simultaneously with the film; in marketing terms, music and screen fed off each other as much as they do within the film itself.

In addition to the references to David Bowie in *Trainspotting* the book, especially in the title of the last chapter, Bowie's willingness to collaborate with Boyle may well stem from his contribution of the entire musical sound track – in the form of the cocaine-fuelled *Station to Station* – to that other heroin film, *Christiana F.* (Edel, 1982). Bowie proved to be instrumental in gaining the approval of Iggy Pop and Lou Reed, with both of whom he had collaborated, for permission to use some of their output. All three were known to have a relationship with various drugs, and their work musically underpins the film's relationship with heroin. All three are referenced in the dialogue, and not in any sycophantic terms. Sick Boy says of Reed's 'stuff': 'it's not bad, but it's not that great either' (p.16). As far as Lizzy is concerned, Tommy makes the wrong decision in preferring an Iggy Pop concert to marking her birthday. And Diane, in her youthfulness, confuses Iggy Pop with Bowie's creation Ziggy Stardust and confidently asserts that they are out of date anyway and Renton should move on.

Bowie stands behind several features of the film. He probably also brought Brian Eno to the film with his *Deep Blue Day*, played as Renton swims down to collect his suppositories. Bowie's relationship with Andy Warhol associates him with the distressed, multicoloured images of Diane in her bedroom. Begbie's encounter with androgyny in the London club is in keeping with Bowie's influence. Neither of these details is in the book. There is clearly a tribute to Bowie in Renton's internal monologue on the bus to London as he reflects on 'final hits and final hits. What kind was this to be?' He goes on: 'Some final hits are actually terminal one way or another, while others are merely transit points as you travel from station to station on the junkie journey through a junkie life' (p.96). Sadly, the last sentence hit the cutting room floor. Bowie's talent for collaboration and his prolific creative genius for crossing art forms should bring him far more credit than he is given for his contribution to *Trainspotting* the film. Crucially, in Welsh and Bowie, Boyle found himself working with material whose creators were enthusiastic about reworking their output.

The rest of the music forms a body and has a structure of its own. The Britpop pieces by Pulp, Blur, Elastica and Sleeper ostensibly belong to the early 1990s – the 1996 audiences were brought up on them – and there are several references back to the 1980s. The 30-somethings in the audience would recall their own youthful romances to Blondie's *Atomic* in the early 1980s; Sleeper's cover version begins while Diane is on screen for the first time and plays throughout the apparently simultaneous sex scenes, any aspect of which the audiences could, in good humour, identify with. Pulp's *Mile End* complains about dodgy accommodation as Renton sets about a career in the scamming business. Elastica's *2.1*, played in the club where Begbie meets the transvestite, is an update from Heaven 17's *Temptation* way back in the Volcano.

Then there is the techno-dance music by Bedrock and Ice MC belonging to the very period of the launch of the film; their pieces are dated 1996 in the accompanying cd. Primal Scream's piece is even titled *Trainspotting*, and the audience goes out to Damon Albarn's *Closet Romantic*, sounding like an old-fashioned cinema organ and with lyrics, a listing of several James Bond titles which, if the song wasn't written and played for this film would be cryptic indeed. Without attaching itself directly to the storyline, the music makes an unmistakeable progression through history. Within a broad musical framework the audiences were living their recent past, their present, and were moving into the next phase, all within the film. It was thrilling. Boyle wanted the film to 'pulse', like you do in your 20s.

Far from Will Self's put-down remark that the film is like a pop video, by which, presumably, he meant that it is little more than animations to go along with the interests of the music industry, as Murray Smith points out, 'It would be hard to overestimate the "value added" by the songs to the meaning and emotional force of the film'.[78]

What Sort of Film?

Trainspotting the film crashes through the assumption that social comment, satire, feel-good, surreality, grim reality, storytelling, slapstick, good music, death and box office success can't be contained in one artistic expression. It's a good trick if you can pull it off. What's the secret?

Firstly, it is fiction. No straightforward history or academic treatise, however meritorious, could have done it. Fiction employs the intellect, the imagination, and emotions, demanding a response from the reader/audience. Fiction always intersects with reality at some point. Reality in this case is, variously, the heroin experience, youthful bravado and folly, and ambition. *Trainspotting* pulls us through defiance, dismay, desperation, despair, fun, anxiety, pain, sadness, loyalty, disloyalty, death, sex, and profound optimism. All this is reality; *Trainspotting* relates to it all.

Fiction can contain great truths. Good fiction does not tell its audiences what to think or believe. To paraphrase what Lou Reed said of one of his songs, it isn't for heroin, it isn't against heroin, it's about heroin. Heroin is there. *Trainspotting* doesn't ask how heroin gets there, nor makes any comment to the effect that it shouldn't be there. It doesn't ask why people are drawn to heroin, they just are. *Trainspotting* works as a discursive, metaphorical, descriptive, incomplete Junkie's Progress. You didn't have to know a junkie, or be particularly close to the scene, to be very well aware that heroin and HIV/AIDS was one of the great issues in public life in the 1990s, and seeing the film created opportunities to discuss it. It also works as an assertion of youthful *joie de vivre*, or lust for life. A whole generation could relate very strongly to it. Far from being weakened by being an adaptation of a book, without doubt it benefitted from having a hinterland. People knew that this was no cinematic confectionery.

Trainspotting also caught a political 1990s zeitgeist. It is a parody and a satire of Thatcherism for a generation that was just about to comprehensively reject it in the 1997 general election. It was also the first genuinely popular and contemporary presentation of the creed as problem-free and fun; and here it is carried by a likeable exponent. In our first close-up of Renton he looks directly at the camera – you, the audience. As he goes out, looking forward to using the proceeds of the illegal deal and theft he says he is going to be 'just like you', the audience. We thought the film was about heroin – now it requires reflection and some intellectual processes not to be caught up in the onward rush and find oneself, with Renton as our model, implicitly endorsing free-market thinking against one's previous instincts. To the mid-late 1990s audiences, this was subtle and edgy.

Secondly, the film itself was ruthlessly marketed as a hot, branded, consumer item, obeying all the laws of market capitalism. It was a good return on investment: costing $3m, by 2008 it had grossed more than $64m. In 1996, already the book and the play were feeding each other. Now came the film at the cinema, the video, the DVD, and, later, special editions with scenes deleted from the version for general release, and interviews with the makers; the posters, the t-shirts, and the screenplay in book form, complete with more interviews; all interconnected. Furthermore, it made everyone concerned with the production a good deal wealthier, not only financially but profiles, careers and prospects were also considerably enhanced. The cultural impact and the commercial success, enormous in both cases, went hand in hand. People were more than happy to buy into the *Trainspotting* phenomenon, both financially and metaphorically.

So it is not completely transgressional. Indeed, on this view it subverts its own transgressional message: capitalism has neutralised criticism of itself. Duncan Petrie says that '*Trainspotting* becomes the ideal Blairite product, conspicuously displaying its "coolness" via a hip edginess masquerading as transgression, but ultimately affirming the self-conscious, self-regarding and starkly depoliticised state of contemporary British society'.[79] Welsh immunised himself from such comments by asking not to be expected to be consistent in an inconsistent world. As Murray Smith summarises, it was 'punchy, slick and commercially savvy'.[80] It certainly fed discussions in the pubs and online.

Whatever one's own judgement of the quality of the film, its sheer success at the box office secures for it a significant place in the history of cinema, not only in the decade of its release.

Danny Boyle, Director

It is a mark of Boyle's genius that he was creative in so many aspects of the film. He stands out not as a dictatorial director, an *auteur*, but as an inspirational leader of a capable and creative team. His later career helps throw some light on his early work. Boyle now has almost a couple of dozen films to his credit as director (and other involvement in many others), some of them flops. What made him a household name in UK, however, was not a film but his direction of the opening ceremony of the London Olympics, 2012. Cutting across stereotypes, he's the professed leftwinger, chosen by the Tories to open the London Olympics and the republican who offered the queen the opportunity to play a Bond girl on the night (she was pleased to do so), to her great advantage.

He did more than save us from what otherwise might have been state propaganda or useless commercial gimmickry. His triumph was to launch and celebrate a new sense of Britishness, updating what had been an England-centric harking back to the days of Empire. With style, panache, stunning displays and sheer showmanship, he recorded a People's History of all the British Isles and celebrated the vibrant, multi-cultural country Britain has become, with its strong state institutions such as the welfare state, the National Health Service, and the BBC. He also straddled the arts, giving music great prominence. He gave the mantra of the government of the day: 'We're all in this together' a meaning that was never intended by its cynical creators. He later refused to do interviews in which he would have soaked up the glory, and he declined a peerage because he believes in 'equal citizenship'.

Looking back, we can see that *Trainspotting*, and some of his other films, is in the same creative vein and contains similar themes: this is everyone's story; everyone has a right to be heard, regardless of social status; even in the midst of dangers and problems, life is greatly to be celebrated; many things are true, and one truth does not necessarily contradict another; it doesn't do to moralise; and serious content and intellectual rigour can sit alongside whacky, off-the-wall entertainment. Of course, there are some sleights of hand; they are part of the entertainer's craft. Everyone had something to identify with in the Olympic opening ceremony, as in *Trainspotting*. People are entertained, challenged, uplifted, and have something to talk about. History has more than vindicated Welsh's decision to entrust his own creation to Boyle for transformation into another medium. We are all grateful that their meeting in the Glasgow Film Theatre, way back in 1994, went so well.

Reviews of and Comments on Trainspotting the Film

'A dark and ironic take on young junkies at their anti-social worst, directed with terrific energy and style, a witty subversion of the usual documentary approach to such subjects, and excellently acted by its ensemble cast.'

Gritten, David (ed) (2008). *Halliwell's Film Video & DVD Guide*. London: HarperCollins.

'Spends far too much time with its nose pressed up against the glass of American cinema, desperate for a piece of the action, but merely fogging up the screen with longing. Until British cinema kicks this habit, it will continue to churn out films such as this, which bear the same relation to real filmmaking the drugs do to real pleasure. It's utterly empty: a cold turkey, despite the fancy trimmings.'

Tom Shone, *Sunday Times*, quoted in *Halliwell's* (ibid).

'An extraordinary achievement and a breakthrough British film'
Derek Malcolm, *Guardian*, quoted in *Halliwell's* (ibid).

'For all its brilliance, the film finally feels sour and hollow.'
Sheila Johnston, quoted in *Halliwell's* (ibid).

'Clockwork Orange for the 90s.'
Variety, quoted in *Halliwell's* (ibid).

'A shocking, painfully subjective trawl through the Edinburgh heroin culture of the 1980s, Irvine Welsh's cult novel is hardly an obvious choice for the team who made *Shallow Grave*. Yet the film is a triumph. Audaciously punching up the pitch black comedy, juggling parallel character strands and juxtaposing image, music and voiceover with a virtuosity worthy of Scorsese on peak form, *Trainspotting* the movie captures precisely Welsh's insolent, amoral intelligence. Amoral, but not unthinking, and certainly not unfeeling. Nihilism runs deep in this movie, emotion cannot be countenanced, only blocked off by another hit, another gag, but the anarchic, exhilarating rush of the highs can't drown out the subsequent devastating lows – these are two sides of the same desperation. Danny Boyle's intuitive, empathetic direction pushes so far, the movie flies on sheer momentum – that and bravura performances from Bremner's gormless Spud, Carlyle's terrifying Begbie, and, especially, McGregor's Renton, who supplies a low key charismatic centre. This may not have the weight of 'Great Art', but it crystallises youthful disaffection with the verve of the best and brightest pop culture. A sensation.'

TCh (2011). *Halliwell's Filmgoer's and video viewer's Guide 9th edition*. London: Grafton Books.

'*Trainspotting* – film of the year. Already! *Trainspotting* is probably the most important film about modern Britain in nearly a decade... a harrowing social document, but free from that grim, kitchen-sink misery... like *Naked* [Leigh, 1993]. Best of all, it succeeds where attempted 'yoof' films like *Shopping* [Anderson, 1994] failed, in showing some of the exhilaration, the *fun* of transgression... and it *looks* brilliant in a way that British films never do; there's no washed-out grainy colour, and there are no long pauses or shots of people staring into space.'

NME Monthly, March 1996. Published by Vox, *IPC Magazines*

'Church of Scotland spokesman, the Rev. Bill Wallace, had this to say to the Daily Telegraph: 'It is sad that this is the best filmmakers can turn their minds to.'

Alona Wartofsky, in *The Washington Post*, July 21, 1996.

'[*Trainspotting* has a] shallow, joyless ring... it embraces a new soulless addiction to materialism... it is fitting that Renton's face blurs as the voice-over proclaims his intentions to become an anonymous, unremarkable consumer.'

Dyja, Eddie (2017). *Studying the British Cinema: The 1990s*. Leighton Buzzard: Auteur. p49.

'This is an important and original film, which because of its popularity will provide some enduring stereotypes of drug addicts, both for themselves and for the general population. Psychiatrists who ignore this film would do well to remember that the dominant image in society of electroconvulsive therapy comes not from the public information literature of the Royal College of Psychiatrists, but from *One Flew Over the Cuckoo's Nest* (1975). The film has begun a debate about today's drug users ('Generation why not?') who are 'not crazed radicals, not junkies on a slow decline into the gutter, but discerning consumers who decide exactly how much they want to take, when, where and how often'.[81] Psychiatry should contribute to this discussion.'

Byrne, Peter: *Trainspotting* and the depiction of addiction. *Psychiatric Bulletin* 1997, 21:173-175.

Bob Dole today denounced what he termed the glorification of heroin and other drugs by the entertainment industry and led a high school gym filled with teen-agers in chanting a new slogan that he presented as the center of his drug-fighting strategy: 'Just don't do it.'

Mr. Dole said President Clinton shared responsibility with the entertainment industry for the surge in drug use by teen-agers. He said the President displayed 'moral confusion' for having joked... about his youthful experimentation with marijuana.

'There can be no question that the trendiest trend of our popular culture is the return of drug use,' Mr. Dole told his young audience, gathered for a morning assembly at a Roman Catholic preparatory high school... 'Stars too young to have seen the devastation of drugs in the 1960's now seem intent on repeating it. The marijuana leaf and the heroin needle have become the symbols of fashionable rebellion.'

Mr. Dole, in a theme of his Presidential campaign, blamed the entertainment industry and the White House for the turn of events. He picked out two contemporary movies – 'Pulp Fiction' and the British film '*Trainspotting*' – that he said promoted "the romance of heroin."

Adam Nagourney: *Attacking Drugs, Dole Takes On Entertainment Industry*: New York Times, 19 September, 1996

(Bob Dole later said he had not seen *Trainspotting*.)

'[*Trainspotting*] combined a darting, bracing, stylistically innovative mode of storytelling usually found in the American Indies with an inner-city British landscape traditionally documented in stolid social-realist terms. *Trainspotting* was both surrealistic and naturalistic, fantastical and gritty, hip and harrowing. It trod a dangerous thematic tightrope and did so with a confidence and panache that took the breath away.'

Xan Brooks (1998). *Choose Life: Ewan McGregor and the British Film Revival*. Glasgow: Chameleon Books. p93.

The Trainspotting Phenomenon

The *Trainspotting* phenomenon (the book, the play and the film) addressed an issue – heroin abuse and HIV/AIDS – that urgently needed to be discussed between generations, politicians and professional disciplines. 'Trainspotting' became a byword for transgression, for bucking convention, for coolness. Variations were easily recognised: 'nerd-spotting', 'politician-spotting', and so on. On becoming a cultural icon, it caught the mood of the moment such that politicians rode its bandwagon. It gave Scotland a voice in its own right. It was not the language of Hollywood, nor of London. It was modern, urban, disrespectful, and undeniably and authentically Scottish. It woke up overseas audiences to the existence of Scotland as distinct from England. Claims that it singlehandedly made the case for the 1997 referendum on devolution to Scotland are overstated, but it certainly joined in a Scottish clamour that was getting noisier.

We are indebted to Irvine Welsh for his original work. The whole *Trainspotting* phenomenon could not have come to fruition, however, without the creative contributions of, in chronological order, Robin Robertson, Harry Gibson, Giles Havergal, Ian Brown, Andrew MacDonald, John Hodge, and Danny Boyle and their production team.

Postscript

Welsh has often been asked what he thinks of the 'gentrification' in Leith since his day. He puts one answer into Sick Boy's mouth in *Porno*, purportedly around 2002: Newly returned from London, he says that 'grand old thoroughfare [Leith Walk] look[s] much the same as ever... like a very expensive old Axminster carpet. It might be a bit dark and faded, but it's still got enough quality about it to absorb society's inevitable crumbs.'[82] His aunt Paula has asked him to take over her pub Port Sunshine, which is a thin disguise for the actual Port o' Leith pub, where Welsh used to meet his writing group:

> The place is a potential gold mine, just waiting for a make-over job. You can feel the gentrification creeping up from the Shore and forcing house prices up and I can hear the tills ringing as I give the Port Sunshine a tart-up from Jakey Central to New Leith Café Society... Leith is on the up. It'll be on the Tube line before Hackney... I'm walking down into the new Leith: the Royal Yacht Britannia, the Scottish Office, renovated docks, wine bars, restaurants, yuppie pads. This is the future and it's only two blocks away. The next year, the year after maybe, just one block away. Then bingo![83]

Well, he wasn't so far wrong. The pavement on the west side of Constitution Street, catching the morning sun, has been broadened and nicely slabbed, and there is indeed a clutch of cafés in the immediate vicinity, tables and seating outside in the new style. It's all very far from when the Port o' Leith was known as the dockers' bank, where some of them 'deposited' their week's wages on Friday evenings after work before getting home. In the first years of this century you would think Leith was a suburb of Ocean Terminal, the shopping mall built on the site of Henry Robb's shipyard, of very recent memory. Now Leith is on some tourist maps issued in Edinburgh, but only showing the streets on the west side of the Water of Leith where there are more attractions and open spaces.

'Gentrification' or 'yuppification' are curious terms. They carry negative, disapproving connotations. If the question is: has Leith shaken off its roughness and become generally more wealthy? The answer, on the whole, is yes. However, in the council's Leith ward 25 per cent of the children live in poverty, and there are 3,700 working people in poverty. Despite the excellent projects of the Port of Leith Housing Association, around the city private landlords own more than the council and social landlords combined and property and rent prices have soared throughout the city, including Leith. The march of austerity and neo-liberalism, combined with the centralising tendencies of the government at Holyrood, leave the council vulnerable to exploitative and inappropriate developments. One jewel in the crown is Lothian Buses, municipally owned and regularly winning awards.

In the referendum of 2016 Edinburgh Northern and Leith constituency voted 78 per cent to remain in the European Union, one of the very highest proportions in the UK. This reflects a very cosmopolitan community. One hears many people saying that Leith is a good place to live, and the community spirit is often quoted as the main reason. The well-established annual Leith Festival in the second week of June is a showcase for diverse talents, and the Festival organises a good many events at other times of the year.

Leith is a happier place than it was in the *Trainspotting* days, but the use of illegal drugs remains a problem and a scandal. Almost a thousand people died in Scotland as a direct result of a drug overdose in 2017, the highest since records began and the highest per capita level in the UK and Europe. This is five times higher than traffic fatalities. Around one half of them are aged over 35, thus putting them into what is publicly referred to as 'the Trainspotting generation'. Opiates and opioids – opium, heroin, methadone – were implicated in almost 90 per cent of cases. The deaths of many drug-dependant people arising out of a combination of complex and longstanding medical problems, often associated with poor diet and rough living, are not recorded in these statistics. It is reckoned there are about 61,000 drug-dependant people in Scotland.

The legal situation of the drug scene is unchanged from the 1980s: heroin, along with several other Class A drugs, is illegal, and prison awaits those caught with anything more than a tiny amount which is clearly for immediate personal use. But public awareness has improved and support systems for drug dependency have been put on a proper footing. New agencies are now properly funded out of public health budgets. Social care charity Turning Point Scotland offers a service in Leith aimed not only at harm reduction and recovery support but it also addresses some root problems. Since substance abuse, including alcohol, is associated with several indicators such as homelessness, poverty, and mental health, it offers a range of services under one roof: needle exchange, acupuncture, cooking, gardening, peer support, and building up of self-confidence through one-to-one and group sessions. Working alongside NHS medical staff is a multidisciplinary team of practitioners and peer volunteers who have 'lived experience' of recovering from addiction, who are prepared to listen and give support. Working with the Scottish Ambulance Service, staff are notified of non-fatal overdoses in the area, and they will call at the home of the person following discharge from hospital offering support and advice along with life-saving Take Home Naloxone.

A bewilderingly complex range of novel psychoactive substances is available, from local dealers and the dark web. With supply chains stretched longer than they were, drugs at street level are of very uncertain quality. For a period, dealers can earn a reputation for supplying reasonably good gear, and thus recruit a loyal customer base, but the market-place is highly unstable so nothing lasts for long. You can get drugs in prison, though the range might be limited. Prison can be a difficult place to try to stop using. One person with experience says 'The only time you are likely to be offered a free hit is when you're trying to quit, and those around you want to bring you down to their level.'

There are presently explorations to provide 'safe spaces' or 'consumption rooms' for the taking of drugs, but problems are caused by the illegality of the substances coupled with an antipathetic consensus throughout wider society. Dr Roy Robertson, at the forefront of compassionately treating drug dependency since the 1980s in Muirhouse and Professor of Addiction Medicine in the University of Edinburgh Usher Institute, supports this proposal.

The situation regarding HIV in Scotland has changed dramatically since the days of *Trainspotting*. With much earlier diagnosis and more effective treatment, only a handful of HIV+ people in Scotland now develop AIDS. Retro-virals normally permit a healthy and long life. Gay and bi-sexual men are around half of Scotland's new diagnoses, while hetero-sexuality is the transmission route for just over 30 per cent. Drug injection as a transmission route accounts for most of the remainder, although this percentage has recently risen significantly since the low of 5 per cent in 2014. The increase is probably explained by the eventual emergence of a group of hard-to-reach drug injecting people in Glasgow city centre. The calculation is that of Scotland's almost 6,000 people with HIV, around 13 per cent are unaware of it. In 2017 there were 368 new diagnoses of HIV.

In Scotland PREP (Pre-Exposure Phrophylactic) can be prescribed subject to some eligibility criteria. This is different from England, where it is not available on prescription. If used as prescribed it can reduce the risk of acquiring HIV through sex by 90 per cent, and through injecting by

70 per cent. The first eight months of this regime are encouraging; take-up is higher than was expected, and there is evidence that users are accessing other supports and means of preventing infection – in other words, it is helpful in getting people to be positively engaged in and responsible for their own life-style and health. It is expensive, but part of the argument is that not to judiciously prescribe it incurs greater expense in the long run.

It is part of the thesis of this book that problematic drug use is a health and social inequality issue, and the associated stigma is due in large part to the criminalisation of the substances. The collision between intra-venous drug injecting and HIV in Muirhouse was a collision waiting to happen. If we keep focussing on a deficit model, we will keep getting the same results. Education, prevention and harm reduction, along with the creation of a more equable society, are more important than ever.

Meanwhile in Muirhouse, where things went so wrong so fast in the 1970s and 1980s, there are great changes afoot. The worst of the 1960s buildings have been demolished, and in what is the largest public house building programme in the UK (possibly the largest in Europe) the area is in the throes of exciting new developments. The dreadful shopping centre is disappearing, to be replaced by a sort of civic square, where local businesses and a variety of community enterprises will be encouraged to take premises. Avoiding the mistake half a century ago, there is a mix of house and flat ownership and tenancy, with the involvement of the local Muirhouse Housing Association and some private developers, whose role is carefully co-ordinated with everything else. Taking advantage of the desirability of Edinburgh in the national housing market, the intention is to attract a full range of people to come and live in Muirhouse. It is conveniently placed for the city and the airport, and the nearby Silverknowes Foreshore is an attractive part of the neighbourhood.

There is a strong community spirit, underpinned by a locally produced booklet 'Never Give Up' – it looks like a direct take from the Persevere motto of Leith, from where many of the older residents came – which traces the developments of the scheme from the days when it was farmers' fields in the early years of the last century, through the bad years of the 1970s and 1980s to the present. Throughout there is a sense of solidarity and good purpose. Newcomers from around the world are actively welcomed, and local groups act if there is any sign of racism or other hostilities. Craigroyston Community High School is in new premises, as is the Health Centre. Walking round the area now, one sees several cultural and community facilities, all well used. There is a palpable sense of strength and well-being. Muirhouse has the opportunity to get the best from hard experience and co-ordinated, creative, well-funded redevelopment. The next story of social malfunction in Edinburgh will not emanate from Muirhouse.

Trainspotting the brand is here to stay. Now that a variety of establishments, from tourist boards, to the literati, to psychiatrists and medics, to Leithers themselves, we're still waiting for the politicians, all recognise the importance of Welsh's seminal work, *Trainspotting* will be associated with Leith in much the same way as Lewis Grassic Gibbon's *Sunset Song* is associated with the Mearns and Emily Bronte's *Wuthering Heights* is associated with the Yorkshire Pennines. There have been sequels and updates: Welsh has said he has killed off Renton, Sick Boy, Spud and Begbie in his most recent book, *Dead Men's Trousers*[84] although only one of them actually dies; Harry Gibson's play is still being staged around the world; and there is Danny Boyle's sequel, *T2 Trainspotting*[85], loosely based on the book's sequel *Porno*. But the brand doesn't depend on sequels and updates. The heroin story is universal, which explains its world-wide appeal, but it always takes place somewhere, in someone's neighbourhood, in someone's family. *Trainspotting* took place in Leith.

Tim Bell
Leith, April 2018

GLOSSARY

Glossary of terms and vocabulary in *Trainspotting* by Irvine Welsh

ace	winning card
affie	afternoon
Ah	I
ain	own
alko *(noun)*	an alcoholic
Approved School	a semi-secure school for children with significant behaviour problems; correctly known in Scotland as a 'List D' school since 1968
arrays	arrows: darts
arse *(verb)*	to consume
Augies	St Augustine's Roman Catholic School
auld	old
aw	all/oh
aw aye	oh yes
awfay	awful
ay	of
ay oop	expression from northern England meaning 'hello'
aye	yes
ayesur	'yes sir'; a sign of deference and obedience associated with Catholics and lower working class
bag off	pair up
bairn	baby, child
baith	both
bam / bampot	stupid *or* wild person
bang	fuck
banged up	imprisoned
bar	pounds (cash)
Barrowland	former ballroom, now gig venue in street-market area of Glasgow
barry	excellent
baws	balls
beamer	a blush
bell	telephone call *(noun)*; to ring, to telephone *(verb)*
ben	the other room in a house
bevvy	abbreviation of *beverage*; drink, always meaning alcoholic drink
billy	bully
Billy Whizz	speed; after a cartoon character who moves at super-human speed who appeared in the *Beano* from 1963 (*see also* 'heap big medicine man')
birl	spin
biscuit-ersed	anxious; fragile
bit	house / place to live; short period
blaw	something to smoke: tobacco or hash
blether	informal *and/or* inconsequential conversation
blootered	drunk
boak	vomit
boatil	bottle (*see also* **bottle**)
boatum	bottom
Bobby Sands	elected Member of British Parliament while in prison; the first to die in prison in hunger strike in protest of British 'occupation' of Northern Ireland
bog	toilet
bollocks	testicles; *also* rubbish

bonnie — nice, pretty;

boot — (ugly) woman

boozer — pub (bar)

bothir — trouble

bottle *(noun)* — courage; determination

bottle oot *(verb)* — duck; avoid, too scared to do something

Bowtow — local nickname for Newhaven

box — head

brar — brother

brass — money

brassic — without money; *abbreviated from brassic lint ie a medical dressing, then rhyming slang with skint*

bread — money

Brownie points — points awarded for good effort in the Brownies, the junior Girl Guides – widely mildly ridiculed as meaningless reward for small but genuine effort

buftie — gay male; *pejorative term used by macho straight men*

bugger — person: *(mildly offensive term)*: describes anal intercourse, the action and the person.

bung — loan *or* gift

burd — bird: girl *or* girlfriend

C — cancer

cairds — cards, playing cards

cairry-oot — takeaway food *or* drink

cauld — cold

Charlotte Square — concentration of finance offices in 1980s; former venue of Edinburgh International Book Festival

chaser — half pint of beer to go with a nip of whisky

chib / chibbed — knife / knifed

chippy — joiner

chist — chest

choc-box — anus

chory — light-fingered stealing; shoplifting

chuffed — pleased

chum *(verb)* — accompany

City — City Hospital, specialising in infectious diseases; adapted for early HIV surgery and Milestone House hospice was built within the grounds

civvy street — civilian life

clathes — clothes

clock *(verb)* — register

close — alley-way; *traditional in Edinburgh; so-called because they were closed for security reasons at night*

cmoan — *see* moan

collies — drugs; *abbreviated rhyming slang with dug (dog)*

connin(g) — deceiving

cookin(g) — preparing heroin for injection

cop (out) — opt out

Coronation Street — well-known TV soap opera based in northern England

Corstorphine — suburb on Glasgow Road, Edinburgh

coupon — face

cowp (ower) — tip (over); unbalance

crack — talk, conversation

crack (it) — solve (a situation, problem)

Craigy — Craigroyston High School

crash — sleep

craw (shoot the) — go; *crow (shoot the)*

cruising — surveying and searching for a response

cry — call, name

cuntya / cuntcha / cuntchy — you cunt

cut (gear) — drugs mixed with other substances

daein	doing	eftir	after; *also afternoon, after-*
dahnt	don't *(London accent)*		*wards or later*
Daniel Stewart's	Edinburgh private school	eighty	80 shilling – beer brand name
		ersed	can't be bothered
dead	very	(cannae be)	
deek	look, see	Eton	very expensive private
deid	dead		school in England, often
didnae	didn't		used to symbolise the top of
dig *(verb)*	approve, understand		the established, privileged
dippet	unintelligent		classes
disnae	doesn't	Export	brand of Scottish beer
dive	wretched place	ey / eywis	always
divvi (up)	divide (up)	fae	from
doaktir	doctor	Famous Five	five members of the famous
dole	government unemployment		Hibernian team in 1950s
	benefit. *from Anglo-Saxon:*	faw	fall
	pity, or pity-money, charity.	feart	afraid
	Modern use refers to entitle-	felly	fellow: man, partner
	ment, not charity	Fenian	Irish nationalist; can also
dole-mole	person taking unemployment		carry a derogatory, offensive
	benefit		reference to Irish Catholics
doll	mildly sexist term for a female	fi	from
donks	a long time; *variation of yonks*	first foot	the tradition of stepping over
doon	down		a threshold for the first time in
doss	stupid, useless		a New Year
dough	money	Fit ay Leith	Foot of Leith Walk; heart of
down	widely used to relativise Lon-	Walk	Leith; landmark road junction
	don and Scotland	fitba	football
	geographically: 'up' to Scot-	fiver	five-pound note
	land and 'down' to London	flat-top	hairstyle of the period
down (go / send)	go / send to prison	flick knife	knife with a single, easily openable blade,
downer	bad experience / bad mood	flunky	condom
draftpak	cardboard case of beer cans	flush	with enough money
drag *(noun)*	bore	follay	follow
dreich	cold and wet *(weather)*	foostie	fusty – dry, unused,
drift	direction		old-fashioned
DS	Drug Squad	fuck-all	nothing
E	ecstasy tablets	fucker	disliked person; *strong and*
early doors	early, in good time		*crude*
Edinburgh Academy	Edinburgh private school	fursht	first
		gadge	person

gaff	flat (apartment)	haud oot	hold out: withhold; unforth-
gaffer	boss		coming; *for example with*
gagging (on)	*see* ganting		*heroin or cards*
gam	blow-job: oral sex	heap big	childish parody of North
game (on the)	working as a prostitute		American Indian speech
ganting (on)	desperate (for)	heap big	a doctor – clearly using the
gaunnae	going to	medicine man	parlance of Little Plum, a
gear	goods		North American Indian boy
George	Edinburgh private school		who appeared in a cartoon
Heriot's			strip in the weekly comic
gie / gied	give / gave		*Beano* from 1953, published
gift of the gab	the art of conversation		by DC Thomson of Dundee.
giro	money-order – form of pay-	Heavy	a type of beer
	ment of dole money; cashable	heavy	serious, difficult
	through Post Office or bank	heckers laik	part of a rhetorical question
git	get		anticipating the answer 'no';
git doon (*tae*)	get down (*to*)		easily recognised expression
glaikit	stupid		from northern England
gled	glad	heebie-jeebies	in an uncontrolled state
gless *verb*	glass; *injure someone with a*	heid	head
	broken glass	heid-banger	crazy guy
goat	got	hen	woman; *Scots slang*
goat – gittin	provoking me; *'getting my goat'*	het up	upset, anxious
ma goat		Hibbee	fan of Hibernian Football
gob	mouth; *also* spittle		Club
Goose Green	Battle in the Falklands War	hing-oot	person who hangs about with-
	(1982)		out purpose
graft	hard work	hireys	money
grand	a thousand	hissel	himself
grannied	comprehensively beaten	hoachin	heaving; a lot of something
grass	an informer	hoarse	(racing) horse
gub	hit; beat	hoats	sexual arousal
guttered	put into the gutter	(the hoats)	
gypo	gypsy	hoor	whore
H	heroin	hostelry	pub, bar *(archaic designation)*
hame	home	hotchin (with)	full (of), jostling (with)
Hampden	Hampden Park; Scottish Foot-	how?	why?
	ball Association's national	hud	had
	stadium; 'the Hampden roar':	Hun	nickname for Rangers FC
	strong consensus		(Glasgow) *qv*; drawing atten-
handfae	handful		tion to its close association
hassle	trouble		to Georgian kings and their
haud oan	hold on: wait		

German origins, the British Union, and Protestantism

hunner — hundred

Hurricane — nickname of a well-known snooker player

inside — *can mean* in prison

intae — into; heavily involved (with)

ivir — ever

J D — Jack Daniels (whiskey)

jack and jill — pill

Jack Jones — alone

jack up — shoot up – take heroin intravenously

Jam Rag — sanitary towel

Jambo — fan of Heart of Midlothian Football Club, widely known as 'Hearts'. Reference to Queen of Hearts, who ate jam tarts, reduced to Jambo

jaykit — jacket

jelly — Temazepam, a prescribed sedative and tranquilliser

jist — just

Jock — universal nick-name for Scottish people

Jock Tamson's bairns — children of the mythical Jock Tamson; an inclusive view of all Scots

Joe Baxi — taxi

Joe McBride — ride (*see* ride)

joint — a place; *or* a marijuana cigarette

junk / junkie — drugs / person who uses heroin or methadone

kb — knock back: refuse, reject

keely — ordinary fellow

keks — underpants

ken / kent — know / knew; known

kick — reject, avoid; break an addiction

kin — can

kit and kaboodle — everything (*army expression*)

knob — penis

knock (out of) — steal; shoplift

labdick — police; *probably an acronym of 'Lothians and Borders' Police, the police force covering Edinburgh in the 1980s, with 'dick' deriving from American slang*

lag (*noun*) — prisoner

laldy (give laldy) — sing loudly

lashing (oafay) — pouring (*off of*); can also mean a beating

lassie — girl: *conventional Scottish*

lam — erection

Lee Marvin — starving *rhyming slang*

Leithy — Leith Academy

lemon — girlfriend

like(s) — *colloquial form of speech roughly equivalent to:* 'as it were'

likesay — *an extension of* likes *without adding to or changing the meaning*

Links — Leith Links; public park in Leith

lippy — cheeky; saying too much

lit on — disclose; divulge

loupin — jumping; horrible

magic — very good

main man — man of the moment; man for the situation

mainlining — injecting direct into a vein

mair — more

maist — most

make — manage; arrive at; succeed

mantovani/ manto — *rhyming slang*: mantovani > fanny > girl

Merchant — a class of post-Reformation institutions with the clear

	implication of commercial success and prosperity
Merrydown	brand name of a cheap cider
Methadone / methy	methadone; a controlled drug, prescribed with the aim of replacing heroin
mibbe / mibbes	maybe
mind	remember
minge	female pubic hair
moan or cmoan	come on: hurry, or pay attention
mobbed	full
Morningside	by reputation a wealthy middle-class suburb of Edinburgh
Mr Cadona	proprietor of amusement arcades
Murrayfield	prosperous Edinburgh suburb and name of the Scottish Rugby Union main stadium
n	and
naebody	nobody
nane	none
nash	go away quickly
National Certificate	post-school qualification, vocational and practically-orientated rather than academic
nick (noun)	police cell or prison
nip	short drink – often whisky
nippy	annoying; or quick, neat
nivir	never
no	not
nonce	sex offender
nondy	stupid
noo (the noo)	now: the present moment or for a moment
nowt	nothing
nuffink	nothing; London accent
nutter / nutty	crazy guy / crazy
oafay	off of: from (see ootay)
oan	on
oantay	onto
OD	over-dose
Old Firm	Celtic and Rangers football clubs, both in Glasgow and traditionally dominating domestic football
one oaf	one-off; a single occasion
oor	our
Oor Wullie	archetypal Scottish boy in a cartoon strip
oorsels	ourselves
ootay	out of (see oafay)
ootay order	out of order: not in accordance with the rules
Orange	Orange Order; organisation representing Protestant supremacy in Northern Ireland
orlright	alright; (London accent)
ower	over
Oxbridge	conflation of Oxford and Cambridge; often used to indicate an elite
pad	place to live
pagger	fight
palsy-walsy	friendly in a shallow or false way; deliberately phoney version of pally
panel	repeated hitting
para	paranoid
Paris bun	Hun (see Hun); rhyming slang
patter	talk, conversation
Percy	Persevere, the pub; abbreviation
perr	poor
perty	party
piece ay pish	easy
pig	police
pish	urine; also alcoholic drink
pished	drunk
pished oaf	pissed off; angry or disappointed
pishin hissel	laughing enough to lose bladder control

pisshead	drunkard
pit oot	put out, exclude
pits (the)	the bottom, the lowest possible
pitten	putting
pleb	common person
plukey-faced	face with spots
poakit	pocket
pockling	pocketing; to put in one's pocket
poke	a sexual act
polis	police
Polmont	Young Offenders' prison in central Scotland
poof	gay male; *pejorative term used by macho straight men*
poppy	money
pox-box	a vagina as a carrier of sexually transmitted disease
puff (*or cream puff*)	huff; offended
puff (on your)	alone – by yourself
puff	breath; *therefore* life
punt (on the)	dealing
punter	ordinary person; *one who expects to get what he pays for*
pus	face
QT (on the)	quietly, discreetly
quack	doctor
rabbiting	talking at length
radge	wild, crazy, useless
Rangers	Rangers FC (Glasgow); traditionally a bastion of Protestantism
rat-arsed	drunk
ride	sexual encounter (*rhyming slang with Joe McBride*)
rid-heided	red-haired
Ritz	video hire chain
rock n roll	dole; *rhyming slang*
root	erect penis
Royal Ed	Royal Edinburgh Hospital, specialising in psychiatry
Royal Scot	Royal Scottish Fusiliers: a Scottish Regiment in the British Army
s	is *or* its (it's)
sais	says
Salisbury Crag	high cliff; *prominent feature within Edinburgh; rhyming slang for* skag
sap	naïve; foolish (person)
Saughton	local name for Her Majesty's Prison, Edinburgh
schemie	someone from a Council-built housing scheme – either a pejorative term, or a matter of pride
scoobied	from cartoon character Scooby Doo, who never knows
score (*noun*)	situation
score (*verb*)	succeed; acquire
scrambled eggs	legs; *rhyming slang*
scran	food
script	prescription
shaft	fuck
shan	bad; terrible
Sherman Tank	Yank: American; *rhyming slang*
shiteing, shiters	fearful
shit-stabbing	anal penetration
shoatie (*keep*)	keep look-out; keep watch
shoodir	shoulder
shooting gallery	place to shoot up; *adapted from normal meaning similar to 'rifle range'*
shooting up	injecting (drugs)
shows	amusement arcade
skag	heroin
skaggy-bawed	too much under the influence of heroin for sexual functioning

slag	rubbish; *can mean* an easily available *or* sexually promiscuous person, *usually without taste or style*	swallay *(noun)*	swallow (*of liquid, usually alcohol*)
slagging off	giving verbal abuse, talking badly of someone	swedge	fight
		swedge	fight, battle
slavering	slobbering	swedgin	verbal abuse
smack	heroin	tae	to
smack-head	heroin user	tae	too; also
smert	smart	tan	drink heavily
Smoke, the	London	tan	to hit in an aggressive blow
snookered	unable to proceed	tap (up)	cadge
snuff (it)	die	tapped	tapped in the head – *ie* got it wrong
snug	traditionally the small room in a pub	tattie / couch tattie	potato / couch potato: one who sits passively watching too much television.
soap-dodger	Catholic nick-name for Protestant	tatties (mince and)	minced meat and potatoes – a simple basic traditional meal
sound	ok	tea leaf	thief;
specky	(person) wearing spectacles	Telford College	Further Education College specialising in the trades north-west of city centre.
spesh	Special (beer)		
split	leave		
sprog	young one		
squaddie	basic-grade soldier	telt	told
square go	straight fight	temazapan	prescription medication for the treatment of insomnia
stane	stone		
Stanley knife	brand name of short-blade retractable working knife	tenement	block of flats
		tenner / ten-spot	ten-pound note
steamboats; steaming	drunk; *from having a drink on the steam boats going down the Clyde from Glasgow*	thair	there *or* their
		thame	them
stey	stay; *to mean* living (somewhere)	the bottle	courage
		the day	today
stick (to give some)	to beat (someone) with a stick, punishingly	the morn	tomorrow
		the morn's morn	tomorrow morning
stoap	stop		
stoat the baw	stot (bounce) the ball: *euphemism for* under-age sex	the night	tonight
		the now (the noo)	at present; for a while; soon, shortly
stoatir	stotter; a fine example, particularly a bruise	thegither	together
stowed oot	full	thin	than
sub	subsidise; *ie* lend	thit	that
suss *(verb)*	suspect; realise	thoat	thought
swag	stolen goods	thumb (by)	hitch-hiking

ticker	heart	US	useless
tidy *adjective*	good, strong performer can also mean attractive *(normally referring to a person)*	us	me; *widely used instead of first-person singular*
tin flute	suit; *rhyming slang*	use / using / user	take heroin / person who takes heroin
tipple	realise what is happening	vallies	Valium tablets (*a prescribed medication typically produc-ing a calming effect*)
tod – oan ma tod	by myself		
toke	inhale a cigarette or a spliff	voddy	vodka
toon	town (*meaning Edinburgh*)	wad	pack, stack (of money)
Tories	The Conservative Party: *the dominant political party in 20th British politics; with its origins in the aristocracy, land-ownership and commerce*	wan / wahn	one (Glasgow accent)
		wanker	person who masturbates: a futile *and/or* manipulative person
toss (give a ..)	masturbation: *usually neg-ative: eg* 'I don't give a toss' *means* 'I don't care')	washhoose	washhouse – a communal place for washing clothes and traditionally a female stronghold
toss-bag	condom	wasnae	wasn't
trades	trades fortnight, a traditional two-week holiday for indus-trial workers in Edinburgh, in the first two weeks in July	waster	useless person
		wee	small, little
		Weedie	Glaswegian (*person from Glasgow*)
Tron	a focal point on Edinburgh High Street, traditional gathering-place for New Year celebrations before the official New Year public party was introduced in 1991	wey	way
		whae	who
		whair	where
		whin	when
		whinge	whine, complain
		whit	what
tube	useless, helpless (person)	white doves	ecstasy tablet with imprint – a temporary currency
twat	female genitalia *or* annoying (person)	wick (on [my])	annoying
um	him / them	wid	would / we would
umpteenth	a non-existent number, thus suggesting a number beyond counting	wide	off-centre; non-conforming;
		wide-o	wide person (*see above*); per-son often looking for trouble
up	widely used to relativise Lon-don and Scotland geograph-ically: Scotland is 'up' from London	widnae; wouldnae	wouldn't
up the kite / stick	pregnant	wifie	woman
		windae	window
uptight	excessively anxious	Windsor Group Hotels	euphemism for Her Majesty's prisons

wis	was	yis	alternative to *youse*
wisnae; wusnae	wasn't	YLT	Young Leith Team; *a movement or gang in Leith – the distinctive YLT logo is widespread throughout Leith as graffiti*
wog	offensive, derogatory term to describe a black person		
Woolies	Woolworths; cheap general store	yon	that one
workie	working person; usually a labourer	yonks	a long time
		youse	*plural of* you
wurd	word	yuppie	Young Upwardly-mobile Person – usually used pejoratively
ye	you		
yin	one	yuv	you've
yir	you are *or* your	zit	spot on skin

Bibliography

Section I

Mullay, A J (1991). *Rail Centres: Edinburgh*. Birmingham: Ian Allan Ltd.
Mullay, A J (1993). *Leith Central: The Station Nobody Wanted: Back Track* vol 1, part 1. Truro: Pendragon.
Munro, John Neil (2013). *Lust for Life! Irvine Welsh and the Trainspotting Phenomenon*. Edinburgh: Polygon.

Section II

Blackburn, Simon (1999). *Think*. Oxford: Oxford University Press.
Davies, Luke (1997). *Candy: A Novel of Love and Addiction*. New York: Ballantine Books.
Ellis, Bret Easton (1991). *American Psycho*. New York: Vintage Books.
F., Christiane (2013). *Zoo Station (a memoir)*. San Francisco: Zest Books.
Heylin, Clinton (2005). All Yesterday's Parties: *The Velvet Underground in Print, 1966-1971*. La Vergne, Tennessee: Ingram Publisher Services US.
Mcnair, Sandy (2011). *Carspotting: The Real Adventures of Irvine Welsh*. Edinburgh: Black and White Publishing.
Schoene, Berthold (ed) (2010). *The Edinburgh Companion to Irvine Welsh*. Edinburgh: Edinburgh University Press.
Selby, Hubert, Jr (1979). *Requiem for a Dream*. London: Marion Boyars Publishers Ltd.
Stellin, Susan and MacIndoe, Graham (2016). *Chancers*. New York: Ballantine Books.

Section III

Devine, T M (2002). *The Scottish Nation: A Modern History*. London: Penguin.
Devine, Tom (ed) (1991). *Irish immigrants and Scottish society in the nineteenth and twentieth centuries: proceedings of the Scottish Historical Studies Seminar, University of Strathclyde, 1989–90*. Edinburgh: John Donald Publishers.
Jamieson, Stanley (1984). *The Water of Leith*. The Water Of Leith Project Group, Edinburgh.
MacKenzie, Hugh (1995). *Craigroyston Days*. Edinburgh and London: Mainstream Publishing.
Marr, Andrew (2007). *A History of Modern Britain*. London: Macmillan.
Mowat, Sue (1997). *The Port of Leith: Its History and People*. Edinburgh: **John Donald Publishers.**
Scott Marshall, James (1986). *The Life and Times of Leith*. Edinburgh: John Donald Publishers.
Townshend, Charles (2006). *Easter 1916; The Irish Rebellion*. London: Penguin Books.
Valentine, David Stewart (2007). *Leith Lives*. Edinburgh: Porthole Publications.

Section IV

Booth, Martin (1996). *Opium: A History*. London: Simon & Schuster Ltd
Bryce, David, with Pia, Simon (2005). *Alive and Kicking; A Story of Crime, Addiction and Redemption in Glasgow's Gangland*. Edinburgh and London: Mainstream Publishing.
Carnwath, Tom & Smith, Ian (2002). *Heroin Century*. London: Routledge.
Chatterley, Marion (2016). *Reflecting theologically on the impact of HIV in Edinburgh with particular reference to infected people, health and social care professionals, Scottish churches and local agency, Waverley Care*. PhD thesis, University of Glasgow.

Coyle, Helen (2008). *A tale of one city – a history of* HIV/AIDS *policy making in Edinburgh – 1982 –1994.* PhD thesis, University of Edinburgh.
De Quincey, Thomas (ed Milligan, Barry) (2003). *Confessions of an English Opium Eater.* London: Penguin Books.
Jay, Mike (2010). *High Society; Mind-Altering Drugs in History and Culture.* London: Thames & Hudson.
Kohn, Marek (1992). *Dope Girls; The Birth of the British Drug Underground.* London: Granta Books.
Plant, Peck and Samuel (1985). *Alcohol, Drugs and School-leavers.* London: Tavistock.
Robertson, Roy (1987). *Heroin,* AIDS *and Society.* London: Hodder & Stoughton.

Section V

(various authors) (2005). *One City.* Edinburgh: Polygon.
(various authors) (2010). *Crimespotting.* Edinburgh: Birlinn.
Borthwick, David (2010). *Welsh's Shorter Fiction* in *The Edinburgh Companion to Irvine Welsh;* Edinburgh: EUP
Kelly, Aaron (2005). *Irvine Welsh.* Manchester: Manchester University Press.
Morace, Robert (2001). *Irvine Welsh's Trainspotting.* New York: Continuum International Publishing Group.
Morace, Robert (2007). *Irvine Welsh.* London: Palgrave MacMillan.
Parks, Tim (2014). *Where I'm Reading From: The Changing World of Books.* London: Vintage
Royle, Nicholas (2015). *The Art of the Novel.* Cromer: Salt.
Stellin, Susan and MacIndoe, Graham (2016). *Chancers.* New York: Ballantine Books.
Tolstoy, Leo (edited and translated by Pevear, Richard and Volokhonsky, Larissa) (2009). *War and Peace.* London: Vintage.
Wright, David (translator): Chaucer, Geoffrey (1985). *The Prologue of The Summoner's Tale; The Canterbury Tales.* Oxford: Oxford University Press.

Section VI

Scullion, Adrienne (2010). *Welsh and the Theatre* in *Edinburgh Companion to Irvine Welsh* ed. Schoene: Edinburgh. EUP
Sierz, Aleks (2001). *In-Yer-Face Theatre; British Drama Today.* London: Faber and Faber Ltd.

Section VII

Booker, Christopher (2004). *The Seven Basic Plots: Why We Tell Stories;* London. Continuum.
Brooks, Xan (1998). *Choose Life; Ewan McGregor and the British Film Revival.* London: Andre Deutsch Ltd.
Browning, Mark (2001). *Danny Boyle; Lust for Life.* Gosport: Chaplin Books.
Hodge, John (1996). *Trainspotting; A Screenplay.* London: Faber and Faber.
Kuhn, Annette and Westwell, Guy (2012). *Oxford Dictionary of Film Studies.* Oxford: Oxford University Press.
Page, Edwin (2009). *Ordinary Heroes; The Films of Danny Boyle.* London: Empiricus Books.
Smith, Murray (2002). *Trainspotting.* London: British Film Institute.
Stollery, Martin (2000). *Trainspotting: Directed by Danny Boyle.* London: Longman.

Endnotes

1   All references refer to *Trainspotting* (1993) published by Secker and Warburg.
2   Letter in *Edinburgh Evening News*, 3 December 1985.
3   Letter in *The Scotsman*, 22 September 1983.
4   *Edinburgh Evening News*, 7 January 1989.
5   Quoted in *Lust for Life!* p.98 see bibliography.
6   Presumably a reference to the blue police uniform.
7   https://digital.nls.uk/scottish-theatre/slab-boys/index.html accessed on 31 May 2018
8   'Right away' means 'well away' or 'far away', not 'immediately'.
9   Quoted in *All Yesterday's Parties...* see bibliography.
10 Sandhu, Sukhdev. *Stretch out and wait*: in *The Guardian Review* 24 December 2011
11 These places are included in The Proclaimer's song *Letter from America*.
12 *Carspotting*, p.193 see bibliography.
13 From *Lesson*: Robert Garioch 1909–1981
14 'Where they make a desert they call it peace.' Bitter words by Tacitus, put into the mouth of a tribesman defeated by the Romans at the battle of Mons Graupius, AD83.
15 *Glue*: Irvine Welsh; Jonathan Cape (UK), WW Norton (USA), 2001. Page numbers refer to UK edition.
16 *The Acid House*: Irvine Welsh; Jonathan Cape, 1994.
17 *Marabou Stork Nightmares*: Irvine Welsh; Jonathan Cape (UK), 1995, WW Norton (USA), 1996. Page numbers refer to UK edition.
18 Irvine Welsh: *Made in Edinburgh* in *The Guardian* 17 February 2018
19 *Opium: A History*: see bibliography.
20 k.b.: abbreviation of to 'knock back' ie to refuse or reject.
21 *Alcohol, Drugs and School-leavers*: see bibliography.
22 *Edinburgh Evening News*, 6 December 1984.
23 AIDS – *The Facts*, pub SAM, 1984, as quoted in Coyle p. 68 see bibliography.
24 *The Scotsman*, 28 November 1985.
25 Dawson, Carole: *Babies of the AIDS capital*: *The Sunday Telegraph*, 13 April 1986
26 *Edinburgh Evening News*, 30 June 1987
27 *Edinburgh Evening News*, 13 September 1989
28 From a leaflet produced by SARA: Scottish AIDS Research Appeal, 1991
29 From a flyer produced by Waverley Care Trust, 1991, as a fund-raiser for their projected hospice.
30 Wilson and Ramsay (1990): *"Invisible" Caring in Edinburgh*, an essay contained in *Women, HIV and Drugs: Practical issues*. Henderson (ed).
31 *The Herald*, 7 January 2004.
32 *The Herald*, 8 January 2004.
33 *The Herald*, 10 January 2004.
34 Ibid.
35 Ian Bell: *War of Words*; Sunday Herald, 11 January 2004.
36 (various authors) (2005). *One City*. Edinburgh: Polygon.
37 (various authors) (2010). *Crimespotting*. Edinburgh: Birlinn General.
38 Quoted in *The Guardian*, 19 August 2012.
39 Wright, David (translator): Chaucer, Geoffrey (1985). *The Prologue of The Summoner's Tale; The Canterbury Tales*. Oxford: Oxford University Press.
40 *War and Peace*; Pevear and Volokhonsky p.xii see bibliography.
41 Ibid p. xiii.

42   *Daily Record* 5 February 2017
43   *Alcohol, Drugs and School Leavers*; Plant, Peck and Samuel see bibliography.
44   The Scotsman 24 March 2018
45   See bibliography.
46   *The Guardian* 22 May 2018
47   France, David: How to Survive a Plague. Picador 2016
48   *Welsh's Shorter Fiction* in *The Edinburgh companion to Irvine Welsh* p.32 see bibliography.
49   This analysis owes much to Aleks Sierz: *In Yer Face Theatre: British Drama Today.* Faber and Faber, 2001 pp.243, 244.
50   Ibid p.232.
51   Billington and Nightingale both quoted in Sierz p.64.
52   http://www.irvinewelsh.net/theatre/item.asp?id=6&t=Trainspotting accessed on 28 November 2012.
53   *4-Play*: Irvine Welsh p.12 see bibliography.
54   Critics quoted in *In -Yer-Face Theatre*: Aleks Sierz, Faber & Faber 2001 pp.59, 60.
55   *The Herald*, 5 May, 1994.
56   Ibid Sierz p.60.
57   http://www.bushtheatre.co.uk/post/archive_treasure_n07_trainspotting/ accessed on 28 November 2012.
58   *Weslh and the Theatre* in *The Edinburgh Companion to Irvine Welsh* p.80 see bibliography.
59   Irvine Welsh (2001). *4 Play* London. Vintage.
60   http://www.sharonpollock.com/pages/Reviews/Entries/2006/10/12_Trainspotting.html (accessed 02/03/2011).
61   http://www.dailyinfo.co.uk/reviews/feature/833/Trainspotting (accessed 02/03/2011).
62   http://www.backstage.com/review/la-theater/trainspotting-roger-mathey-elephant-theatre/ viewed on 11 February 2015.
63   http://www.literature.hss.ed.ac.uk/2014/01/a-look-back-at-trainspotting-in-the-theatre-out-of-the-blue-leith/ accessed on 17 December 2014.
64   *The Herald*, 13 September 2016
65   *The Guardian*, 19 September 2016
66   All quotations from the screenplay are found in *Trainspotting: A Screenplay*; John Hodge. Miramax Books (Hyperion, New York) 1996.
67   *Danny Boyle Lust for Life* p.9 see bibliography.
68   Hermann and Rieck (1979) *Wir Kinder vom Bahnhof Zoo.*
69   Davies, Luke (1998) *Candy: A Novel of Love and Addiction.*
70   Selby, Hubert, Jr (1978) *Requiem for a Dream.*
71   *The Jungle Book*, Disney 1967.
72   *The Seven Basic Plots* Christopher Booker p.86 see bibliography.
73   *ibid* p138.
74   *Lust for Life*: Iggy Pop first released 1977.
75   *Perfect Day*: Lou Reed, performed by Velvet Underground, first released 1967.
76   NME Monthly, March 1996; pub ipc Magazines, p18
77   Brooks, Xan (1998). *Choose Life*. Chameleon Books p88.
78   Smith, Murray (2002). *Trainspotting*. London: British Film Institute. p65.
79   Petrie, Duncan (2010). *Trainspotting, the film* in *The Edinburgh Companion to Irvine Welsh*, ed Berthold Schoene. Edinburgh: Edinburgh University Press. p52.
80   Smith, Murray ibid p14.
81   Cook E. (1996) generation why not? *Independent on Sunday* 28 January 1996.
82   *Porno*: Irvine Welsh, Vintage (2003) p.44.
83   Ibid pp.45, 47.
84   *Dead Men's Trousers*: Irvine Welsh, Jonathan Cape (2018).
85   *T2 Trainspotting*, Boyle, 2017.

Luath Press Limited

committed to publishing well written books worth reading

LUATH PRESS takes its name from Robert Burns, whose little collie Luath (*Gael.*, swift or nimble) tripped up Jean Armour at a wedding and gave him the chance to speak to the woman who was to be his wife and the abiding love of his life. Burns called one of the 'Twa Dogs' Luath after Cuchullin's hunting dog in Ossian's *Fingal*. Luath Press was established in 1981 in the heart of Burns country, and is now based a few steps up the road from Burns' first lodgings on Edinburgh's Royal Mile. Luath offers you distinctive writing with a hint of unexpected pleasures.

Most bookshops in the UK, the US, Canada, Australia, New Zealand and parts of Europe, either carry our books in stock or can order them for you. To order direct from us, please send a £sterling cheque, postal order, international money order or your credit card details (number, address of cardholder and expiry date) to us at the address below. Please add post and packing as follows: UK – £1.00 per delivery address; overseas surface mail – £2.50 per delivery address; overseas airmail – £3.50 for the first book to each delivery address, plus £1.00 for each additional book by airmail to the same address. If your order is a gift, we will happily enclose your card or message at no extra charge.

Luath Press Limited
543/2 Castlehill
The Royal Mile
Edinburgh EH1 2ND
Scotland
Telephone: +44 (0)131 225 4326 (24 hours)
email: sales@luath. co.uk
Website: www. luath.co.uk